A CRITICAL APPROACH TO YOUTH SECTOR PEACEBUILDING
Dialogue, Politics, and Power

Andy Hamilton, Mark Hammond, and Eliz McArdle

With a foreword by Candice Mama

First published in Great Britain in 2025 by

Policy Press, an imprint of
Bristol University Press
University of Bristol
1–9 Old Park Hill
Bristol
BS2 8BB
UK
t: +44 (0)117 374 6645
e: bup-info@bristol.ac.uk

Details of international sales and distribution partners are available at policy.bristoluniversitypress.co.uk

© Bristol University Press 2025

British Library Cataloguing in Publication Data
A catalogue record for this book is available from the British Library

ISBN 978-1-4473-7342-1 hardcover
ISBN 978-1-4473-7343-8 paperback
ISBN 978-1-4473-7344-5 ePub
ISBN 978-1-4473-7345-2 ePdf

The right of Andy Hamilton, Mark Hammond, and Eliz McArdle to be identified as authors of this work has been asserted by them in accordance with the Copyright, Designs and Patents Act 1988.

All rights reserved: no part of this publication may be reproduced, stored in a retrieval system, or transmitted in any form or by any means, electronic, mechanical, photocopying, recording, or otherwise without the prior permission of Bristol University Press.

Every reasonable effort has been made to obtain permission to reproduce copyrighted material. If, however, anyone knows of an oversight, please contact the publisher.

The statements and opinions contained within this publication are solely those of the authors and not of the University of Bristol or Bristol University Press. The University of Bristol and Bristol University Press disclaim responsibility for any injury to persons or property resulting from any material published in this publication.

Bristol University Press and Policy Press work to counter discrimination on grounds of gender, race, disability, age and sexuality.

Cover design: Nicky Borowiec
Front cover image: Alamy/eye35.pix

Contents

List of figures and tables	iv
List of abbreviations	v
About the authors	vi
Foreword by Candice Mama	vii
1 Introduction: A critical approach to youth sector peacebuilding	1
2 Working with young people in a contested society	16
3 Power and legitimacy: entering the world of the peacebuilder	34
4 Prewrapped peacebuilding	52
5 A peacebuilding typology	69
6 Morphology: an analytical tool for peacebuilding	86
7 Four viewpoints on youth sector peacebuilding	99
8 A new model of youth sector peacebuilding	121
9 Radicalising youth sector peacebuilding	133
10 Peace activism with and by young people	146
11 Conclusion: Reclaiming a political practice	164
Appendix	168
Notes	170
References	171
Index	196

List of figures and tables

Figures
2.1	Conversation as the cog which drives the other three youth work processes	32
3.1	Field of youth sector peacebuilding	43
3.2	Practice capital versus economic capital	46
4.1	Cooper's (2012) adaptation of Hurley and Treacy's (1993) sociological model of youth work	54
6.1	Features of a kitchen	88
6.2	A multipurpose home office	89
6.3	The sorting process in action	94
6.4	Continuum of national identity	96
6.5	Continuum of political identity	96
6.6	Post-qualifying experience	97
7.1	Demographics of viewpoint 1	104
7.2	Demographics of viewpoint 2	109
7.3	Demographics of viewpoint 3	113
7.4	Demographics of viewpoint 4	117
8.1	Hamardle model of youth sector peacebuilding	122
8.2	Viewpoint 1 as politicising dialogue	123
8.3	Viewpoint 2 as harmonising dialogue	125
8.4	Viewpoint 3 as harmonising action	128
8.5	Viewpoint 4 as politicising action	130
10.1	Drivers of effective youth participation	150
10.2	Lundy's (2007) model of participation	153
10.3	Andersson's (2017) typology of youth political participation	156
10.4	Methodologies for the Hamardle model	162

Tables
4.1	Cooper's (2012) political models of youth work	56
5.1	Dichotomies of reconciliation	72
5.2	Distinctions of multiculturalism	81
6.1	Practitioner demographics	95
7.1	Selection of distinguishing statements for viewpoint 1	101
7.2	Selection of distinguishing statements for viewpoint 2	105
7.3	Selection of distinguishing statements for viewpoint 3	111
7.4	Selection of distinguishing statements for viewpoint 4	114

List of abbreviations

BGFA	Belfast Good Friday Agreement
DE	Department of Education for Northern Ireland
EMU	Education for Mutual Understanding
EU	European Union
GAA	Gaelic Athletic Association
IRA	Irish Republican Army
MHPSS	Mental Health and Psychosocial Support
P4Y	Peace4Youth
PSNI	Police Service of Northern Ireland
RUC	Royal Ulster Constabulary
UN	United Nations

About the authors

Andy Hamilton is Research Associate with the Taking Boys Seriously project at Ulster University. His doctoral research investigated how informal educators approach peacebuilding with young people in Northern Ireland and stemmed from over a decade of experience as a practitioner and trustee in the community youth work sector. Andy's research interests include equity and equality in education, gender and masculinities, participatory action research, youth in contested societies, and applied social and political theory. He has published in the *Irish Journal of Sociology*, *British Journal of the Sociology of Education*, *Pedagogy, Culture & Society*, and *Action Research*.

Mark Hammond is Senior Lecturer in Community Youth Work at Ulster University. He has worked in the field of youth work and peacebuilding for over 30 years with various statutory and voluntary sector youth work agencies. His PhD study explored the purpose of youth work and the processes in which it engages. Mark's research interests are varied and include, peacebuilding and community relations, the purpose of youth work and underlying processes, faith-based youth work, and mentoring. He has a passion for learning and teaching and seeing the development of students in the academic, professional, and personal journey.

Eliz McArdle is Senior Lecturer in Community Youth Work at Ulster University. She is a member of the Centre for Youth Research and Dialogue and enjoys collaborating with practitioners in developing new models of practice, including the LIFEMAPS model of how youth work builds mental health, a model of Irish Medium Youth Work, and the place of conversation at the heart of youth work. Eliz developed a suite of training, research, and support for youth workers delivering peacebuilding projects with young people as part of the European Union PEACE II and PEACE IV programmes. Eliz is Course Director for the BSc (Hons) Community Youth Work full-time programme.

Foreword

Candice Mama
Author, Speaker, Forgiveness Advocate

Although I understood the conflict that had happened in Northern Ireland, it was only when I was invited to speak at the 20th anniversary of the 1998 Belfast Good Friday Agreement that I truly saw and experienced the active steps towards peace being taken. I was inspired by how much the youth were involved in these efforts, leading to my continued work within Northern Ireland. Witnessing the resilience and determination of young people to forge new paths forward has left an indelible mark on me.

As someone who has been engaged in peacebuilding from a young age, I resonate deeply with the themes explored in *A Critical Approach to Youth Sector Peacebuilding: Dialogue, Politics, and Power.* This book is a vital contribution to understanding the role of young people as catalysts for change in societies emerging from conflict. The authors, Andy Hamilton, Mark Hammond, and Eliz McArdle, provide a comprehensive framework that combines theoretical insights with practical applications, challenging conventional approaches and encouraging critical engagement.

This text emphasises the potential for transformative change by recognising and harnessing the political agency of young people. It encourages viewing youth not merely as beneficiaries but as co-creators of peace, capable of driving societal transformation. The authors illuminate how storytelling, empathy, and dialogue can dismantle barriers and foster reconciliation, reflecting my own experiences of the power of personal narratives in peacebuilding.

The book underscores that peace is an ongoing process requiring creativity and courage. It invites practitioners, policy makers, and educators to embrace the complexities of peace work and to empower young people as leaders. In my work, I have seen how these principles can transform communities, making this book an essential resource for anyone committed to fostering peace.

I am honoured to write this foreword and recommend this book to readers passionate about peacebuilding. May it inspire you to listen more deeply, engage more critically, and act more compassionately in the pursuit of a peaceful future.

1

Introduction: A critical approach to youth sector peacebuilding

> Everybody's got a bias, and everybody's got an agenda of some sort. (YW29)

This book intends to establish the language of *youth sector peacebuilding* as a global umbrella under which many practitioners can identify and situate their practice, where the dual identities of youth worker and peacebuilder are equally integral. This is not, however, a consensus-building book. The practices of youth work and peacebuilding are in constant conflict, not only with each other but within themselves. Both have rich histories of grassroots activism and community-level leadership, yet as both have become increasingly professionalised, they have been co-opted by state departments and philanthropic bodies who bring their own agendas (de St Croix, 2016; Richmond and Tellidis, 2020). In response, this text seeks to interrupt common-sense ideas of peacebuilding that have been enshrined in youth and peace policy and filtered into practice. Our intention is to reinvigorate critical engagement around approaches to peacebuilding with young people, appealing to multiple communities of practice involved in this work.

The chapters of this book combine existing scholarship, social and political theory, new research conducted by the authors, and our own personal and professional histories. These are the lenses through which we analyse, critique, and make sense of peacebuilding work with young people. We expect readers will find places of both resonance and jarring with how we frame and critique contemporary dynamics of youth sector peacebuilding. This synergy and clash of ideas is the crux of a critical practice alive with opportunities and open to the forging of new paths.

This chapter begins with three short stories that offer snapshots into the authors' positionalities in writing this text. This leads into a brief context of Northern Ireland, also referred to as the north of Ireland.[1] The authors use both these terms, acknowledging the contested nature of constitutional language. This is the setting for our research and acts as an illustrative case study for peacebuilding with young people in contested societies around the globe. An introductory outline of youth work and peacebuilding as key terms is then presented, concluding with an overview of the proceeding chapters.

'I'm in that picture' by Mark Hammond

In the early 2000s, while working in the YMCA, I co-designed a peacebuilding programme for around 20 community activists, youth workers, teachers, and police officers. Within each learning session, the group focused on various aspects of peacebuilding and community relations, such as gaining different perspectives on history and culture, facilitating contentious dialogue, understanding conflict, and creating awareness of others' views, feelings, and beliefs. This powerful cocktail of identity and perspective gave rise to poignant and intimate discourse against the backdrop of suspicion and derision found in the wider community and Northern Irish society.

One such cathartic activity was entitled 'Where were you when?'. The activity involved participants viewing conflict-related pictures from the previous three decades known colloquially, and euphemistically, as 'the Troubles'. These pictures were laid out on the floor and the group would walk around the room and pick up a picture that spoke to them. The pictures represented Northern Ireland in good times and bad, with photos of idyllic scenery and children playing, as well as more violent imagery of rioting and the aftermath of bombings. These juxtaposing images were set to provoke memories, the sharing of stories, and personal reflections. The group was split into small groups to tell their story and share their memory. While we knew this exercise had potential potency, the outcome was even more revealing. After half an hour I asked the group what they made of the exercise and how they heard the others' story.

There was a quietness in the group's response. It seemed the exercise had achieved its cathartic aim. Some from each group began to speak emotionally about their memories of the Omagh bomb, the 1998 Belfast Good Friday Agreement, contested Drumcree Orange walks/marches, or the expansive north Antrim coasts and their holidays away from it all. One of the men, a police sergeant with over 25 years of experience, spoke through the quiet reflections in the feedback. He simply said, 'I'm in that picture'. He showed the picture he had chosen to the larger group. It was a police officer on fire lying on the ground behind a police Land Rover, and another officer trying to quell the flames. David said something like 'That's me there, I am dragging him away from danger'. Suddenly, this cathartic yet somewhat academic exercise got real.

We paused as David told his story, those gathered listened attentively, whether Loyalist, Republican, Unionist, Nationalist or other. Police (the Police Service of Northern Ireland [PSNI] replacing the Royal Ulster Constabulary [RUC] in 2001) officers had not been in many gatherings like this one. The Republican movement did not recognise nor trust the police because of their involvement in the conflict and the fact that it was more than 90 per cent Protestant. Although perceived as partisan, yet without full acknowledgement, the PSNI had also been involved, as agents of the state, in policing contentious Protestant Orange Order walks/marches since the early 1990s. Alongside this, the Patten (1999) report had recommended and brought about significant changes to the status quo. The police were and probably still are hated by many in the two main traditions. They were alienated from the rest of the community and their story rarely heard. David's story was now heard.

The atmosphere in the room enveloped a deep sense of empathy, not enmity, as David spoke of what it was like to be hated by both traditions and find himself under threat of violence from both sides. While not a unique story, it was one that was rarely told or spoken out loud in a diverse grouping such as this one. Those listening were tearful and some, for possibly the first time, were enabled to talk about their loss, shame, and pain, because another human, no longer a police officer, had opened up. As the group reflected on David's experience, they were able to not only listen but empathise and converse about their perspective, their experience, and their hopes. Dialogue was being realised where each person was respected not out of politeness but because they saw the other as human.

For me, this was a breakthrough moment, not only in my career, but it was a cathartic realisation that the humanness of the encounter had burst a bubble. I had lived and worked in communities where the police had been involved in unjust, sectarian incidents. I had perceived them as partisan, some had used power with impunity, and, at times, rather than keep the peace, they had exacerbated the violence. As a youth worker I had witnessed how badly they had treated young people, and I knew police officers with sectarian, bigoted attitudes. A just, stable, and non-partisan police service was, from my perspective, far from realised. However, my attitude was beyond academic and lacked objectivity. My bias had dehumanised the police and had not seen the personal cost. David's story opened me to the possibility that for change to happen, listening, hearing, and talking must be the objective.

The empathy, mutual understanding, and opportunity for open dialogue which ensued as a result of David's story started to break down the barriers and at least in that room something new happened. While not the panacea for a divided society, this story illustrates that change in intractable conflict often comes out of relationships and open conversation with the other. From my perspective, this dialogical engagement, which allowed storytelling from the heart, was a meagre start in transforming the conflict into something else. When David said 'That's me in the picture' it made me think that in the north of Ireland, we are all in the picture.

A place apart, placed apart by Eliz McArdle

Border people are an oddity. You need wily ways to manoeuvre across borders – to see opportunities from the separation of people and places;

always on the lookout with shady stories to tell, but mostly told in hushed tones. Secrecy, silence, and darkness are overshadowed by stoicism, but nevertheless, they lurk in the background.

I am from Monaghan. The county of Monaghan is at the base of Ulster, one of the four provinces on the island of Ireland. At the time of partition in the 1920s, the state of Northern Ireland was devised of six counties of Ulster, leaving Co. Monaghan, Co. Cavan, and Co. Donegal in Southern Ireland. Monaghan was and is still a county of Ulster but part of the new Republic of Ireland.

But you don't belong, and you don't fit. The accent jars. 'Are you from the North?' was the usual refrain of your fellow countrymen trying to work out how different you were from them. With narrowed eyes and suspicious mouths, you felt the gaze of 'your own people' who didn't know you and didn't trust you.

It wasn't difficult to see how different you were when you crossed the border 'to the North'. You lurched along the border, zigzagging forwards and backwards from South to North along a road that knows no manufactured borders – there were 'approved roads' and 'unapproved roads'. Move swiftly and without hesitation, to avoid your car being hijacked to transport a bomb or as part of an ambush. You passed through the architecture of roadblocks, and green corrugated iron walls to match the khaki green of soldiers and armoured tanks. Searches and marches, customs posts and RUC stations. You knew you didn't live like this and that you didn't understand this life.

I left Co. Monaghan. The idea grew in me that this was a place that was left behind and the people were left behind. No investment, no infrastructure, nobody wanted to be on the border and no discernible future could be moulded from this. So, I left and crossed the border. But even though I left this place, the place has not left me. The sense of being outside of things stays and your practice grows from this. I don't truly know war from the inside and don't truly feel part of one side or another. This is where I stand – on the fringe. I mediate, I harmonise, I make peace. This is my foundation for practice.

In 2002, I interviewed a young man for a research project on young people and social exclusion. I met him in the Woodvale area of North Belfast, a largely Protestant area on the interface with the Catholic Ardoyne and in the midst of a protracted and painful dispute locally called the Holy Cross dispute. The entire area was tense and hostile. I was specifically interviewing young people from Protestant backgrounds about their experiences of social exclusion. I walked along the short hallway to a small room. I opened the door, and the young man stood up. I said, 'Hiya, I'm Eliz McArdle. How are you doing?'. He visibly recoiled. The strange accent took him by surprise. It took only three or four seconds for him to collect himself and settle into his seat, ready to talk of his life on Twaddell Avenue. He spoke excitedly of riots, the lads, his hatred of school, and his pride in marching. He was frank and candid in conversation. I was struck by the ease with which he had talked to me. It was as though he suspended our introduction in his mind and held it in limbo. He spoke to me as though I knew his life. To him, I was a Protestant. For him, I was like him. There was no other logical explanation for a Southern Catholic interviewing a young Protestant from the Shankill. Just being there gave enough legitimacy without having to show that you belong.

This is life on the fringes of belonging; where you are welcomed in unexpected places and exiled from others. The encounters are full of contradictions, and in the contradictions, there is room for refining and redefining who we are and where we belong.

A closet Catholic and confused Protestant by Andy Hamilton

I was eight years old when I was first asked if I was Catholic or Protestant. My answer would have surprised my parents. The town I grew up in was over 80 per cent Protestant and the church I was dropped off at each week for Sunday school taught that the Pope was an anti-Christ. When I responded, 'I haven't told anyone but I'm Catholic', my inquisitor, another eight-year-old boy who was kitted out in a Celtic soccer team tracksuit, said, 'Good, me too'. Many eight-year-olds would have known that Catholics supported Celtic and Protestants supported Rangers, but even at that young age, I was utterly disinterested in following football. I was completely unaware of this cultural signifier of religious and political identity. My answer was not a lucky guess. Rather, I was sincerely and unwittingly confused.

In a society where religion had become a euphemism for one of two competing political and cultural identities, whether you were Protestant or Catholic was a high-stakes question. My Sunday school teachers, alongside the religious elements of my primary school education, had successfully engendered within me a sense of the eternal significance of religion. They failed drastically however in their messaging that Protestantism was 'the way'. Somehow, I had concluded that *really* believing in God and having a sincere faith meant being Catholic. Reflecting now, I think this was because others around me declared they were Protestant but did not go to church nor think much of God. I was a closet Catholic in an all-Protestant family, too embarrassed to tell everyone that I believed in God. I was, of course, not Catholic at all. I simply thought Catholic meant being a 'true' Christian – a centuries-old theological dispute and ideological debate that has fuelled many brutal wars and is intertwined in the history of conflict and division in Ireland, North and South. At eight years old in 1999, a year on from the ongoing optimism of the Belfast Good Friday Agreement, I was naive to that reality. Later, when testing out with my older sister what she would say if I told her I was a Catholic, she swiftly put me right and I was no longer under any illusion.

This memory is so poignant because the dynamics of naivety and unfolding awareness about the place where I live and my position within it have been repeated many times, often accompanied by that same sense of confusion. The first time I went to Ballysillan, a loyalist working-class area in North Belfast, I was struck by how visibly Protestant it was – the union flags, painted kerbstones, sectarian graffiti, talk of band parades and casual references to Ulster Defence Association (UDA) – a paramilitary organisation. Aged 15 and volunteering at a youth centre alongside my middle-class peers, I felt out of place in the same streets my mum had grown up in. For much of my childhood and early teenage years, I was unaware of my privilege and subtle forms of sectarianism where difference was avoided, and distance maintained from those communities considered to be 'stuck in the past'. I began trying to make sense of my prejudice and partial understandings, alongside a growing consciousness of the class dimension of conflict legacies where working-class communities have often been scapegoated by their middle-class neighbours.

As a youth worker, I gradually came to see how confusion and dissonance could be a source of learning. When young men spoke enthusiastically about respective Loyalist and Republican cultural traditions that I knew little of, I would position myself as the learner, curious to see the world through their lens. While my youth work experience has brought many rich and meaningful conversations about difference and division, rarely was my practice explicit about connecting the personal with the political and supporting young people to recognise and embrace their political agency as peacebuilders. Throughout this book, my bias is towards promoting a politicising peacebuilding practice with young people. This is not because it reflects my approach as a practitioner, but rather because it was so often missing from my youth work.

Northern Ireland: an illustrative case

Northern Ireland, with a modest population of fewer than two million, has had colossal geopolitical significance for the UK, Ireland, the wider European Union, and the United States since its borders were established in 1921 (Sanders, 2019; Lagana, 2021). This British-Irish two-state solution was an uncomfortable compromise made by political actors with the intent of quelling violence. The six north-eastern counties of Ireland were hewn off as part of the UK while the remaining 26 counties were liberated from British colonial control giving rise to the Irish Free State (Browne and Bradley, 2021). Decades of growing enmity between pro-British versus pro-Irish actors, fuelled by conflictual and contested histories stretching back to the 16th century, erupted into almost 30 years of violent conflict in the latter part of the 20th century (Ruane and Todd, 1996). This period of terror, known colloquially as 'the Troubles', was marked by civilian killings, political assassinations, abductions, routine bomb threats, paramilitary action, army occupation, police collusion, displacement, and everyday violence (Dillon, 1991; McKittrick and McVea, 2012; Feeney, 2014; Gilmartin and Browne, 2022). Every aspect of social, cultural, religious, political, personal, and economic life was impacted by the Troubles (McAtackney and Ó Catháin, 2024). Hope of a new reality was birthed on Good Friday, 10 April 1998, with the signing of the Belfast Good Friday Agreement (British and Irish Governments, 1998). The agreement was supported by most of the local political parties and significantly by the two largest opposing political parties of the time. It was a landmark deal that was the product of formal and backchannel talks with the leadership of paramilitary groups as well as political parties convened by the British and Irish governments (Stanton, 2021). The United States played a significant role in negotiations and peace talks, as did the European Union, which in 1995 had launched the first of a series of peace programmes in Northern Ireland and the border counties of Ireland (Mitchell, 2000; Lagana, 2021). The monumental support from major Western powers was matched by local convictions towards peace when the Belfast Good Friday Agreement was put to a referendum in Northern Ireland and a huge majority (71.1 per cent) voted in favour of the deal (Whyte, 2002).

Northern Ireland and its populace have since endured many partial and fraught attempts to embed political stability through a power-sharing form of government (McGarry and O'Leary, 2016). Young people who have grown up during peacetime are socialised in a context of conflict legacies which have a powerful influence on social, political, and cultural identities (McAlister et al, 2014; Townsend et al, 2020). These legacies include segregated social housing and education, separate cultural and sporting traditions, contested histories, mistrust of policing, residual paramilitarism, disputed language rights, and occasional sectarian rioting (Gray et al, 2023). Visible signs of the violent past are most prominent in working-class communities. Murals painted on gable walls include depictions of masked paramilitary men as well as memorials of Republican and Loyalist icons. Lampposts are adorned with either the flag of the UK or Ireland and paramilitary flags and emblems are on display. Armoured police vehicles patrol the streets, sectarian graffiti is commonplace, and corrugated iron structures act as 'peace walls' separating predominantly Nationalist communities from predominantly Unionist communities (Morrow, 2019; Welch, 2020). More subtle forms of separation are expressed through seemingly arbitrary choices over which shops to go to, which factories to work in, which routes to take, and which destinations to holiday in (McMullan, 2018). These 'hidden barriers' persist, engendering a deeply ingrained sense of territorialism (Coyles et al, 2023).

A preeminent concern is the constitutional status of Northern Ireland as remaining part of the UK or being returned to Ireland to be governed as a part of the Irish Republic (Murphy and Evershed, 2022). The handling of Brexit – the UK's exit from the European Union following the 2016 referendum – catapulted Northern Ireland back into international headlines reminiscent of the height of the Troubles. This time there were fewer (although still some) images of exploded petrol bombs and clashes between young people and police in riot gear. Instead, the primary focus was on legal language and maps attempting to explain the quagmire of Northern Ireland with a historically contentious border facing new challenges (Hayward, 2021). Northern Ireland was the only part of the UK which would remain physically connected to a European Union (EU) country – Ireland. This raised a raft of unsettling implications around hard borders, monitoring the flow of goods and people, security concerns, and the integrity of Northern Ireland's status within the UK (Hayward, 2018; Hayward and Komarova, 2022; Rosher, 2022; Coulter and Shirlow, 2023).

The binary between Nationalists who want a united Ireland and Unionists who want to remain part of the UK has been increasingly challenged. The Alliance Party have sought to depoliticise the constitutional question, focusing instead on building a cross-community voter base (Tonge, 2020). The surge in Alliance seats in recent local assembly elections suggests a growing centre ground (Coakley, 2021). The growth in Alliance, however, does not resolve the constitutional question. Despite shifting demographics away from a clear Unionist majority in Northern Ireland, some political analysts have reinforced that constitutional change is not a foregone conclusion (Coulter et al, 2023). Others have noted that changes in demography, the ramifications of Brexit, and the historic 2022 local assembly election results where Sinn Féin, the largest Nationalist party, won the role of First Minister for the first time, are both psychologically and politically significant (Diamond and Colfer, 2023). These may prove important moments on the route towards an Irish border poll which the 1998 Belfast Good Friday Agreement made provisions for.

The next chapter further unpacks the nature of Northern Ireland as a contested society. Throughout this book, we draw on experiences and examples from the Northern Ireland context. This book is not a comparative analysis nor a comprehensive overview of peacebuilding with young people in different political and cultural contexts. Rather, Northern Ireland offers an illustrative case that invites the reader to consider parallels and applications to their own geopolitical reality. Like many other illustrative cases of contested societies, such as Bosnia and Herzegovina, Kosovo, Ukraine, Tajikistan, Israel–Palestine, Hong Kong, South Korea, South Africa, Rwanda, Sierra Leone, Timor-Leste, and Colombia, to name a few, Northern Ireland is a place of strategic geopolitical importance. It is a place where some have had their citizenship brutally denied and violated and where lines between victim and perpetrator are disputed and hard to draw. It is a place haunted by violence where the trauma experienced by past generations is passed onto children. It is a place that continues to experience paramilitarism and is marked by deep divisions and segregation. It is a place where women have been courageous peacebuilders; where mothers and fathers have struggled for peace; where some feel compelled to continue or return to armed struggle. It is a place where communities have created pathways both in and out of violence; where many want to move on; where political impasses are frequent; and where systems of segregation remain deeply rooted. It is a highly stratified place where poorer communities face the consequences of past and enduring violence much more readily than their wealthier neighbours. It is a place where international actors play significant roles in peacebuilding programmes and where much hope is placed on young people as those who will carve a new way forward and break with historical waves of recurrent political violence.

Many of these features of conflict will resonate in societies where native populations have been displaced and struggles for recognition, rights, redress, and justice persist. Through an analysis of youth workers' priorities with young people in Northern Ireland, this book seeks to stimulate critical thinking on how we approach peacebuilding work with young people in such contested situations, and how this work can reach more emancipatory goals.

Peacebuilding and far-right extremism

While the perspectives on peacebuilding discussed and critiqued in this book are based on research in Northern Ireland as an illustrative case of ethno-territorial conflict, there are parallels with societies encountering the violence of far-right extremism. Ireland, North and South, has experienced a decade-long global rise in far-right racist ideology and violence which has destabilised many countries and transnational institutions that pride themselves on democratic values (James McAdams and Piccolo, 2024). Often it has been said of Northern Ireland that sectarianism is a transferable orientation, not far removed from notions of ethnic supremacy rooted in the racist othering and scapegoating of minority groups (McVeigh and Rolston, 2007; Doebler et al, 2018).

Media portrayals of *culture wars* highlight, and contribute to, a growing polarisation in political perspectives. Issues of immigration, housing, taxes, benefits, religious practices, and national identity become the ammunition of such culture wars that penetrate the social fabric. Mass appeals to feelings of insecurity and anger at the perceived threat of 'outsiders' and a global 'elite' who are deemed distant from everyday people, activate a siege mentality of protecting the interests of homogeneous social groups (Joppke, 2023). It is beyond the scope of this book to offer a detailed and nuanced analysis of tactics deployed by far-right actors. The book does, however, provide critical insights into different peacebuilding approaches pertinent to working with young people immersed in a digital world of unleashed populist propaganda and potent online influencers whose content fuels real-world violence (Nilan, 2021; Gaudette et al, 2022). In situations of growing polarisation and intolerance between left- and right-wing political ideas and activism, some may be drawn to strategies of harmonisation and a return to a more measured centre ground. Others may gravitate towards strategies of politicisation which seek to tackle head-on the appeal of fundamentalism to those who feel disenfranchised, by promoting political participation and robust spaces for critical thinking and dialogue, as well as activism inspired by principles of equity and inclusion.

Defining peacebuilding and youth work

Throughout the book, we deliberately avoid offering definitions of peacebuilding and youth work. These are approached as contested terms, which cannot be fully delineated in succinct definitions. As such, we explore the parameters of youth work and peacebuilding based on the multiple and at times contradictory ways in which practitioners seek to make sense of their work.

While seeking to avoid definitions, it is useful to make several broad distinctions. Galtung's (1975) well-known differentiation of peacekeeping, peacemaking, and peacebuilding is instructive. Peacekeeping has been summarised as 'keeping enemies apart' (McCandless, 2010: 201). The primary emphasis is on deescalating tensions, containing conflict, and appealing to the pursuit of political goals through non-violent means. Peacemaking is a negotiation phase which is often both public-facing and secretive where backchannel talks take place between paramilitary groups and state leaders. The goal of peacemaking is ceasefires and ultimately a long-term peace agreement. Reaching a conflict settlement prepares the way for a subsequent era of peacebuilding where strategies are employed to address conflict legacies and embed a sustainable peace.

The imagery of *building* peace has been called into question (Verwoerd, 2021). It supposes an overly determined approach with 'precise control by [a] builder, clear plans, working with inanimate objects' (Verwoerd, 2021: 240). In contrast, the peace worker's experience, much like Mark's reflection at the beginning of this chapter, involves 'messy, unpredictable, humbling realities of facilitating dialogue and enduring relationships between human beings' (Verwoerd, 2021: 240). Verwoerd therefore proposes the notion of *cultivating peace* as a metaphor more in tune with these processes.

Peacebuilding is an imperfect term. It is, however, for our purposes appropriately broad in the field of peace and youth research and practice to provide a common heuristic. The term grew to prominence in the 1990s, propelled by United Nations (UN) reports, notably the 1992 Agenda for Peace report, which introduced 'peacebuilding' as a tool to be used by the UN (Boutros-Ghali, 1992). The Brahimi report (UN, 2000) later referred to peacebuilding as 'activities undertaken on the far side of conflict to reassemble the foundations of peace and provide the tools for building on those foundations something that is more than just the absence of war'.

The concepts and critiques developed throughout this book are most relevant to the notion of peacebuilding as an activity with young people on the *far side of conflict*. Other priorities will take precedence in work with young people in the context of an active war zone, which is beyond the scope of this book to examine.

Youth work: an ill-defined practice

Turning to youth work, drawing on our own experiences and extant literature, we acknowledge this to be a disparate and ill-defined practice that assumes different forms in distinctive contexts (Coburn and Gormally, 2017; Hammond, 2018). Practitioners do, however, tend to gather around a collection of common characteristics. These include:

- voluntary participation;
- informal education;
- empowering young people;
- fostering association;
- democratic participation;
- embedding equity, diversity, and interdependence;
- promoting the welfare of young people (NYA, 2000; Jeffs and Smith, 2005; Batsleer, 2008; Banks, 2010; Davies, 2015).

These principles will likely resonate with peacebuilders. Youth work and peacebuilding are natural companions in conflict societies and youth workers are often uniquely placed to engage young people in difficult and meaningful peace work (Grattan and Morgan, 2007). Debate, however, envelops the interpretation and application of these principles. Youth work has found purpose in diverse contexts, including centre-based, street work, schools work, youth justice, faith-based initiatives, and social care settings (Williamson, 2015; Cooper, 2018; Davies and Taylor, 2019). While a rich diversity of practice occurs within and across borders, broad propensities of practice have evolved in regional contexts. A distinction is found in youth work approaches grounded in educational theories compared with those that place greater emphasis on theories of human psychology and development. Subsequently, a continuum exists between youth work as primarily educational and youth work as welfare.

In the UK and Ireland, youth work is founded upon notions of informal and non-formal education. Similarly, across Europe, informal and non-formal education with young people is well recognised and resourced by bodies such as the Council of Europe and European Union. While there is ambiguity over differences in the notions of informal and non-formal learning, generally informal education can be characterised as incidental everyday learning which takes place without a curriculum. This is contrasted with formal education that works to a pre-specified curriculum. Non-formal education sits between informal and formal and involves a process where young people negotiate a flexible curriculum of learning with youth workers (Fordham, 1993).

In the United States, youth work is largely premised on an approach called *positive youth development*, with a focus on building resiliency in young people. Psychological and social support are integral to these approaches (Cooper, 2018). The Australian youth sector is a complex interplay of social care, informal education, recreation, and crime prevention. Policies and approaches vary from state to state within a federated political structure (Cooper, 2018).

Youth work in the global south, and particularly within Commonwealth countries, has largely been influenced by principles of informal and non-formal education inspired by UK youth work (Cooper, 2012; Corney et al, 2023). However, these principles and approaches are not a British invention. Rather, the participatory and emancipatory pedagogies which underpin a critical disposition to informal/non-formal education are expressed in the work of, among others, Brazilian educator and activist Paulo Freire (1921–1997) (Hatton, 2018). Freirean critical pedagogy features prominently in youth work literature, integrating dialogue with democracy as an emancipatory form of education that opposes didactic methods (Freire, 1970; Batsleer, 2008; Beck and Purcell, 2010; Seal, 2016). Critical pedagogy has been defined as 'a democratic process of education that encourages critical consciousness as the basis of transformative collective action' (Ledwith, 2020: xii). As such, critical pedagogy is rooted in social contexts of inequality and seeks to inspire collective agency and action to challenge and subvert systems of oppression. Social pedagogy is a related term which has been used as a substitute for *youth work* in some European countries. It has been proposed as a way of uniting the disparate applications of youth work as informal education, social care and welfare, and positive youth development by focusing on a rights-based approach to non-formal education leading to action for change (Corney et al, 2023).

Critical and social pedagogy as foundational theories of youth work tend to emphasise a focus on politicisation where young people are encouraged to engage in politics and democratic decision-making processes (Beck and Purcell, 2010; Batsleer, 2013). Forrest (2010: 68) depicts such a political approach to youth work as fostering '[a] level of collective empowerment [that] seeks to problematise the world, and to activate individuals into challenging existing social policies and political decisions'. Critical notions of participation, beyond mere taking part in activities, are predicated on a democratic youth work practice that seeks to analyse power relations and harness the collective capacity of young people to bring about a fairer and more inclusive society (Podd, 2010). Such processes which build agency, voice, and political thinking and action are the lifeblood of grassroots social change (Beck and Purcell, 2020).

However, as critiqued in subsequent chapters, a preoccupation with delivering a highly effective, efficient, and uniform youth service has encroached upon the professional autonomy of practitioners (Taylor et al, 2018). Subsequently, aspirations towards social change *with* young people are replaced by a de facto social control *of* young people (Husband, 2020). This book explores the emancipatory potential of youth sector peacebuilding. In doing so it also considers how a more restrictive and less ambitious agenda may 'keep the peace' at the expense of a more radical and politicising practice.

The book in brief

Youth sector peacebuilding is a hugely valuable practice in conflict societies that deserves greater recognition and a more expansive scholarship. This book is our contribution to the literature that offers new conceptual, theoretical, and practical frameworks to stimulate ongoing critical thinking and action. Chapter 2 elaborates on Northern Ireland as an illustrative case drawing out the dynamics of living in a contested society. Four fault lines of division are examined – law and order; education; religious and cultural experience; and equity. The second part of Chapter 2 explores the transformative role youth work can play in contested societies with an emphasis on key processes of conversation and dialogue; relationship building; youth participation; and experiential learning.

Chapter 3 introduces two 'theories of practice' that invite a deeper analysis of the political, social, and cultural contexts which shape the policy and practice climate of youth sector peacebuilding. Drawing on Lave and Wenger's work, we situate youth sector peacebuilding as constellations of communities of practice across the globe. Practitioner communities of practice interface with policy communities of practice. Regimes of competence that delineate legitimate practice are developed and renewed in interactions between 'old-timers' and 'newcomers'. Building on the communities of practice lens, Bourdieu's ideas frame an analysis of power relations in the field of youth sector peacebuilding. This critique presents taken-for-granted ideas and approaches of youth sector peacebuilding as an outworking of the economic, social, cultural, and symbolic power of the state.

Chapter 4 offers a critique of youth work and peacebuilding within a neoliberal policy and practice landscape. The chapter outlines tendencies towards quick fixes and 'one-size-fits-all' approaches that result in decontextualised and depoliticised practices which are at odds with youth work as an empowering and participatory practice. Drawing on literature from critical peace studies, similar dynamics are observed where top-down approaches jar with notions of locally owned and community driven peace processes. While these critiques of youth work and peacebuilding are not new, the chapter outlines how youth sector peacebuilding is doubly subjected to these limitations. This highlights the need for new thinking and language to push back against the hollowing out of dynamic and politicising approaches.

Chapter 5 presents a contemporary typology of peacebuilding approaches that practitioners variously draw upon. The typology covers six areas, delineating debates and tensions across the domains of reconciliation; intergroup contact; human rights; justice; citizenship; and wellbeing. Familiarity with these concepts and the different trajectories of practice they give rise to is an important preliminary to Chapter 6.

Chapter 6 is a transitional one, which marks a pivot from analysis and application of existing literature to the introduction of new concepts. It outlines the process of Q methodology, which was used in the research the book is based upon. The methodology is merged with a discussion on the conceptual approach of morphological analysis. This sets up a morphological analysis of youth sector peacebuilding which is presented and unpacked in subsequent chapters.

Chapter 7 presents the findings from our research which reveals four distinct, yet overlapping, viewpoints on youth sector peacebuilding:

- viewpoint 1: critical thinking and dialogue;
- viewpoint 2: mutual understanding;
- viewpoint 3: social cohesion and restoration;
- viewpoint 4: political engagement and social justice.

These viewpoints are animated through direct quotations from the youth work practitioners who participated in the research. The voices of our research participants are also found at the start of each chapter, with a direct quotation following each chapter title.

Chapter 8 presents our new Hamardle model of youth sector peacebuilding. It invites the reader to identify their positionality and bring to consciousness different orientations towards peacebuilding practice with young people. Notably, distinctions between harmonisation or politicisation and dialogue or action are discussed. This new framework and language for thinking critically about youth sector peacebuilding is applicable to nearly all contexts in which peacebuilding work occurs with young people.

Chapter 9 connects the Hamardle model of youth sector peacebuilding with the critical insights of Lave and Wenger, and Bourdieu from Chapter 3. The prevalence of harmonising approaches to youth sector peacebuilding at the expense of more politicising approaches is critiqued as a consequence of state power over policy and funding directives. An analysis across the four quadrants of the model is presented. This is intended to support youth sector peacebuilders to move beyond harmonising, common-sense approaches and develop a language for advocating with policy makers to embrace a more radical and politicised practice.

Chapter 10 compels the reader to consider the foundations of youth activism in peacebuilding. Rather than young people being framed as recipients of peace programmes with prescribed outcomes, this chapter calls for the authentic participation of young people as co-creators. Several models of participation are discussed, and examples of youth activism and leadership are outlined. The chapter challenges the misrepresentation of youth as lethargic, disinterested, and disengaged from political thinking and action. Chapter 11 then concludes the book with a synthesis of key takeaways and a discussion on implications for the future of youth sector peacebuilding.

2

Working with young people in a contested society

> Not just learning about the past but trying to deconstruct it and give young people a kind of critical consciousness to be able to make different choices in the present. (YW28)

Introduction

Peacebuilding is complex with competing agendas and differing perspectives. In Northern Ireland, also referred to as the north of Ireland, there have been numerous initiatives, projects, and programmes to address the conflict and its legacy. The north of Ireland has been in conflict for hundreds of years with the more recent spate of violence being euphemistically referred to as 'the Troubles'. From the late 1960s to 2022, these 'Troubles' resulted in over 3,700 deaths (CAIN, 2023a). In the 25 years since the 1998 Belfast Good Friday Agreement there has been less mortality and morbidity, but the peace is fragile. This chapter, after exploring the historical context of the Troubles, will elucidate how this contested society is impacted by the conflict using the ethnic frontier lens (Wright, 1987) and reflect on the indicators of division that still exist. The ultimate section of the chapter will highlight the youth work processes by which practitioners seek to address this protracted ethno-territorial conflict (Byrne and Nadan, 2011). In focusing on Northern Ireland as a case study and exploring the key issues the authors seek to illustrate how apparently intractable conflict can be approached through the processes found in youth work practice.

Although more than 25 years have passed since the signing of the 1998 Belfast Good Friday Agreement, Northern Ireland still shows evidence of deep division in this deep-rooted conflict. In this place, tension is evident along the fault lines of politics, religion, and national identity, and thus dominated by a relationship of antagonism (Morrow, 2011). This sociopolitical and religious conflict has been referred to as an ethnic frontier (Wright, 1996), which is marked by the inability of either of the significant groups to dominate or control the other. Wright suggests Northern Ireland is characterised by an uneasy strain between two competing nationalisms within its boundaries (cited in Chapman et al, 2018). With two dominating sides, the conflict persists. Wright (1987) sought to analyse the characteristics of this conflict by comparing it to other intractable situations. In his seminal work, he argues that an ethnic frontier is not unique to Northern Ireland. He examines the political and historical context of Northern Ireland, contrasting its conflict with postwar Europe and ethnic conflict within such contexts as Germany, Poland, Moravia and the racial tension of the southern states of the United States. While the application of the ethnic frontier lens was initially applied to these conflicts, there is some cross-over to conflicts which exist today along socio-religious, ethno-political lines and even the culture wars of the last decade.

Also referred to as political ethnicity, the ethnic frontier is divided by 'competing notions of nationhood' (Morrow, 2011: 302). In the north of Ireland, this competition for political attention relates to Islanders' allegiance to either Britain (Unionists or Loyalists) or to the Republic of Ireland (Nationalists or Republicans). Drawing on the work of Roel Kaptein, Morrow and Wilson (1996) contend that in this contested space the result is rivalry. In a context of rivalry, antagonism becomes 'indistinguishable from revenge while peace becomes inseparable from victory' (Morrow, 2011: 306).

Historical context

While this is not an historical book it is useful to understand something of Northern Ireland's history to sharpen the focus for the subsequent chapters. The development of Northern Ireland as a state is contested and did not begin at its inception in 1921. Northern Ireland exists as a 'distinct and devolved' (Morrow, 2011: 308) entity that was 'born in violence' (McKittrick and McVea, 2012: 4). Centuries prior to the implementation of a compromising solution to create a land border in Ireland in the early 1920s, antagonism and rivalry between native Irish Catholics and settler British Protestants proliferated, undergirded by the politics of empire and imperialism. Critical commentaries emphasise the violence of this process where 'British settler-colonialism in Ireland … [was] a means of controlling the indigenous population' (Browne and Bradley, 2021: 8). Through this process of facilitating the mass settling of British citizens in Ireland from 1609 onwards, Britain socially engineered an ethnic frontier where 'empire had left identifiably different groups sharing the same territory' (Morrow, 2011: 303).

Fundamentally, conflict between Nationalists and Unionists reflected divergent perspectives on British imperialism in Ireland (Morrow, 2017), manifested in 'two competing national aspirations' (McKittrick and McVea, 2012: 2). Nationalists became increasingly committed to complete Irish independence following a series of failed Home Rule bills brought to the Westminster parliament in 1886, 1893, and 1912–1914. These bills would have allowed for a devolved Irish government in Dublin to manage domestic affairs while remaining part of the United Kingdom of Great Britain and

Ireland. Unionists in Ireland vocalised their aversion to Home Rule. They mobilised to prevent the British government in Westminster from establishing Home Rule in Ireland, fearful this would threaten the link with the Union and act as 'a prelude to complete Irish independence and the ending of Protestant and British domination of Irish affairs' (McKittrick and McVea, 2012: 3). Violence ensued in 1916, beginning with the Easter Rising in Dublin where several Republicans participated in armed insurrection against British rule in Ireland. The violent response of the British state appeared an overreaction and played an important role in inciting the Irish Republican Army's (IRA) War of Independence from 1919 to 1921 (McKittrick and McVea, 2012).

The Government of Ireland Act (1920) set in motion the partition of Ireland. The act was a fourth attempt at establishing Home Rule, legislating for two devolved institutions in Ireland, one in Dublin and the other in Belfast. Six of the nine majority Protestant north-eastern counties of Ulster were 'carved out of the rest of the island of Ireland' and designated as Northern Ireland (McBride, 2019: 353). These six counties of Northern Ireland were established as a constitutional part of the UK in 1921, separate from the other 26 counties. Nationalists, making up an overwhelming majority of the population of the 26 remaining counties, rejected the Home Rule system of devolved government. The IRA's War of Independence continued into 1921 until a treaty established the Irish Free State, which subsequently was declared as the Republic of Ireland in the 1948 Republic of Ireland Act (O'Toole, 2010). Partition of Ireland was a pragmatic solution to appease the competing constitutional desires of the population and an effort to contain mounting violence (McBride, 2019). Tensions, however, proliferated between Nationalists and Unionists in the newly formed Northern Ireland.

The creation of Northern Ireland crystallised the ethnic frontier where religion became a marker of competing national identities that were forced to co-exist (Morrow, 2015a). Partition instigated a rupture for northern Catholics who experienced 'exclusion from the wider Irish community' (Ruane and Todd, 1996: 51). Meanwhile, the Protestant political class in Northern Ireland sought to embed British loyalties and, as William Craig stated, a 'Protestant Parliament and State' (cited in Cochrane, 2013: 27). These two distinct communities of Catholic/Nationalism and Protestant/Unionism have become embedded binaries in Northern Ireland, where 'identity is everything precisely because it is so vulnerable' (Morrow, 2020). The pre-eminence of a 'two communities thesis' (Hayward and McManus, 2019) has been influential in framing peacemaking and peacebuilding in Northern Ireland.

Antagonism is the mark of relationships in an ethnic frontier (Morrow, 2011; 2015b), and in Northern Ireland, suspicion, mistrust, and fear were instilled from the outset (Wright, 1987). From the time of partition to the

1960s, unease, skirmishes, and bubbling resentment were apparent across the island, particularly in the north (Darby, 1983). Following almost five decades of mounting tensions since the formation of Northern Ireland, the 'sectarian powder-keg … exploded in 1969' (Jeffs et al, 2019: 38). Three decades of terror ensued and while those killed were overwhelmingly male, every stratum of society was affected (Smyth and Hamilton, 2003). Ending the violence involved covert meetings between representatives of paramilitary organisations, political parties, and the British and Irish states, as well as public interventions of community, political, and religious leaders to condemn violence and appeal for peace (McKittrick and McVea, 2012). The IRA's 1994 announcement of a ceasefire marked cautious optimism of a decade where peacekeeping and peacemaking efforts gained traction. Paramilitary ceasefires were, however, subsequently revoked, and the death toll was continuously being added to, fuelling the scepticism of those disillusioned with the rhetoric of peace.

Amidst a backdrop of ongoing and often indiscriminate violence, political leaders from Ireland, Britain, and Northern Ireland produced what became the Belfast Good Friday Agreement (BGFA), approved by referendum on 10 April 1998 (British and Irish Governments, 1998). The agreement conferred power to the citizens of Northern Ireland to decide by majority vote whether to remain part of the UK or unite with Ireland. Building on previous intergovernmental negotiations and agreements between the British and Irish governments, the BGFA embedded the right of citizens to hold dual nationality as British and Irish, regardless of any future change in the constitutional status of Northern Ireland. The BGFA also provided new mechanisms for a democratically elected devolved government in Northern Ireland. Through the BGFA, a form of power-sharing was devised to ensure a single majority could not monopolise executive power, as had been the case for unionism since the creation of Northern Ireland. Under the new arrangements, power would be shared between unionism and nationalism, with the largest parties on both sides of the ethnonational divide appointing the First and Deputy First Minister for Northern Ireland (Hamber and Kelly, 2018).

Key issues for this ethnic frontier

From this historical backdrop and implicit within Wright's (1987) analysis of Northern Ireland as an *ethnic frontier* are four key issues: law and order, education, cultural and religious experience, and equity. Each of these issues is woven into the fabric of society and show themselves as indicators of division, evidenced in documents such as the Northern Ireland peace monitoring reports. These six reports (Nolan, 2012; 2013; 2014; Wilson, 2016; Gray et al, 2018; 2023) along with other tracking research (Morrow, 2019; Lundy et al, 2021) illustrate the depth of division which still exists in this contested society. Outlined here are some of the indicators of division which emanate from a past steeped in bloodshed, political wrangling, and intercommunity antagonism. These issues are examined to illustrate the complex nature of Northern Ireland as an ethnic frontier.

Law and order

It is no coincidence that the Department of Justice was the last to be devolved to the Northern Ireland assembly, by the British government, in 2010 (DoJ, 2023). This move illustrated the polarising tension that law and order and a theme like justice attract in the north of Ireland. In ethnic frontiers, law and order is a primary concern (Wright, 1987). This is evident in contested societies where a majority of the population aligns with the state while for others the legitimacy of the state, including the legal system, is challenged. Law and order have been at the epicentre of the conflict in Northern Ireland, with both of the major communities holding differing views about its place and power. Traditionally the Unionist community viewed policing as a necessary protection against terrorism. Both Nationalists and Republicans tended to view the legal system and policing as state-sponsored with Protestant and Unionist bias. To address this partisanship, the police service, under the BGFA, was obligated to reform. The Patten (1999) report made strong recommendations and conditions for reform of the then Royal Ulster Constabulary including the change of its name to the Police Service of Northern Ireland (PSNI) and reconfiguring its recruitment policy. The result was structural and policy reform aiming for a more inclusive police service to be representative of the whole community. While progress has been evident, challenges remain. For example, the PSNI board is made up of all the main political parties and recruitment policy has changed, yet violent fringe elements persist against the police (Gray et al, 2023). In February 2023, an attempted murder of a senior police officer is evidence of continued tension regarding the place of the PSNI in Northern Ireland society. Furthermore, the recruitment policy to create a more balanced police service appears to have flatlined with officers of a perceived Catholic background currently around 33 per cent (PSNI, 2024). Young people's experience of law and order and policing is fraught beyond that of ethno-territorial conflict, and their views are often mismatched to the older population (Gray et al, 2018; Murray et al, 2019). Policing, and law and order more generally, are still contested in this divided society and represent a key indicator of division.

Education

The education system in Northern Ireland has been segregated since the inception of the state in 1921 (Begley, 2019). This divided education system is indicative of yet another issue in an ethnic frontier (Wright, 1987). In the Northern Ireland context, segregated education is the norm, with most children and young people attending a state school, which is predominantly Protestant, or a Catholic Maintained school that is partially funded by the state. Only 7 per cent of students and pupils attend integrated schools (Devine et al, 2023), which have been designed to cater for young people from all religious backgrounds. Although young people seem to be enthused about integrated education (Devine et al, 2023) this percentage has plateaued, but it is predicted to increase in the coming years.

The lack of integration across the education system is indicative of wider socio-political issues. Segregated housing is a marked factor for many living in Northern Ireland, with approximately 90 per cent of social housing being in single identity communities (Community NI, 2019). Alongside this, teacher training at higher education level is instructed separately (Begley, 2019). In such a context, education remains a sector which is segregated at similar levels to the voting pattern, based in segregated communities and taught, in the main, by teachers who have been educated in segregated academic institutions. Milliken and Roulston (2022) suggest such segregation creates a systematic separation of teachers where educational institutions mostly employ from their own tradition. They suggest that parental choice of a particular school further cements the division which already exists. Moreover, they argue that the resultant duplication of this segregated system of choice is economically costly (Milliken and Roulston, 2022). Perhaps, this is a cost of 'choice' in a society where mixing with the 'other' is difficult given the underlying tension and antagonism (Morrow, 2011). The reality is somewhat of a contradiction when compared across recent attitudinal surveys. In the 2021 and 2022 Northern Ireland Life and Times survey (ARK, 2023a), 69 per cent and 68 per cent (respectively) of respondents stated they would prefer to have their children in a mixed religious school.

Religious and cultural traditions

Religious and cultural segregation in Northern Ireland is a third issue evident in Wright's (1987) analysis of Northern Ireland's ethnic frontier. As Byrne and Nadan (2011) suggest, religion serves as a divide which escalates tension. While the conflict in Northern Ireland is not exclusively about religion, religious identity has played a significant part in the division that exists. In the Northern Ireland census (NISRA, 2021), around 80 per cent of the population of Northern Ireland identify as one of the two main religions: Protestant or Catholic. In this context, religious affiliation, as Bruce (2002) suggests, does more than connect people to the sacred and supernatural. Religion in Northern Ireland connects its population to an ethnic and political dimension which ultimately leads its citizens towards an

Irish Nationalist or British Unionist perspective and identity. In Northern Ireland Catholics have traditionally tended towards Irish Nationalism while Protestants lean towards British Unionism. This religious force (Byrne and Nadan, 2011) acts in similar ways in other ethnic frontiers such as Israel/Palestine, Cyprus, and Sri Lanka (Wright, 1987; 1996).

Alongside religious and political affiliations are a set of cultural phenomena related to the divide. Two asymmetrical examples are the place of the Orange Order and Gaelic Athletic Association (GAA) with their historical and contemporary relationship connected to the two main religions in Northern Ireland. Within the Protestant tradition, the Orange Order sees itself as a defender of civil and religious liberties 'committed to the protection of the principles of the Protestant Reformation' (Grand Orange Lodge of Ireland, 2022). While the Orange Order would have had almost 100,000 members in the 1960s there are thought to be fewer than 30,000 today (*Belfast Telegraph*, 2023). Nonetheless, this segregated phenomenon has broad support from the Protestant community and shows how a cultural organisation has significant connections to a single religious community. The Orange Order celebrates the victory of the Protestant King William of Orange over the Catholic King James in 1690. This is celebrated through a five-month-long marching season. The centrepiece is the annual 12 July celebrations, which have had significant attention in recent years due to resistance shown against contentious walks through Nationalist areas. However, while still conflictual there have been some examples of a successful resolution to disputed parades (Gray et al, 2018; 2023). The Orange Order still represents a large sector of the Protestant community. Although it is community-based it has had long-standing official connections with Unionist political parties and the Protestant church (Govan, 2021).

While not an equal opposite, the GAA has its roots within the Catholic tradition. Its foundations are 'based on the traditional parishes and counties of Ireland' (GAA, 2023) and it is an amateur sporting organisation promoting indigenous Gaelic sports. In Ulster (Northern Ireland plus three counties from the Republic of Ireland) the GAA has a membership of around 150,000 (Irish News, 2022). The GAA, while changing, has a partisan and predominantly Catholic membership. Although officially apolitical it has in the past supported political causes such as the Irish Republican hunger strikes of the 1980s (Reynolds, 2017). The GAA and the Orange Order do not have a symmetrical relationship, but they do represent significant portions of each religious community. The asymmetrical relationship between both organisations shows that the conflict and the division is not equal and opposite but symptomatic of a division which, stemming from religion, has also developed into a cultural divide.

Religion, too, has a cross-over into political identities and persuasions, but it seems that religious identity is less important than it once was. This is evident as 92 per cent of census respondents stated their religion in 2011, lowering to 80 per cent in 2021 (NISRA, 2021). On the surface, this diminishing significance of religion shows a secularising trend in Northern Ireland, but it remains high for Western societies. Furthermore, Coulter et al (2023) suggest that while this trend is evident, partisan voting patterns still exist. Nevertheless, a remnant of belief relating to God being supportive of your cause is still evident when conflict is intertwined with religion and nationhood. As Byrne and Nadan (2011: 65) state, 'the most intractable conflicts exist when two ethnoreligious groups with separate identities compete for the same territory'.

Equity

Equity is a fourth issue deemed significant by Wright (1987) in an ethnic frontier. He contends that equity, fairness, and civil rights have been central to the conflict even prior to the inception of the Northern Ireland state. More specifically, the civil rights movement of the 1960s had five key demands regarding more equitable treatment of the minority Nationalist (mostly Catholic) community. These demands related to discrimination in the allocation of housing and government jobs, voting rights, the removal of the Special Powers Act, and the disbandment of the Ulster Special Constabulary. Although the underlying issues of the civil rights movement can be viewed from differing structural or agential perspectives (McGrattan, 2021), both communities had divergent experiences of the equity which was being demanded. While initially socialist and with cross-community support, the civil rights movement became more partisan with traditional Nationalist leadership obliged to abandon 'their conciliatory relationship with unionists' (Wright, 1987: 191). Daily experience of law and order, education, housing, and cultural and religious expression become issues about equity and the rights of each of the two main communities to live fairly and without discrimination. Indicators of division still permeate the society in the north of Ireland (Gray et al, 2023) and each side continues to dispute the others' concerns on equity.

Shifting identities

The indicators of division outlined here illustrate how the key issues of law and order, education, cultural and religious experience, and equity define this contested society of Northern Ireland. However, the picture is changing, with conflicting views and indicators about the future. In assembly elections in February 2020, for example, 20 per cent of the seats were won by those identifying as 'other'. This is a contrast with the 2017 election when 'other' seats were held by only 12 per cent of the assembly. This aligns with the demographic shift, as the Northern Ireland census shows that 21 per cent of the population designate as 'other' (NISRA, 2021). These two indicators of shifting religious self-designation and a change in the voting patterns indicate that while the support for more populist Unionist and Nationalist parties is plateauing, the middle ground is increasing. This shift could be seismic or, as proposed by Coulter et al (2023), has been misunderstood. They suggest that many of those designating as other may well be disproportionately closeted Unionists and could revert to type in any given election.

Alongside these shifts, young people have also been changing. For 20 years, the Young Life and Times surveys (YLT, 2023) have examined the views of young people, monitoring their attitudes towards each other, the 'Troubles', and its legacy. With around 2,000 respondents of 16-year-olds, this annual survey offers a reliable longitudinal source of attitudinal change. Since the inception of the survey in 2003 young people were consistently asked two questions: if they felt relations between the Protestant and Catholic communities are better, worse, or about the same in relation to the preceding five years; and also, how they think they will be in five years' time. Although a change in attitudes may have been expected through time, there has broadly been a similar response to both questions. In the 2023 YLT survey, 43 per cent of respondents thought that things were about the same as in the past (Schubotz, 2023). Regarding perceptions of community relations in the future, only 30 per cent thought they would be better, with 15 per cent of young people thinking that they would be worse. The attitudes of young people seem to have flatlined since the inception of the survey 20 years ago. While not filling the writers with optimism, there have been some changes evident for young people. Rather than being preoccupied with the 'Troubles', young people are more concerned with mental health, education, climate change, and human rights, with only a small number citing Brexit and the Troubles as key concerns (Gray et al, 2023). This attitudinal shift is a sign of change and suggests a movement away from the conflict of the past towards an interest in more everyday contemporary issues for young people.

Partial progress and more of the same

The conflict in Northern Ireland is by no means history, with some indicators of change emerging. These changes include a more stable justice system, an increasing interest in mixed if not integrated education, increased secularisation, and a movement, for young people at least, away from an obsession with the Troubles. Nonetheless, Northern Ireland is still a divided community with more peace walls (walls and fences separating communities to keep peace) than at the signing of the BGFA (Gray et al, 2023). This, alongside a police service with a significant majority from one community background, meagre attitudinal aspirations of peace from young people, and segregation high on almost every level, means that the peace is fragile and slow.

The division is further illustrated by exploring the four issues of law and order, education, cultural and religious experience, and equity. There is little doubt that these issues have had a significant impact on Northern Ireland and give a contextual basis for the conflict. As outlined in Chapter 5, there have been multiple peacebuilding concepts which have informed the responses to these issues. However, youth work, in itself, has been a constant throughout the Troubles and has offered a space for young people to make sense of their world in a place of insecurity, conflict, and violence.

What of youth work?

This context has meant that working with young people has been a priority since the start of the Northern Ireland conflict. While specific peacebuilding measures were a part of youth work processes, the development of policy in the early 1970s showed how the government prioritised the security and wellbeing of young people. The implementation of the Education and Libraries (Northern Ireland) 1972 Order (HMSO, 1972) instituted statutory youth work policy and provision in Northern Ireland. This provision came at a time when no other part of the UK or Ireland had statutory youth work policies. It also coincided with the most intensely violent period of the Troubles. While a policy and pledge for youth provision were in place, the youth work practice was not so well developed. Milliken (2020) recognised the naive role that youth work had in the early stages of the Troubles. He posits that while youth workers had worthy intentions, there was little understanding 'of the complexity of the situation or, in the absence of any reliable research, the nature of what amounted to effective practice' (Milliken, 2020: 439). It is evident that peacebuilding theory and practice was underdeveloped but so too was youth work. Peacebuilding approaches are discussed elsewhere in this book, but the rest of the chapter will outline youth work processes and theory and how they support the development of peace.

Youth work as a distinctive approach

Although youth work has been the focus of sometimes fierce debate (Davies, 2010) and ill-defined, as stated earlier, there is broad agreement that, at least within the UK and Ireland, it is a distinctive approach – different to other practices in working with young people (Taylor, 2017; Davies, 2021; Hammond and Harvey, 2021). It is framed conceptually as an educational endeavour of learning and growth, as opposed to a youth welfare or a youth protection pursuit. Youth work imbibes the purposes and processes of informal and non-formal education. While sometimes referred to as social pedagogy (Corney et al, 2023), youth work encapsulates wider ideas and practices, including sports and recreation. Seal (2016) narrows the focus further to an aligned phrase in defining youth work as critical pedagogy. Stemming from the educational movement of Paulo Freire (1921–1997), critical pedagogy seeks to address issues of power in the educational context whereby individuals can address their personal needs and the world which they inhabit. This Freirean critical pedagogy is a core foundation for youth work, which takes account of the dialectic nature of education, born out of conscientisation. While these terms, informal/non-formal education, and social and critical pedagogy, are somewhat synonymous, we use the more generic term of youth work as the general parlance of this book.

The planned, structured nature of non-formal education or youth work offers opportunities to develop skills and competencies (Council of Europe, 2000). However, this alone does not include the full array of 'unpredictable and creative' encounters and situations that can maximise learning for young people (IDYW, 2012: 2). For Jeffs and Smith (2011), the untapped potential for learning lies in informal education as the 'spontaneous process of cultivating learning … through conversation, and the exploration and enlargement of experience'. This focus is less on 'teaching' activities and more on 'crafting experiential learning opportunities, facilitating critical dialogues, or engaging in projects that allow young people to process their academic, familial and activist lives' (Baldridge, 2020: 620).

While youth work includes elements of non-formal education, it is the embedding of informal education as a philosophical stance and an operational imperative that makes the youth work approach distinct. Seal and Frost (2014: 1) describe the approach as operating through words and ideas – 'it is the conversations (words) we have and the meanings (ideas) which we help people create in their lives that define us'. This work happens with and through relationships. Tiffany (2001: 94), in exploring the essence of relationships, proposes that 'a connection or association exists or is formed, between two or more things, people or ideas'. However, the interpersonal dimension of relationships recognises how 'something tangible and meaningful exists between people' (Tiffany, 2001: 94), emphasising care within the connection.

Youth work writers stress the equal power relationship between the youth worker and the young person. The youth worker starts where the young person starts and moves forward (Davies and Merton, 2009). In this approach, the worker tips the balance of power in favour of the young person (Davies, 2021) and, more controversially, the young person exercises their active and ongoing choice to engage (Ord, 2016; Williamson, 2020; Davies, 2021). These conditions for engagement establish clear intent for the purpose of youth work, laying fertile ground for power to be held and ignited within and by the young person.

Further to these features of youth work, various defining characteristics have been outlined (Jeffs and Smith, 2010; Ord, 2016; Davies, 2021; Hammond and McArdle, 2024). These characteristics are defined as the necessity of focusing on young people; the voluntary participation of young people; the creation of spaces for young people to associate with each other and significant adults; fostering democracy; and emphasising the education and welfare of young people. However, along with these features and defining characteristics are processes which enable young people to learn informally.

Youth work processes

Although there has been limited writing explicitly on youth work and peacebuilding, the literature emphasises skills, ideologies, and attitudes to promote peace (McMullan, 2018; Hamilton, 2022; Hamilton and Hammond, 2023). There is an overlap in these ideas to the processes which generic youth work employs. While the defining characteristics and features of youth work demonstrate purpose, the processes by which youth workers engage add another dimension to the peacebuilding practice. Youth work offers versatility and is uniquely placed to engage young people in contested societies in a way that is distinct from other educational or social activities in which young people participate. As such, the youth work processes discussed in the following sections add complementary dimensions to peacebuilding parlance and practice.

In a study by one of this book's authors (Hammond, 2018), four key processes emerged from researching the perspectives of 32 youth workers in Northern Ireland. These four key youth work processes were: relationship building; conversation and dialogue; participation; and learning through experience. The study found that youth workers engage in these four processes to produce personal development and learning outcomes for young people and form the basis for youth work practice. The research respondents suggested that because of the informal nature of youth work's educational endeavour, these processes are essential in engaging young people on an equal basis. Each process in turn is explored in the following, with a more significant focus on the major finding that conversation and dialogue ultimately drive the other processes.

Relationship building

In the study, the importance of building relationships with young people was not seen as a purpose but as the foundation for further work with the young person. It facilitates the building of skills and trust while at the same time supporting young people to learn. For some, relationship building generated the 'space for change' to bring about transformation. The research suggests that youth workers regard the relationship with young people as a 'journey' and favoured the idea of 'accompanying' young people on their terms rather than working to presupposed agendas or predetermined outcomes. These perspectives aligned with the youth work literature (Tiffany, 2001; Williamson, 2020) and the allied ideas of Freire (1970), Rogers (1967), and Büber (1970), where positive relationships are viewed as central to the learning process. Relationship building is a central process which enables depth in learning and creates the spaces for new thinking to begin. De St Croix and Doherty (2023) affirm this relational aspect of youth work as a process which they suggest creates fluid associations between youth workers and young people.

Conversation and dialogue

The process of conversation and dialogue is inextricably linked with that of relationship building. While conversation leads to relationships with young people, building a relationship is equally a way of enabling the conversation to move deeper. This connection between dialogue and building strong relationships enables transformative learning (Mezirow, 2003). The focus for youth work practitioners is to enable young people to use conversation and dialogue to help them make sense of their experiences, batting ideas and thoughts forward and back to shape insights into their world. The respondents in Hammond's (2018) research talked of how youth work was driven by conversation and created a critical space for young people to clarify their thinking and then devise different ways to act. This idea concurs with that of Freire (1996) as he suggests that critical thinking is a process of conscientisation where those who are in a state of passive acceptance and conformity are made aware of their views and actions through dialogue and conversation. The process of conversation and dialogue has the potential for transformative encounters with young people. As will be seen, this powerful process is well documented with scholars emphasising its varying tenets.

Participation

Of the four processes explored in Hammond's (2018) study, participation is perhaps the most easily recognised, yet, evidence suggests, the least understood. Youth workers had a wide range of perspectives on participation, with the continuum of expression ranging from 'just taking part' and the notion of choice, to deeper insights on power relationships, control, and decision-making by young people. The youth workers' vocabulary in the study included ideas about young people having their say in the issues that affect them – 'having their voices heard', 'control', 'ownership', and 'power'. While the literature stresses the political dimension of participation (Arnstein, 1969; Crick, 2004) and its educational process for increasing engagement in the learning experience (Dewey, 2007), the respondents rarely referred to these themes. Instead, few recognised the political dimension in their practice of participative processes. The notion of democracy, as featured earlier in this section, was rarely mentioned by respondents, seldom referred to in terms of power taking and never used as a process for political education.

Learning through experience

The fourth process examined in the study was that of learning through experience. Dewey (1997) posits that at the heart of learning is the experience of the learner and that this experience is not in isolation from context nor from the relationships with others. While not all respondents in Hammond's (2018) study demonstrated a full understanding of the role of experience in their youth work, they recognised a connection between experience and learning. With a relationship between the youth worker and the young person, the worker can enter a participative dialogue and assist the young person in making sense of their experience. In youth work this experiential dynamic enables young people to learn from each other as well as from the activities in which they engage. The theoretical basis for experiential learning of this nature is promoted by such theorists as Piaget, Vygotsky, Kolb, and Dewey (Cooperstein and Kocevar-Weidinger, 2004). It is rooted in adult and lifelong learning and 'casts the individual as a central actor in a drama of personal meaning-making' (Fenwick, 2000: 248). This 'meaning making' enables the young person to find personal agency in their social interactions.

The significance of conversation and dialogue

Hammond's (2018) research demonstrates the reciprocal relationship between these four key youth work processes. Deeper analysis showed that the process of conversation and dialogue was deemed paramount. Some respondents talked of conversation in inspirational terms while others initially glossed over the process but subtly showed how they frequently engaged young people in dialogical ways. The data included many examples of the process and practice of conversation. Often, the process of conversation and dialogue was inextricably linked to that of relationship building. The connection between relationship building and conversation demonstrates the interdependence of both processes, which are symbiotic in nature and iterative in function – building one from the other. This reflects the connection made by Mezirow (2003) in deciphering how dialogue and building strong relationships work to enable transformative learning. He outlines the vital part which relationship building plays in creating a critical discourse with the learner.

Dialogue and conversation were referred to as a process to get beyond the initial rapport and engage young people to think and develop things for themselves. The literature indicates that moving beyond the initial phase of chit-chat and banter is essential in moving into a more intentional and purposeful engagement with the young person (Ord, 2016). Furthermore, deepening the discourse aligns with Jeffs and Smith's (2005) view of conversation and the level of engagement that is needed to help facilitate change. They promote the idea of 'trusting in conversation' in order to be with the young person 'rather than seeking to act upon them' (Jeffs and Smith, 2005: 31). The respondents in Hammond's (2018) study recognised that this type of conversation fosters a two-way relationship and brings about understanding and learning.

While respondents illustrated a deftness in the practice of conversation and dialogue, few explicitly mentioned theoretical perspectives, models, or concepts. Their responses did, however, align with ideas found in the writings of Freire, Büber, Mezirow, and Habermas. Developing a critical consciousness is a primary focus of Freire's (2007: 40) view of dialogue, whereby 'critical understanding leads to critical action'. The focus for the youth work practitioners was reflective of this in enabling young people to think more deeply about themselves and in turn change or act upon their new self-conceptualisation. The youth worker's role, as suggested by one respondent, is to draw out what the young person is saying and challenge them to do something better while another suggested that it is through conversation that young people change. This emphasis on change certainly aligns well with the action orientation which Freire (1970) advocates.

The equalising of power in dialogue emerged as the most critical condition to achieve some of the philosophical outcomes of conversation. In the first instance, the power, status, and hierarchy between the youth worker and the young person was significant. A dominant assumption of the respondents was that theirs was a different type of learning relationship than the assumed hierarchical relationship of formal educators. The young person would have 'complete ownership', one respondent said. This high aspiration delineates the notion of power tipped in favour of the young person (Davies, 2021) within the learning process and juxtaposes youth work against the formal education of schools. The ideas of Martin Büber resonated with the aspirations of the respondents who thought of conversation as a two-way process which endeavours to find mutual ground. This philosophical perspective reaches for what Büber (1970) suggests is the 'space between' and intimates a levelling out of a potential power imbalance between talker and listener. The reciprocity and equality of which Büber writes was evident in much of what was said by the respondents. Where status does not easily allow for equalised power, the youth worker's skills are invoked to boost the position and power of the young person.

Dialogue, listening, and the use of empathy created greater equality between the young person and the youth worker (Hammond, 2018). This approach is not about telling but actively listening and hearing the young person. One respondent said that 'it's actually hearing what they [young people] are saying not just nodding your head' that brings about the change. This concurs with Mezirow (2003), who argues that conversation involves high levels of interpersonal skills and insight. He denotes these skills as involving 'having an open mind, learning to listen empathetically, "bracketing" premature judgment, and seeking common ground' (Mezirow, 2003: 60). For a young person, having power over their own choice and direction in dialogue further enhances the dialogical features of the equalised conversation. Another respondent illustrated the point by framing conversation as a process where 'you're not really in control', whereby directionality in conversation is the preserve of the young person. While no respondents explicitly referred to Habermas' (1987) ideas, the aspiration for constraint-free conversation (Ewert, 1991) was evident from all the respondents. It is the absence of constraint in equal and shared conversation that can enable open learning to take place. Habermas (1984) acknowledges that this is a sophisticated form of dialogue that necessitates a high degree of maturity on behalf of the participants to create open and honest discourse. If young people are infantilised, then the power balance will remain with the adult worker and the growth and ultimate transformative learning will be stunted. Equalised power in conversation can build a dialogical encounter with emancipatory qualities for reflective learning. Freire (1970) suggests that, alongside creating a critical consciousness, dialogue is about achieving greater equality between the learner and the educator. He suggests that it is not one working for the other, but it is an equal partnership and a co-learning environment which is being created.

Bakhtin (1986) argues that learning is dialogical and two-way. Dialogue of this nature, Freire (1970) suggests, is to emancipate in a way that emphasises and creates ownership of the learning. Starting with the young person, enabling them to determine the issues and find the answers for themselves was an emancipatory notion expressed by most respondents as they spoke of the purpose of conversation. The dialogical can build more comprehensive understandings of self or other phenomena, and in doing so can reveal or build some new truths. Bakhtin (1981) states that truth is not owned by one person but 'it is born between people collectively searching for truth, in the process of their dialogic interaction' (Bakhtin, 1981: 110). One respondent spoke of conversation for discovery 'because young people are able to learn about themselves'. The truth-making can then lead to action, which was

Figure 2.1: Conversation as the cog which drives the other three youth work processes

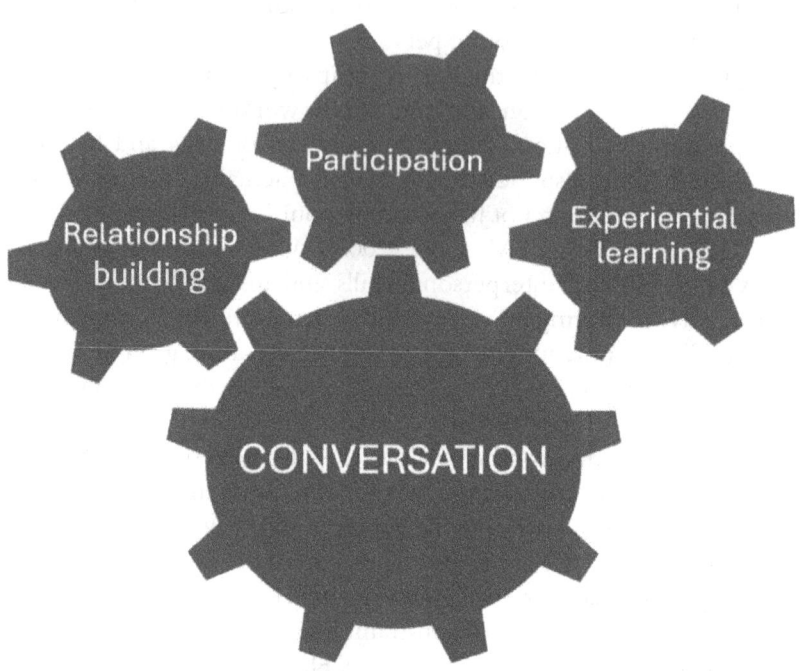

widely recognised by the respondents as an outcome of conversation. This type of learning partnership Mezirow (2003) deems to be transformative.

Hammond's (2018) analysis placed conversation as the central cog (Figure 2.1), which drives other key youth work processes. This demonstrates a shift in emphasis, away from the centrality of relationships and relationship building, often heralded as the central purpose of youth work, to conversation and dialogue. Thus, creating a critical consciousness for young people. However, it is the nature and characteristics of this dialogue which can either open or close learning and emancipatory possibilities. It is this critical conscientiousness that enables young people to learn something different about themselves and the world which they inhabit.

Conversation and peacebuilding

While conversation and dialogue emerge as a central process to youth work, there is also strong evidence that such a methodology is key to peacebuilding. In the study upon which this book is based, Hamilton (2022) highlights that critical thinking and dialogue was found to be a significant peacebuilding process. While Hamilton's study does not find that dialogue is exclusively the ideation of peacebuilders, it does have prominence. His study shows that peacebuilders engaging in youth work gather around four viewpoints (detailed in Chapters 7 and 8). These perspectives illustrate a diversity of approaches to peacebuilding. However, in viewpoint 1 a desire for political engagement through dialogue was found to be a dominant ideation among peacebuilding practitioners with a depth and breadth of peacebuilding and youth work experience. Aligning with a similar finding in Hammond's (2018) study, practitioners in this viewpoint held that dialogue and critical thinking bring about greater potential for personal and political change. Hammond also found that dialogue created space for critical thinking (Hammond and McArdle, 2024). Perhaps engaging in dialogue, where difficult conversations can take place, will bring about the change or peace which young people need and often crave. In the next chapters, the approaches utilised by peacebuilding youth workers and the theory and literature which inform such practice will be explored.

Conclusion

This chapter has demonstrated that to maintain and sustain a positive peace all societies must develop and invest in law and order, education, cultural and religious experience, and equity. In societies with competing claims to territory and power, that Wright (1987) names as ethnic frontiers, these four domains face seismic ruptures and manifest as both symptoms and causes of conflict that periodically erupt into violence. Northern Ireland is an exemplar ethnic frontier and a pertinent case of protracted conflict with parallels to other contested societies. From this case, we draw out insights which will be of interest to peacebuilders around the world. Youth work can play a transformational role in peacebuilding. This is due to the processes by which it engages young people, the central one being conversation/dialogue.

3

Power and legitimacy: entering the world of the peacebuilder

The people on the ground need to be pushing for change rather than having one or two per cent of the population at the top dictating everything down for the majority. (YW20)

Introduction: clash of the titans

For ideas to persist, they need weight and legitimacy. And what greater weight than the promise of history? Ireland is a land of indigenous tribes who have co-existed through a sophisticated system of social laws and systems of justice. Historically, where harm was caused by one neighbour to another, feudal laws were an agreed process to repair the damage caused within the relationship and make reparation for the pain inflicted. The emphasis was not on punishment but on the repair and restoration of community through healing. This system of restorative justice was replicated across the globe in Native American tribes, aboriginal lands, and India, and was to be rekindled for contemporary living in Northern Ireland. At the turn of the 21st century, following the signing of the 1998 Belfast Good Friday Agreement, the issue of so-called 'punishment' beatings and shootings in Republican and Loyalist communities was relentless and intransigent. Restorative justice was revived as an alternative to this violent 'penal' system.

Around the same time, a tsunami of money came flooding in. And with money comes power. The Downing Street Declaration was signed in 1993 following peace talks between the British and Irish governments and the political parties in Northern Ireland. Then, the ceasefires of 1994 by the Irish Republican Army and the Combined Loyalist Military Command were announced and hopes to solidify peace in Northern Ireland were shored up by an injection of cash. In September 1994, the European Commission announced that it would add £47 million to the International Fund for Ireland, followed closely by the European Parliament contributing another £40 million (CAIN, 2023b). Then came the introduction of the European Union (EU)'s PEACE I programme of 1995 to 1999, for Northern Ireland and the border regions of Ireland, which contributed €667 million (€500 million provided by the EU, €167 million from the UK and Irish governments) (Bush and Houston, 2011). And with four iterations of peace programmes across the region to date, the investment so far is a cool €2,265 million (Gomersall, 2024). The money was staggering, with the ability to change communities, change direction, and change the very language of peace.

This chapter questions how one titan idea gains dominance over another; how political actors and grassroots activists position themselves in the peacebuilding landscape; how legitimacy is built and won; and how these can influence the direction of peace. These struggles are played out in the arena of everyday peacebuilding practices with young people (Berents, 2018). The competing influences of top-down economically driven approaches against more historically and culturally rooted indigenous perspectives mark out core tensions for practitioners to grapple with. In analysing these tensions, the chapter draws on two complementary 'theories of practice'. Both theories are concerned with how human practices, in this case, youth work and peacebuilding, are structured in such a way that makes the practice meaningful and provides a sense of how things ought to be done. These theoretical lenses raise questions over who defines and controls the peacebuilding agenda. Themes of identity, competence, power, and reflexivity in peacebuilding are examined.

First, Lave and Wenger's (1991) work on communities of practice is discussed as a way of capturing the everyday interactional processes by which peacebuilding practice is embodied and learned. This is followed by an overview of Bourdieu's (1990; 2014) thinking tools, which invites a deeper analysis of asymmetrical power relationships and struggles within and surrounding the field of youth sector peacebuilding.

Learning the craft of youth sector peacebuilding

Lave and Wenger (1991: 98) define communities of practice as: 'A set of relations among persons, activity, and world, over time and in relation with other tangential and overlapping communities of practice.' Communities of practice offer a powerful sense of belonging to participants as sites where meaningful activities are co-constructed and collective identities formed. Youth sector peacebuilding is not a single community of practice but rather a 'constellation' of communities made up of practitioners situated in local, regional, and international contexts. Their mutual engagement in the domain of peacebuilding work with young people, which involves a shared repertoire of concepts, approaches, processes, ideas, actions, stories, information, and discourses, is the basis of their participation in these communities of practice (Wenger, 1998).

Participation is not enforced. Members only tend to stay if they have a stake in the practice, that is, they desire to contribute to attaining and defining 'regimes of competence'. These regimes of competence are the commonly understood standards that deem a practice effective

(Wenger-Trayner and Wenger-Trayner, 2014). Communities of practice are not reliant on consensus. Often, they are sites of disagreement and challenge as participants continually negotiate and re-negotiate the purpose of their practice and how to legitimately pursue it. Applying this lens to youth sector peacebuilding focuses attention on how regimes of competence are generated, reproduced, or challenged. Of interest is not a single definition of youth sector peacebuilding but rather the multiple ways in which people engage in the practice and how it is reproduced by both newcomers and more experienced practitioners.

It is through participation in a community of practice that competence and expertise are developed. Lave and Wenger (1991) depict interactions between 'newcomers', 'near peers' and 'old-timers' as the space through which meaning is made and learning happens. Newcomers learn the practice from 'near peers' who are only slightly ahead of them in the learning process, and from old-timers who are established in the community, through a process of 'legitimate peripheral participation'. It is a process of testing, trialling, and learning ever more complex tasks. By participating in 'peripheral tasks' and observing others within the community of practice, newcomers learn how to handle difficult situations – where to prioritise time, which relationships to invest in, how to cultivate viable 'shortcuts', and how to depict success. In other words, they are accepted into the community freed from the burden of expectation placed upon an experienced practitioner while simultaneously being invited to contribute in a meaningful way to the practice, which is always in the process of becoming. Learning arises through interaction with the world and others. The journey towards full participation is enacted through sustained engagement and assuming increasing levels of responsibility, decision-making, and autonomy, surrounded by peers and old-timers (Wenger, 1998). In learning and negotiating the culture and assumed ways of operating within a community of practice, newcomers add to conventional wisdom and generate new relationships with people and bodies of knowledge which shapes the development of the practice. A shared vocabulary and discourse evolve, which helps to signify membership in a community of practice where practitioners gather around common challenges and dilemmas.

This book examines how practitioners conceptualise youth sector peacebuilding through the lens of communities of practice. We have observed tendencies for relative newcomers to gravitate towards a particular approach to peacebuilding that embraces the predominant policy paradigm. Subsequently, a certain stability is added, preserving and reproducing the dominance afforded to a particular enactment of peacebuilding with young people. As well as supporting the continuity of practice, we also seek to interject new models and critical perspectives that serve to unsettle the reproduction of approaches that prioritise (inter)personal over social transformation.

Negotiating meaning in practice

Negotiating meaning is fundamental to communities of practice and involves inseparable processes of *participation* and *reification*, where one relies on and enriches the other (Wenger, 1998; Farnsworth et al, 2016). Participation, as indicated already, includes interaction, mutual engagement, and active membership. Reification refers to how ideas, concepts, processes, and information are codified and packaged as artefacts and units or bodies of knowledge. A 'theory of change', for instance, devised as part of a youth peacebuilding programme, is a reification of the practice. An evaluation form is a reification of what is considered a meaningful measurement of the practice. A governmental peacebuilding strategy is a reification on a large scale, which points to schemes of proposed activities to achieve overarching aims and outcomes. Through reification, abstract representations are injected with a concrete quality and status which informs participation in practice.

Reification is a process of adding symbolism to specific practices as a shorthand, making it more manageable for 'novices' and 'experts' alike to learn evolving processes. Such reification gives form and substance to particular understandings, which subsequently become a point of reference for negotiating meaning. Or, as Wenger (1998: 58) puts it, 'we project our meanings into the world and then we perceive them as existing in the world, as having a reality of their own'. A spiralling process of reification and participation is the basis of negotiating meaning, which in turn constitutes a practice. Neither participation nor reification are static but constantly unfolding and evolving. Implementing a theory of change (reification) by facilitating group work sessions with young people (participation), for instance, necessarily involves interpretations of the theory, which impact upon the theory itself. The 'power of reification' stems from its 'succinctness' and 'portability' in representing complex ideas and processes and helping to coordinate action and comprehension within and across communities of practice (Wenger, 1998: 61). However, reification also risks ambiguity and oversimplification of deep understanding and tacit knowledge that requires direct participation in the practice itself. Therefore, 'reification always rests on participation: what is said, represented, or otherwise brought into focus always assumes a history of participation as a context for its interpretation' (Wenger, 1998: 67).

Our research codifies multiple perspectives on peacebuilding with young people, generating a reification of practice approaches. In Chapter 8, we map these perspectives onto a model of youth sector peacebuilding. The model introduces new language and conceptualisations of practice, offering a basis for new forms of reflexivity for both newcomers and experienced practitioners. As a reification, it will be most useful as a framework for negotiating meaningful practice when considered in relation to participation in peacebuilding practice with young people. Our model is intended to raise questions over how certain reifications in the form of youth and peacebuilding policy are created in such a way that they 'force people more or less towards certain interpretation' despite being 'never fully deterministic' (Farnsworth et al, 2016: 147).

The policy and practice tug of war

The domain of youth sector peacebuilding exists within a universe or *landscape* of interrelated communities of practice. Notable in our research is the interdependence of distinctive practitioner and policy spheres. *Boundary objects* are utilised to enable connections across these communities of practice. A peacebuilding policy, a funding application, or a contractual offer of funding each act as a boundary object, connecting practitioners with a policy community of practice made up of policy makers, administrators, managers, and evaluators. These documents represent multilayered and historical relations between practitioners, the organisations they are part of, and those who enable access to funding.

Wenger (1998: 80) emphasises that the enterprise pursued by a community of practice is shaped collectively by the participants and 'is never fully determined by an outside mandate, by a prescription, or by any individual participant'. Where policy making seeks to dictate practice, practitioners draw on conventional wisdom that underpins meaningful engagement with young people and carve out their own approaches. Such approaches invariably deviate from the assumptions and discourses of policy. Over time, however, as conventional wisdom has assimilated the outcomes and accountability requirements of funders, practices morph, and what once was peripheral moves to occupy a more central position. This is exemplified in the proliferation of vocational qualifications that have become a staple of peacebuilding. Youth work practitioners mould their participatory, voluntary, and informal approaches to fit more structured, regulated, and formal programmes of learning premised on securing a minimum number of 'completers' (de St Croix, 2018; Knox et al, 2023). While Wenger reinforces that 'no practice subsumes another' (Farnsworth et al, 2016: 149), the interdependence of practitioner and policy communities of practice construct social relations imprinted with power hierarchies.

A framework for analysing power: plugging into Bourdieu

Lave and Wenger's theory of communities of practice does not set out to theorise power relations, although it does acknowledge how power arises through the construction of *regimes of competence* in communities of practice exercised by 'those who have legitimacy to enforce it – or who can successfully challenge it' (Farnsworth et al, 2016: 153). In response to a limited focus on distributions of power in communities of practice, this text has adopted the 'plug and play' approach as advocated by Wenger-Trayner (2013), referring to the combining of theoretical lenses to enable a more holistic analysis. Wenger-Trayner purports Bourdieu's theory of practice to be a 'good candidate for plug and play' due to the shared emphasis on practice, with distinctive entry points. Bourdieu is primarily focused on 'structural power relations and their reproduction at scale' (Farnsworth et al, 2016: 152).

The opening sections of this chapter have focused on *communities of practice* to ground the use of social theory in the process of being and becoming a practitioner. Youth sector peacebuilding has been characterised as a constellation of communities of practice around the globe that have formed through mutual engagement in peacebuilding work with young people. Themes of legitimacy and competence have been emphasised, raising questions about who has the authority to set the parameters on what constitutes effective peacebuilding work with young people. Intersections and interdependence with a policy community of practice add further complexity to how predominant narratives and practices are shaped and reproduced through time. Bourdieu's theory of practice introduces additional concepts to critique power and peripheral players in youth sector peacebuilding, ultimately pinpointing which and whose agendas are driving youth sector peacebuilding and to what ends.

Making practical sense: lessons from Bourdieu

Writing prolifically throughout the second half of the 20th century, Pierre Bourdieu (1930–2002) developed interdependent analytical 'thinking tools' germinating from his anthropological work. These tools are useful for thinking critically about youth sector peacebuilding. While a deep exploration of Bourdieu's work is beyond the scope of this book, an overview of his key ideas provides a context for our analysis. Following Bourdieu, we refer to the field of youth sector peacebuilding. This field exists within the larger field of peacebuilding, which in turn intersects with multiple other fields including that of international relations and the political field.

Bourdieu sought to refute theories that employ overly deterministic or excessively autonomous accounts of human behaviour. Therefore, he developed theoretical constructs that incorporate and account for contradiction. He strives to convey the illogical, imprecise, and iterative *logic of practice* that should be preserved in studies of the social world, noting the organic nature of practices that are never fixed but morph over time, space, and context (Bourdieu, 1977). This resonates with Lave and Wenger's understanding of practice as the site where meaning is continually negotiated. Practices such as peacebuilding are not the product of linear input–output mechanisms that can be fully represented through a set of underpinning principles or encapsulated in a model. While conscious and rational strategies form part of the field of peacebuilding, Bourdieu's logic of practice emphasises how agents draw on a 'practical sense' of how to think, behave, and act in particular settings and scenarios. This practical sense, which generates 'practical knowledge', comes from immersion in the social world and is internalised primarily below the level of consciousness.

Bourdieu (1994) compared this practical sense with a 'feel for the game'. It is similar to how players in a team sport acquire, over time, intuitions about where and when to position themselves and anticipate the moves of others. Such sensibilities are developed by people as they participate in social practices. Youth work practitioners invoke this practical sense during interactions with young people. Through the twists and turns of conversation, new thoughts are sparked on how to engage the group in a meaningful way. A whole programme of activities and incremental participatory processes begins to unfold in their mind's eye. All the while, they hold the space for conversation, listening intently, bringing quieter voices to the fore, managing expectations, and connecting passions or frustrations to future possible actions. They also have an immediate sense of the resources that would be required, who the gatekeepers are, and how they can leverage support to access all that is needed to turn their vision into a reality. Of course, this is only one (albeit simplified) example of the thousands of daily thought processes and actions a practitioner makes as they go about their work.

Attempting to isolate every micro thought and action would make it almost impossible to engage seamlessly in this or any social field. Imagine the incongruence that would occur in conversation when a practitioner notices that a young person is less vocal and stops to make a conscious 'cost–benefit' analysis of the pros and cons of each course of action – say nothing so as not to put the young person on the spot; invite them to speak to make them feel valued; make a generic comment about the importance of hearing what everyone thinks. Agents who attempted this would be in a perpetual state of introspection, caught in a trap of constantly trying to rationalise their next course of action while the rest of the world moves by around them. In practice, such thought processes are largely automated, and action occurs without the need to stop and consciously map out what to do or say next. It is for this reason, Bourdieu (1977: 109) states, 'practice has a logic which is not that of logic'; it is a logic of practical sense-making rather than rational logic models. To describe where this practical sense of the social world comes from, Bourdieu developed the concept of habitus.

Habitus

Habitus, according to Bourdieu, refers to how certain ideas and practices become dominant within a social field and tend to be repeated and reproduced. This concept incorporates but is not exclusively concerned with how human thinking and action emerge from past experiences, generating perceptions of viable courses of action. It accounts for how social structures and relationships inform, although do not fully determine, future trajectories. For instance, while there are a multitude of ways in which a practitioner might approach peacebuilding with young people, from a Bourdieusian perspective, this sense of agency is restricted by certain structures. Practitioners encounter and are restricted by elements of the youth sector peacebuilding field arising from traditions, institutional norms, social relationships, conventional ideas, and core concepts that have given legitimacy to this domain of practice in the past and are carried forward and modified in the present.

Bourdieu (1994: 131) emphasises the 'structuring' dimension of habitus where he defines it as 'a property of actors (whether individuals, groups or institutions) that comprises a structured and structuring structure'. Put differently, habitus is 'structured' by past experiences and early socialisation yet is also forward-looking and plays a central role in 'structuring' future trajectories. It encompasses two primary functions. One is to help us fit into the social spaces we inhabit. The other is to help us move across social spaces and acquire a sense of the codified meanings, relationships, and behaviours that form the 'rules of the game' in fields of practice we are unfamiliar with. These fields include different professions, social classes, ethnic groups, political regimes, and so on. In sum, the habitus is what mediates engagement in the world and provides 'a sense of what is reasonable or unreasonable, likely or unlikely, our beliefs about what are the obvious actions to take and the natural ways of doing them' (Maton, 2014: 57). While every individual embodies a habitus, their habitus necessarily shares certain affinities with others, giving way to a collective habitus. Habitus, therefore, is described as 'subjective but not individual' (Bourdieu, 1977: 86).

Over time we develop 'schemes of perception, conception, and action', or dispositions, which flow from the habitus and help us to navigate, and often reproduce, all the commonly accepted norms and peculiarities within and across fields (Bourdieu, 1977: 86). The habitus is constantly tuning in to the unwritten codes of behaviour and the 'regimes of competence' within particular social spaces. The unconscious internalising of these codes and regimes mediates our sense of belonging as well as our adaptability to participate with relative ease or uneasiness in the various social fields we inhabit. For instance, a person entering the field of youth sector peacebuilding whose habitus cannot conceive of learning taking place beyond the strictures of a didactic formal setting is likely to encounter an emphasis on dialogical and participatory approaches as disorienting. Their habitus conflicts with the field habitus, and their experience is that of a fish out of water (Bourdieu and Wacquant, 1992).

While the empirical research underpinning this book does not explicitly set out to examine habitus, it is acknowledged that habitus is at play in orienting practitioners' thoughts and actions within the field of youth sector peacebuilding. Emphasis is placed on identifying and analysing 'the schemes of perception and appreciation' (Bourdieu, 1990: 73) associated with the habitus. Such schemes of perception are inscribed with varying degrees of value and distinction, creating a source of tension. Certain ways of thinking and being are legitimised and incentivised, while others are discredited and devalued (Swartz, 2013). To this end, habitus must be understood alongside Bourdieu's concepts of field and capital. These play a significant role in structuring how agents make practical sense within the world of youth sector peacebuilding and perceive the parameters of the possible and unattainable.

The field of youth sector peacebuilding

While distinctive practitioner and policy communities of practice were discussed as separate but interdependent, both these communities of practice can be understood within the broader concept of a youth sector peacebuilding *field*. The field of youth sector peacebuilding can be understood as one of many overlapping and intersecting social spaces in which individuals participate. Through these fields, shared and competing interests are pursued (Costa and Murphy, 2015). The field of youth sector peacebuilding could be understood as an intersection of three larger fields outlined in Figure 3.1, drawing on, yet distinctive from, practices that are established in these domains. The social world, from this perspective, is made up of multiple intersecting fields.

Underpinning social fields is a logic of practice, a generic field habitus, or, more simply, a practical common sense. This common sense provides a certain structure where the 'orthodox way of doing things' is sensed and internalised by those within the field (Grenfell, 2014: 4). This common sense is not an inherent property of the field; rather, it reflects a history of social relations where dominant actors have constructed norms that have been embraced by those in less influential positions. In the field of youth sector peacebuilding, neoliberal ideas have infused the common-sense world. This theme is discussed further in Chapter 4.

'With caution', Bourdieu writes, a field can be compared with a *game*, bearing in mind that 'a field is not the product of a deliberate act of creation, and it follows rules or, better, regularities, that are not explicit and codified' (Bourdieu and Waquant, 1992: 98). This game analogy captures the embodied and instinctive nature of participation in fields of practice. Immersion within fields accentuates actors' sensibilities to 'the tempo, rhythms and unwritten rules of the game' (Maton, 2014: 53). Developing perceptions of valuable conduct within the field 'tend[s] to take place below

Figure 3.1: Field of youth sector peacebuilding

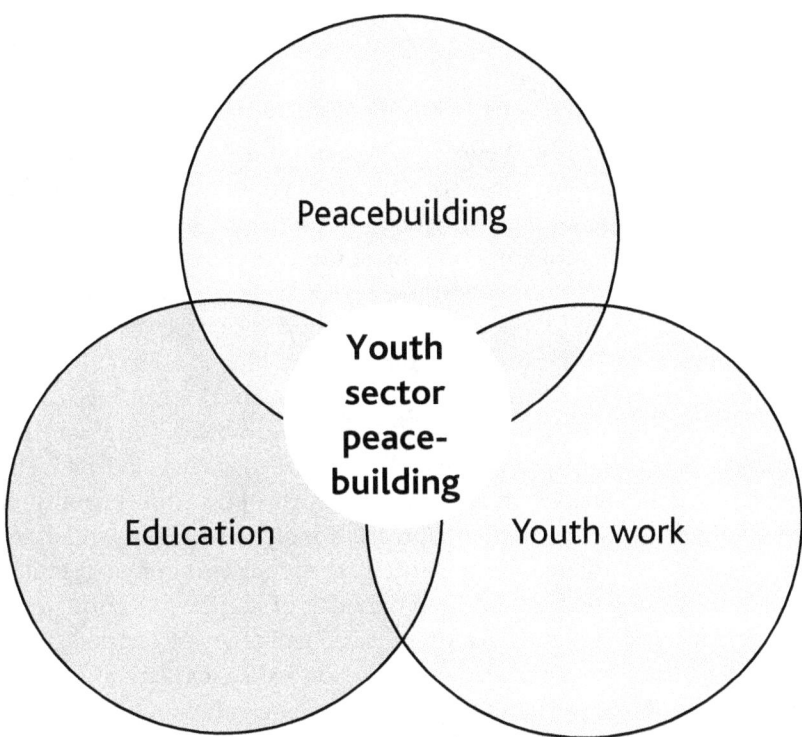

the level of consciousness' (Bourdieu, 1990: 73). This concept of 'below the level of consciousness' is often referred to by Bourdieu as being 'pre-reflexive'. It stands in contrast to 'reflexivity', which involves consciously and critically examining social power relations in the historical development of fields.

In the field of youth sector peacebuilding, the interests of practitioners vary, as do those of researchers, policy makers, funders, politicians, young people, and activists, representing a fundamental source of antagonisms that generate a 'flow of social energy' (Rawolle and Lingard, 2013: 122). For instance, control over the peacebuilding agenda is contested at multiple levels. Individual practitioners and policy makers across different organisations and institutions have different understandings of what should be prioritised in peacebuilding. As illustrated in the introduction to this chapter, influence over the direction of peacebuilding is dependent on the resources at hand and the relative legitimacy attached to those resources. Grassroots peace activists draw on a legitimacy achieved through the historical development of indigenous practices, while state-centric institutions garner authority from the power to accumulate and distribute peace monies. Bourdieu captures such power relations through an analysis of how distinct types of capitals operate within fields.

Capital and legitimacy

Bourdieu identifies four archetypes of capital – economic, cultural, social, and symbolic. Economic forms of capital in youth sector peacebuilding are evident in the vast sums of money poured into peacebuilding from philanthropic organisations and inter-state funds. At an organisational level, economic capital is strengthened through securing funding contracts and ownership of, or access to, assets that support peacebuilding activities such as buildings, buses, and recreational facilities. At an individual level economic capital is experienced in salaries which are often short term due to fixed-term employment contracts resulting from time-bound funding schemes.

Cultural capital is acquired through ways of knowing and being that are recognised as valuable. In an embodied form, practitioners and policy makers both demonstrate cultural capital although their language tends to be distinctive. Policy makers who can articulate the necessity of peacebuilding as central to wider policy concerns in the fields of health, education, justice, the economy, and so on, draw on a particular form of learned cultural capital. They may be particularly focused on using statistics to make the case for greater intergovernmental investment in peacebuilding programmes. Conversely, practitioners are more inclined to speak the language of young people's lived realities, drawing on cultural capital acquired through practice experience and communicating this through stories of personal and interpersonal transformation.

Cultural capital is also 'objectified' or made visible through mission statements, evaluation reports, best-practice models, and social media posts. How organisations and individuals portray themselves through such mediums and the 'reach' and reaction garnered from various audiences is indicative of an objectified form of cultural capital. As well as being embodied and objectified, cultural capital is also institutionalised (Bourdieu and Wacquant, 1992). Key to institutionalised cultural capital are certificates of achievement or awards for excellence validated by bodies that guarantee quality standards. The education system plays a pivotal role in providing a framework within which institutionalised cultural capital operates. This is particularly evident where institutions have developed a tradition of bestowing prestigious awards, a famous example being the Nobel Peace Prize. The distinguished prize is presented each year, as per Alfred Nobel's final will and testament, to the person 'who shall have done the most or the best work for fraternity between nations, for the abolition or reduction of standing armies and for the holding and promotion of peace congresses' (The Nobel Peace Prize, 2023). More localised prizes for youth work and peacebuilding that are less well known on an international stage nonetheless carry significance as forms of institutionalised cultural capital. Such accolades are recognised by others in the field, adding to an individual or organisation's legitimacy as a credible and reputable actor.

Social capital refers to 'the aggregate of the actual or potential resources which are linked to possession of a durable network of more or less institutionalized relationships of mutual acquaintance and recognition' (Bourdieu, 1986: 248). Applied to youth sector peacebuilding, productive working partnerships with recognised and well-established organisations represent valuable social capital. These social relationships within and across youth organisations can be maximised and exploited to enhance other forms of capital. Accessing the social capital of another institution can determine the extent of opportunities to collaborate on larger and more ambitious funding applications, shaping dynamics of inclusion and exclusion across the field.

Finally, symbolic capital is deployed as a concept that takes cognisance of the levels of prestige and legitimacy that accompany other forms of capital (Bourdieu, 1986). It represents the 'esteem, recognition, belief, credit, confidence of others' (Bourdieu, 2000: 166). Each type of capital discussed here – economic, cultural, and social – has a symbolic dimension. This symbolic aspect creates a sense of authority and power; indeed, the term *capital* in each case could be replaced by the word *power*. In the global arena of youth sector peacebuilding, various institutions have accumulated significant symbolic capital through their renown in advancing the field. These include the United Nations, the World Bank, Interpeace, the EU, the International Red Cross and Red Crescent Movement, and the Peace Corps. At a national and local level, organisations with a history of delivering peacebuilding work with young people generate significant symbolic capital. Individual practitioners similarly accumulate symbolic capital through the various ways in which they build and utilise their relative levels of economic, cultural, and social capital within the field.

Each type of capital has specific forms which are intimately connected to the fields whereby they are injected with value. *Practice capital*, for instance, can be understood as a particular type of cultural capital in the youth sector where experience of working with young people and holding specific positions within various organisations are considered desirable assets. Bourdieu focused attention on struggles within fields that emanate from the accumulation of economic capital that dominates over cultural capital on one 'pole' and the opposite position where cultural capital dominates over economic capital on another 'pole' (Bourdieu, 1989). This is illustrated in Figure 3.2 by mapping how youth sector peacebuilding organisations compete for resources, where dominant and 'deficient' forms of economic capital intersect with dominant and deficient forms of practice capital (as a specific type of cultural capital).

Figure 3.2: Practice capital versus economic capital

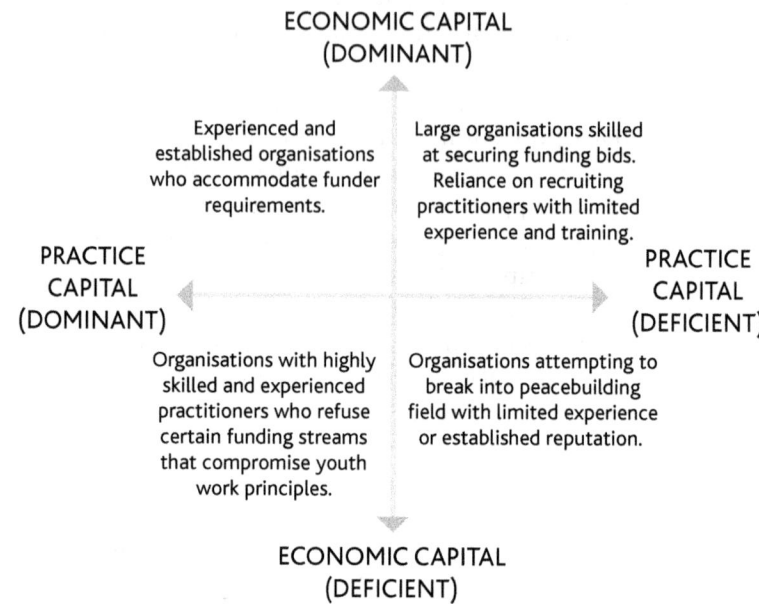

The upper left-hand quadrant signifies the most desirable position where organisations are competent at securing economic capital through funding bids, accommodating funder requirements, and attracting experienced practitioners. The lower right-hand quadrant, by contrast, represents the most peripheral position within the field. It is indicative of organisations attempting to pivot towards peacebuilding work in an attempt to secure new funding streams yet having limited experience or reputation within the field. Those organisations recognised for their expertise yet who deliberately reject funding streams as a form of resistance to imposed economic-driven processes, such as outcomes-based accountability frameworks, may have significant practice capital but diminished economic capital. Finally, those in the upper right-hand quadrant represent organisations that capitalise on the opportunity to secure peace funding yet tend not to attract experienced or qualified practitioners, perhaps due to not being considered an organisation that invests in practitioner and practice development.

Figure 3.2 is an overly simplified depiction of just one set of tensions and struggles within the field of youth sector peacebuilding. It does, however, draw attention to 'the distribution of species of power (or capital) whose possession commands access to the specific profits that are at stake in the field' (Bourdieu and Wacquant, 1992: 97). Far from remaining static, capitals are open to conversion from one form to another (Bourdieu, 1986). An accumulation of practice (cultural) capital can be transformed into funding (economic capital), albeit involving negotiation and compromise that such transactions incur. Similarly, those organisations that have accumulated economic capital can invest in the cultivation of practice capital. Social relations within fields are not only enacted through struggles for accumulating capital but also are constituted through struggles to inscribe value onto particular forms of capital. Bourdieu's (1989) notion of symbolic power further illuminates the processes by which certain groups impose definitions and meanings within the field that become taken for granted.

Symbolic power

Symbolic power is closely aligned with the notion of symbolic capital, representing the accumulation of the various forms of economic, cultural, and social capital. At an interpersonal level, symbolic power is manifested in the elevation of one distinctive perspective and approach to peacebuilding espoused by one group of practitioners as more important than an alternative approach championed by a different group of practitioners. These interpersonal power relations are shaped by larger forces bearing down upon the field of practice. Following Bourdieu, it is this broader level of analysis that we pursue in developing critical insights within the field of youth sector peacebuilding.

The state occupies a dominant position over all fields of practice and exists as 'a power above powers' (Bourdieu, 2014: 197). Bourdieu further explains: 'The accumulation of different kinds of capital by the same central power generates a kind of meta-capital, that is, a capital with the particular property of exercising power over capital' (Bourdieu, 2014: 197). This 'meta' position provides state actors with symbolic power and the ability to set an index of values on the specific types of cultural, social, and economic capital that are most prized (Wacquant and Akçaoğlu, 2017). For instance, funders who support peace initiatives focused on getting young people into work, aligned to a theory of change which proposes economic inactivity of young people is a risk factor for involvement in violence, may be welcomed and further resourced by state actors concerned with embedding social stability. Youth organisations with expertise in delivering employability programmes with young people align their cultural practice capital with the economic capital of the funder to deliver these objectives. In doing so they may be publicly recognised by state departments for their contribution to building peace. This merging of the economic capital of a funding body, the cultural capital of youth organisations, and positive recognition of each by the state leads to further symbolic capital for both the funders and the organisations involved. Conversely, a grassroots organisation that involves young people in political activism that is agitational and continually challenges decisions and omissions made by state departments may be more likely to be held at arm's length by the government. The state then exercises its capacity to legitimise and enable certain approaches to peacebuilding that fit within the 'official' state-sanctioned discourse. Those approaches deemed to be out of step with the state orthodoxy are more likely to be constrained and delegitimised.

Within the scope of our analysis, policy makers and funders within the field of youth sector peacebuilding are understood as being influenced by the logics of practice from bureaucratic state fields. As such, they garner a level of symbolic capital and power that comes from their proximity to the power of the state. This symbolic power manifests in taken-for-granted aspects of the field where, for instance, funding contracts are awarded conditionally with expectations to account for predefined outputs and execution of policy-driven targets. These features of the field are perceived as natural and rational rather than arbitrary conditions shaped by the interests of state actors. For the field of youth sector peacebuilding, the reliance on external funding is indicative of a dependence on those institutions closely aligned to the state-centric field of power. Subsequently, the power to impose value on certain approaches to delivering and measuring peacebuilding can be conceived of as driven by policy makers and inter-state funders.

Core to our argument is that those who have limited access to the types of economic, cultural, and social capital held by policy-making and funding institutions – often young people and practitioners – should be involved as co-creators rather than simply delivery agents and recipients of programmes. This would involve a significant challenge to the existing hierarchies, regimes of competence, and common-sense practices of the field. Such a transformation would see the authority to determine local peacebuilding outcomes and impact measurement becoming a participatory process driven by young people rather than predetermined by policy makers.

Reflexivity: rethinking the thinkable

So far, Bourdieu's ideas have been presented as a theoretical lens that brings into focus the nature of power relations in youth sector peacebuilding. The accumulation, distribution, and legitimising of specific types of capital are at the heart of this analysis. These power dynamics are played out at various levels, with particular attention paid to the disproportionate influence of the state and policy makers over the direction of practice. A key role played by the habitus, which generates dispositions, is habituating participants to the explicit and tacit 'rules' and taken-for-granted ways of being, thinking, and acting in fields of practice. The habitus also can learn to resist the initial inclinations of aligning with the practical logic of fields (Bourdieu and Wacquant, 1992). The opportunities afforded through the cultivation of a *reflexive practitioner habitus* and movements towards youth sector peacebuilding as *a reflexive field* are considered in this section and reoccur as primary themes in subsequent chapters.

One way to think about Bourdieu's notion of reflexivity is that of a meta-analysis, of bringing into focus the unspoken and unthinking actions of agents within a field. For example, embedded in the practical logic of youth sector peacebuilding is the belief that positive evaluations alongside the completion of programmes count as 'proof' of personal and social transformation. It is common for young people to complete evaluation forms with scaled and open-ended questions, often speaking to the glowing success of the programme and the transformational impact it had on their lives and communities. These evaluations are eventually received by the funder who presents the gathered statistics and stories as evidence of impact for the world to see. However, a practitioner working closely with the youth participants may sense that when completing the evaluation forms these young people were 'playing a game within the game'. That is, they were not engaging authentically with the questions. Rather, the young people were responding based on a tacit knowledge that everyone around them (the youth workers, the organisation, the funders) seeks a positive response. Having been credited by the funder for excellent work, it would appear unthinkable for the youth worker to contact the funder and advise them to disregard the evaluations, to retract the public acknowledgement of success, and to make the case that we are all fooling ourselves when we refer to this programme as 'transformational'. Yet this rupture in the normal proceedings of accepting credit for work that aligns with funder requirements presents an opportunity for critically assessing the dynamics of the field. Those who would risk such a seemingly absurd manoeuvre would raise broader questions for the field about the purpose of practice, who sets the agenda, who determines success, and the extent to which radical notions such as 'social transformation' have, in practice, become part of a broader system of social control and conformity.

An individual practitioner is unlikely to make a significant impact in challenging the practical sense of the field. Furthermore, their habitus perceives in advance the limited influence or credit they would receive for acting in such a way, thus disincentivising such unconventional behaviours. To this end, Bourdieu emphasises the importance of the field investing in a reflexive disposition for reflexive knowledge to become instituted as part of the emergent properties of that field. This would require a critical mass of actors participating in 'the systematic exploration of the unthought categories of thought which delimit the thinkable and predetermine the thought' (Bourdieu and Wacquant, 1992: 40). While acknowledging Bourdieu's opposition to 'narcissistic' conceptions of reflexivity that turn 'the analytical gaze back onto the private person of the analyst' (Wacquant, 2008: 223), we emphasise the collective role of practitioners, policy makers, and researchers in developing a reflexive disposition towards youth sector peacebuilding. This reflexive approach is not simply an analysis of individual subjectivities. It requires engaging with notions of field positions, competing interests, relative amounts and distributions of capital, and how symbolic power is exercised within the field. Such reflexivity is central to 'the awakening of political consciousness' (Bourdieu, 1977: 169).

Conclusion

Social theory carries the power to revolutionise the world. Such theories provide tools that frame and facilitate a deeper analysis of power and positionality, of why we and others think, behave, act, and interrelate in particular ways. And in doing so it has the potential to recontextualise perceptions, experiences, and knowledge. Social theory can unlock radical new insights into our social, political, cultural, economic, and historical realities. Such critical insights are both retroactive and prospective, inviting us to re-evaluate past experiences and prior perspectives as well as rethinking current and future trajectories. Bringing together Lave and Wenger's *communities of practice* and Bourdieu's *theory of practice* sets up a critical lens for analysing youth sector peacebuilding.

From Lave and Wenger (1991) a conception of youth sector peacebuilding is derived as a constellation of communities that engage in a shared enterprise. The process of becoming established within the domain of youth sector peacebuilding is mediated through legitimate peripheral participation. Practitioners orient themselves towards existing regimes of competence required to effectively engage in the practice, all the while negotiating and reshaping these regimes. Crucially, the boundary between a practitioner community of practice and that of policy makers represents a key disjuncture or connector. Boundary objects, such as policies, funding applications, and memorandums of understanding, are reifications intended to facilitate the practices of these distinct yet interdependent communities. Boundary objects are a source of tension where policy seeks to impose particular approaches to peacebuilding on the youth sector which are variously accommodated or resisted in youth work practice.

The duality of reification and participation is required for meaningful integration of critical thinking with practice wisdom within youth sector peacebuilding. Where theoretical ideas remain detached from practice, the impact is limited. The ideas and models in this book are presented as stimulus material for practitioners and academics to engage with, interpret, and apply within their own practices, leading to more reflexive critical action.

Bourdieu's notion of habitus resonates with Lave and Wenger's emphasis on the embodied and iterative nature of practice. Dispositions emanating from habitus help orient practitioners to the field and appreciate the types of capital worth pursuing and the social positions available to them. Schemes of perception that both practitioners and policy makers encounter provide a sense of the range of possible ways of legitimately practising peacebuilding work with young people. These schemata, which often go unarticulated, represent a key struggle within the field focused on crediting specific approaches to peacebuilding as more desirable than others. Those most closely aligned with the state are concerned with embedding political conformity rather than incentivising programmes that situate youth as potential challengers of the political system.

While Lave and Wenger are more focused on how people both shape and become shaped by communities of practice, Bourdieu is more attentive to broader power dynamics that influence fields of practice. His notion of symbolic power provides an analytical frame for recognising asymmetrical relations within the field of youth sector peacebuilding. Significantly, the authority to classify as legitimate certain approaches to peacebuilding over others appear as facts of the social world rather than changeable systems. These critiques are applied throughout the remainder of this book alongside a repertoire of concepts intended to help cultivate a reflexive disposition. This reflexivity is geared towards recognising and critiquing orthodoxies and creating openings for new trajectories of practice. Ultimately, these theoretical ideas, when applied in practice, seek to spark redistributions of power away from state actors and towards practitioners and young people.

4

Prewrapped peacebuilding

> There's a neoliberal agenda, it has to be measurable, it has to be quantifiable ... the real measurement is actually in the hearts and the minds of the young people and that stuff – that's beyond measuring. (YW40)

Introduction

This chapter examines a 'double bind' for youth sector peacebuilding arising where tensions from the field of youth work meet with dilemmas from the field of peacebuilding. Namely, a social control agenda imposed on youth work is compounded by a technocratic peacebuilding architecture premised on pre-packaged programme solutions to complex realities. These critiques examine the evolution of youth work and peacebuilding as distinct fields of practice. Subsequently, a neoliberal policy landscape is discussed as influencing the nature and scope of youth sector peacebuilding. The neoliberal mantra of maximising value for money has led to an increasingly top-down, outcomes-driven practice based on targeted programmes and outputs. Demands for increasingly instrumental outcomes and definitive outputs in return for funding have been treated cautiously by many in the youth sector. Constant negotiation of funder requirements and compromising of youth participatory processes has led experienced practitioners to restate core youth work values and underpinning principles (IDYW, 2014; Davies, 2015). Peacebuilders, similarly, often are reliant on funding to resource their practice. This necessitates balancing the expressed and felt needs of communities with navigating reporting and expenditure targets tied to policy objectives inscribed in funding criteria.

As discussed in the previous chapter, despite intentions towards social transformation, the intersecting fields of youth work and peacebuilding are susceptible to subtle exploitation from the state and state-sanctioned funding bodies. Such exploitation comes in the form of converting a practice committed to human freedom and flourishing into one of surveillance, conformity, and control. Later in the chapter, drawing on Northern Ireland as a pertinent geopolitical case, iterations of local policy and its impact on youth sector peacebuilding in the region are examined. This analysis critiques an absence of creative involvement and participation of young people in devising locally owned, nationally significant peacebuilding strategies and democratic processes. Such participatory processes remain a largely untapped alternative to youth as consumers of prewrapped peace programmes.

Youth work: social control versus social change

Youth workers tend to be highly relational in their practice and sensitive to individual young people's immediate personal, social, emotional, educational, and psychological needs. However, where individual needs become the primary focus, any progression towards political orientations of youth work as transformative collective action is elided and substituted with a more individualistic notion of personal transformation (Seal, 2014b). This dichotomy of personal versus political is a recurring tension within the profession (Davies and Taylor, 2019) and youth work continues to grapple with the 'enduring paradoxes of emancipation and control' (Bright and Pugh, 2019: 63). Where statutory funding and services have become commonplace, youth work has often been mandated as part of a broader function of education that socialises young people to become 'good' citizens. Despite this socialising function, many organisations and practitioners have availed of state funding in pursuit of more radical ends with young people at the centre of grassroots social change.

Furlong et al's (1997, cited in Forrest, 2010: 57) analysis of four modes of youth work indicates a progression from social control to social change orientations. While these were originally presented as stages in the historical development of youth work, such modes of practice persist in different settings today:

- *Control* – a deficit approach where young people are regarded as at risk of causing social problems.
- *Socialisation* – concerned with putting young people on the 'right track' to succeed and contribute positively to their social environment.
- *Informal education* – emphasis on experiential learning and supporting young people to be democratic and critical thinkers.
- *Citizenship* – a focus on political engagement and social action.

These typifications are evident in Figure 4.1, which depicts Cooper's (2012; 2018) adaptation of Hurley and Treacy's (1993) sociological model of youth work. Informed by Burrell and Morgan's (1979) sociological take on organisational analysis, the model presents a dialectic between functionalism through the *sociology of regulation* and conflict theories through the *sociology of radical change*. Functionalist notions of consensus with established cultural and social norms are contrasted with conflict perspectives that seek to problematise the status quo and dismantle oppressive structures (Hurley and Treacy, 1993). Within the arena of radical social change, the subjectivist

Figure 4.1: Cooper's (2012) adaptation of Hurley and Treacy's (1993) sociological model of youth work

Sociology of Radical Change

Critical Social Education *(Radical Humanist)*
Youth worker as animateur, enabler, consciousness-raiser, critical social analyst.

Reformist
Young people have ability to analyse and assess alternatives, and to act to change their world if they choose.

Programme: explore personal experience as basis for consciousness raising.

Radical Social Change *(Radical Structuralist)*
Youth worker as radical activist.

Revolutionary
Young people gain skills necessary to act for social transformation.

Programme: indoctrination of young people into revolutionary perspective; rejection of social institutions as oppressive.

Subjectivist ──────────────── Objectivist

Personal Development *(Interpretivist)*
Youth worker as counsellor, supporter, group worker.

Liberal
Young people prepared for active role in society, respect themselves and develop ability to build and maintain relationship.

Programme: Personal responsibility for choices; leadership; good skills for mixing socially.

Character Building *(Functionalist)*
Youth worker as role model and organiser.

Conservative
Young people develop discipline.

Programme: focus energies in constructive way; healthy lifestyles.

Sociology of Regulation

Note: Reproduced with permission

approach orients towards stimulating change through 'changing human consciousness', while the objectivist approach gravitates towards 'changing structures' (Hurley and Treacy, 1993: 6).

Themes of regulation and radical change are also evident in Table 4.1, which shows Cooper's (2012; 2018) political models of youth work (adapted from Cooper and White, 1994). Drawing on political theory, Cooper and White (1994) examined political ideologies and assumptions that infuse different approaches to youth work, revealing disparate purposes and diverse manifestations of practice. Where practice is indicative of 'treatment' or 'reform' it operates at the level of social control. The language of youth 'at risk' is identified with these two approaches. Increasingly, youth policies have tended to fund short-term targeted work that inclines towards preventative and protective measures to address issues such as child poverty and exploitation, social exclusion, academic underachievement, youth unemployment, self-harm reduction, and suicide prevention (Davies and Taylor, 2019; Hammond and Harvey, 2021). This contrasts with 'universal' or 'open access' youth work designed around locally embedded youth centres as community hubs offering ongoing participation and experiential learning opportunities for any young person who chooses to attend. Practitioners in both the voluntary and statutory sectors committed to youth work's iterative, process-driven nature increasingly experience the control agenda through product-oriented demands of governmental funding (Ord, 2016).

Table 4.1 also contrasts radical and non-radical characteristics of youth work as advocacy and youth work as empowerment. Non-radical applications of these approaches tend to operate within existing social structures whereas radical approaches are more inclined to challenge the status quo. Cooper's (2012) adapted models point to the enduring tensions of youth work as a practice of social control or social change. As discussed later in the chapter, the policy context has a considerable influence on the trajectory of practice, creating dilemmas for practitioners as they variously embrace, accommodate, or resist the policy landscape. These dilemmas are similarly felt in the field of peacebuilding.

Peacebuilding: top-down versus bottom-up

The concept of peacebuilding has evolved as a term that reflects the complex and contested nature of peace. Eminent peace scholar Johan Galtung contrasted a platonic ideal form of General Complete Peace with its antithesis, General Complete War (Galtung, 1964). The former imagines a world of endless global peace marked by harmony and human integration with others and the environment. The latter depicts a world of continuous, universal war and strife. This peace-versus-war dualism is characteristic of historical accounts of peace as a zero-sum game, resulting in a 'victor's

Table 4.1: Cooper's (2012) political models of youth work

Name	Political tradition	Human nature	Vision/goals	Values	Language
Treatment	Conservative	Negative	Social harmony	Social cohesion	Deviancy, inadequacy
Reform	Liberal	Reformable	Social mobility	Equal opportunity	Disadvantage, poor social environment
Advocacy (non-radical)	Liberal, social democratic	Reformable	Social contract, individual rights	Rights as due under existing law	Rights, social justice
Advocacy (radical)	Social democratic, socialism	Positive	Gradual social change towards more just and equitable society	Social justice, positive rights, law reform to extend rights	Rights, social justice
Empowerment (non-radical)	Classical liberal/ neo-conservative	Neutral or negative	Small government	Freedom from interference	Empowerment, enfranchisement
Empowerment (radical)	Anarchist	Highly positive	Self-government, grassroots democracy	Equality of social power	Empowerment, consciousness-raising, enfranchisement

Source: Adapted from Cooper and White (1994)

peace' where one side dominates over the other (Richmond, 2005). Such dichotomies fail to account for the realities of many contested societies where competing actors and diverse ethnic groups are compelled to co-exist (Wright, 1987; Cooper et al, 2011). Peace therefore is not best understood as a static condition that can be reached once and for all but as an ongoing process requiring peacebuilding strategies; hence a shift in language from *peace* to *peacebuilding* (Heathershaw, 2008).

Extensive debates revolve around the type of interventions appropriate for addressing the complex web of issues, needs, and aspirations of individuals, communities, and societies emerging from violent conflict. In the field of critical peace studies, the limitations of a 'liberal' peacebuilding agenda have been examined. Liberal peacebuilding has been characterised as a multilayered process involving three interdependent strands of state-building, civil society participation, and embedding democracy (Goetze and Guzina, 2008; Chandler, 2017). Critics challenge the normative connotations of these notions that are interpreted uncritically, incorporating neoliberal dispositions (Richmond, 2011b; Mac Ginty, 2012; Gonzalez-Vicente, 2020). The following sections present a synopsis of these three facets of liberal peacebuilding.

Peacebuilding through state-building

The premise of state-building as an approach to attaining peace rests on a belief that violent conflict swells when states are unable to curtail and control internal and/or external security threats (Daoudy, 2009). Therefore, building peace involves investment in state institutions, equipping them to deter threats of war and suppress eruptions of violence. Chandler (2017) argues that within the peacebuilding-as-state-building approach, naive assumptions abound. A fixed model is imposed by external actors such as the United Nations (UN), where liberal values explicitly determine the notion of institution reform and development. Chandler (2017: 8) characterises the approach as assuming that '[what] was broken could be easily fixed, returning societies to the status quo or establishing a new one on the basis of the liberal institutions of democracy, the rule of law and market efficiency'.

Others contend that the state-building approach often overlooks local and national ownership of peacebuilding processes. The imposition of state-building by an abstract 'international community' tends to obscure fundamental processes of participation, citizenship, and legitimacy in post-conflict settings (Brown et al, 2010). A participatory approach premised on individual agency and collective interests as the basis for building peace poses challenges to traditional notions of state-building that emphasise the role of external actors (Chandler, 2017).

Peacebuilding through civil society

In response to the criticisms of state-building, civil society is attributed special credence in post-conflict liberal peacebuilding. Legitimacy is strengthened by creating space for public opinion to be heard on (often contentious) issues in the peacebuilding process. Scepticism has been raised concerning the influence and agency of civil society to generate critical and emancipatory approaches to building peace within the liberal framework (Paffenholz, 2009; Verkoren and van Leeuwen, 2013). A comparison between radical and more moderate notions of civil society accentuates the tension. Commenting on the writings of Italian Marxist Antonio Gramsci (1891–1937), Ransome (1992) notes that civil society is viewed as the site of social change. This is tempered by widespread submission to the status quo that works against an emancipatory struggle for new social orders to arise. Ideological struggle is fundamental to Gramsci's analysis. This struggle is against the hegemony of the ruling group, where 'a common social-moral language is spoken, in which one concept of reality is dominant, informing ... all modes of thought and behaviour' (Femia, 1981: 24). Such hegemony is to be resisted and opposed 'neither in the factories nor in the streets nor at the military bases but in the sphere of civil society' (Femia, 1981: 192).

A Gramscian radical view of civil society is displaced in the liberal peacebuilding approach by a focus on state-sponsored social cohesion (Paffenholz, 2009; Sriram, 2009; Andrieu, 2010). Chandler (2017) indicates that the emphasis on civil society from the 1990s onwards was motivated by recognising the necessity of a 'bottom-up' approach to peacebuilding to complement external actors' 'top-down' interventions. Contrary to Gramsci's revolutionary notion of civil society, the UN, in Chandler's view, was intent on grassroots voices speaking into the peacebuilding process with an implicit vision of harmonising and legitimising interventions. This contest over the discourse of civil society in peacebuilding mirrors the tensions and contradictions that surface when examining critical research on the purpose of youth work. Both can be viewed within the literature as susceptible to social control agendas where aspirations towards radical social change are sidelined.

Peacebuilding through democracy

Democratic peace can be considered synonymous with *liberal peace*. A primary argument posited by proponents of a liberal peace is that democratic nations are much less likely to experience war and mass violence within or against other democratic countries (Doyle, 1986; Goetze and Guzina, 2008). This logic positions democracy as a critical element of the liberal peacebuilding agenda. Proponents point to democracy as a safeguard against war and conflict, internally and externally (Newman et al, 2009). Critics, however, contend that a deeper analysis and engagement is required with theories and processes of democracy and capitalism. Attention is drawn to the exploitative features and the perpetuation of inequality observed in democratic capitalist states (MacMillan, 2004).

Little (2006: 70) challenges the colonial connotations of liberal peacebuilding where the Western system of democracy is presented as a ubiquitous model of 'good governance', preoccupied with 'the establishment of spaces to allow markets to operate freely'. Many critical peace scholars have therefore concluded that liberal peacebuilding has embraced neoliberal ideals of marketisation and privatisation (Heathershaw, 2008; Richmond, 2009; Gonzalez-Vicente, 2020). Consequently, peacebuilding becomes a project monopolised by political elites that is increasingly removed from concerns with everyday lived experience (Berents, 2018; Mac Ginty, 2021).

Neoliberal trends and alternatives

Vast amounts of literature employ and define the neoliberal heuristic, a broad label encompassing many different forms and modes (Peck and Tickell, 2002). While there are multiple iterations of neoliberalism, broad features and resemblances can be identified that have underpinned currents in transnational, national, regional, and local policy developments. Neoliberal ideology can be traced to the thinking of Austrian economist Friedrich von Hayek and an inner circle of like-minded collaborators converging on economic and philosophic ideas in the 1940s (Harvey, 2005). Property rights, individual freedom for capital accumulation, and a belief in market forces are the impetus for this reimagining of classical liberalism. An expansive welfare state is antithetical to neoliberal ideas. Emphasis is placed on individual responsibility for personal flourishing. Neoliberalism does not, however, equate to a state of indifference. Critics argue that through coordinating and controlling the privatisation of services, the neoliberal state becomes 'more extensive, intrusive, surveillant and centred' (Ball, 2008: 202).

Mapping various conceptions of neoliberalism, Peck et al's (2018: 6) sketch of the term includes 'principles of entrepreneurialism, efficiency, cost control, privatism, and competition … the penal or paternalist management of poverty, the commodification of social life and natural resources, and the (often technocratic) imposition of fiscal discipline'. Proponents have championed these principles as an ideal way to organise society to benefit all and maximise individual rights and freedoms. Opponents critique neoliberalism as a socio-political and economic order that alienates and dehumanises by elevating capital accumulation above concerns for the environment or the welfare of others (Harvey, 2005; Ledwith, 2020). The freedom to pursue personal and private wealth and security is extolled over a more collectivist, egalitarian, and equitable interpretation of freedom.

Critics also raise concerns that neoliberalism leads to a depoliticisation of social policy (Flinders and Buller, 2006). This occurs through appeals to the rationality of scientific conclusions arrived at by notionally independent expert groups and committees, whereby those with political power remove political ideology from politics (Susen, 2014). Such are the manoeuvres of 'a politics that is depoliticized, neutralized, promoted to the state of technique' (Bourdieu and Boltanski, 2008, cited in Susen, 2014: 88). This depoliticised form of governance relies on 'technocratic decision making and/or the self-responsibilisation of individuals, groups, organisations, or whole "stakeholder groups" through adoption of specific technologies of government that rely on scientific expertise, consultants, expert systems, algorithms, metrology, ratings, benchmarking, contingent rewards for approved behaviour, and so on' (Jessop, 2015: 105).

Neoliberal projects utilise the notion of *technocracy* where decision-making is conferred to 'elites' in administration roles who are viewed as impartial. Resultant policies are implied to be universally acceptable based on the guiding principles of efficiency and effectiveness of interventions. Key features of technocratic arrangements are that they 'prioritize bureaucratic rationality', are 'directed from above', and 'pursue the imposition of a single policy paradigm … immune to social context' (Mac Ginty, 2012: 289). Rational and technical knowledge is prioritised, diminishing the role of critical dialogue and a more participative form of democracy.

Debates exist regarding the desirability of pragmatic politics and technocratic forms of governance (Flinders and Wood, 2015). Ledwith (2020: 22) contends, 'without adversarial positioning, policies and practice became flawed by the absence of a structural analysis of inequality and injustice'. Subsequently, the power of decision-making and the distribution of resources is given an illusion of common sense, suppressing political debate (Susen, 2014). Within this technocratic framework, local voices and experiences are further estranged from the peacebuilding process (Mac Ginty, 2012). An emerging alternative to the liberal peacebuilding consensus is post-liberal and everyday peacebuilding. This approach counters many neoliberal assumptions that have permeated policy.

Post-liberal peacebuilding: resistance and the everyday

Richmond (2010) outlines four 'generations' of peace work beginning with conflict management, followed by conflict resolution, giving way to liberal peacebuilding, and finally, an emergent post-liberal peacebuilding. This fourth generation represents a movement to resist the neoliberalising trends that have accompanied the evolution of liberal peacebuilding. While the liberal peace affirms individual agency and an active civil society, critics suggest that the reality is a thin veneer of grassroots participation. Local actors are subject to a peace invented and implemented from above. The essential principles of post-liberal peacebuilding are local ownership, attention to complex local needs, and calibrating power dynamics in the direction of indigenous actors instead of external arbitrators (Richmond, 2010). The notion of civil society in post-liberal peacebuilding invokes notions of resistance and emancipation (Richmond, 2011a). Drawing parallels with radical pacifist movements of the Levellers, Diggers, Quakers, and Gandhi's resistance to British rule in India, Richmond (2011a) suggests that civil resistance can undermine the legitimacy of the ruling elites. This becomes the catalyst for generating new socio-political realities. The 'civil' nature of such resistance is 'based on personal integrity and dialogue, and aimed at producing a compromise' (Richmond, 2011b: 120). Post-liberal peacebuilding invokes notions of civil resistance to challenge the hegemony of an imposed liberal peace. It promotes the agency of citizens to confront elitist top-down approaches to peacebuilding and enact a locally driven peacebuilding process.

Richmond's fourth generation post-liberal approach has also been referred to as the 'local turn' in peacebuilding (Roberts, 2011; Mac Ginty and Richmond, 2013; Paffenholz, 2015). It insists on centring everyday experiences as integral to understanding and intervening in post-conflict environments. Richmond (2011b: 127), drawing on de Certeau's work, explains that 'the everyday represents how individuals unconsciously navigate their way around and try to create space for their own activities while taking into consideration institutions of power'. The everyday is attentive to local needs and contextual realities (Richmond, 2009). Everyday peacebuilding challenges a technocratic pre-packaged, off-the-shelf peace (Mac Ginty, 2008; 2011; 2012; 2014). It pushes back against the imposed status quo in which 'funding schemes and donor demands create an environment where organizations are discouraged from communicating and cooperating for fear of losing funding to a competing organization or being exposed to criticism if a project has failed or not performed' (Firchow, 2018: 16).

Furthermore, the imposition of managerial principles to measure impact and ensure accountability of delivery agencies 'results in a generation of indicators that are measurable and demonstrable, but not necessarily relevant or valid' (Firchow, 2018: 37). Conversely, the everyday peace approach insists the beneficiaries of peacebuilding interventions should construct measures of effectiveness and should be actively involved in designing evaluation metrics (Firchow, 2018). This calls for a radical shift in how peacebuilding programmes with young people are currently designed, funded, delivered, and evaluated. Hybrid forms of peacebuilding have been proposed that emphasise the responsibility placed upon international actors to support peacebuilding efforts and distribute global resources while seeking to rebalance and recentre the voices, experience, and expertise of local people (Mac Ginty and Richmond, 2016). Such balancing, however, is not always evident in situations where neoliberal ideals have become enshrined in youth policy, positioning young people as passive service users rather than active co-creators.

Neoliberalism in the youth sector

Neoliberal influences on youth policy are manifested in propensities towards targeting strategies and the depoliticisation of practice (Taylor et al, 2018; Baldridge, 2020). Often young people are framed in deficit language, as 'at risk' and in need of 'treatment' or 'reform' (Cooper, 2013; Lohmeyer, 2017b). Those targeted tend to be groups deemed as at risk of unemployment or involved in activities regarded as 'anti-social'. Subsequently, youth policy influenced by neoliberalism gravitates towards an emphasis on preparing young people for economic citizenship. In practice this is observed in a growing number of employability programmes, both within peacebuilding and the wider youth sector, with 'at risk' young people. Such programmes task practitioners to embrace and promote an entrepreneurial mindset and industrious disposition. This entrepreneurial and enterprising discourse activates a self-responsibilising narrative focused on 'empowering' individual young people to achieve. A broader critique of social structures and institutions that create barriers and restrict opportunities for these young people is elided (Lohmeyer, 2017b; Taylor et al, 2018).

The notion of meritocracy can be understood as an ally of neoliberalism. This is particularly evident in relation to a policy focus on increasing the employability and aspirations of young people. Meritocracy postulates that natural talents combined with individual effort will propagate success. It supposes that opportunities to succeed exist equally for all regardless of the socio-economic conditions of birth (Sandel, 2021). Others, however, argue that this 'neoliberal meritocratic dream rests on the idea of a level playing field' and overlooks the persistence and inhibiting nature of structural and systemic inequalities (Littler, 2018: 3).

The neoliberalisation of youth work has also reinforced targeting for outcomes. This is guided by managerialist principles that require quantitative evidence to account for the effectiveness and efficiency of agencies and individual practitioners (Bunyan and Ord, 2012; Carpenter, 2017). These targeting strategies discredit forms of practice based on 'open democratic youth work' (de St Croix, 2016: 41), giving priority to short-term programmes built around 'objective-driven performance targets' (Bunyan and Ord, 2012: 24). Increasingly, funders require organisations to develop or work to logic models that depict how a programme intervention will convert resources into effective activities that produce measurable and quantifiable outcomes in response to the needs of young people (Carpenter, 2017).

Interventions tend to be pitched at the level of individual behavioural change facilitated through, for instance, one-to-one mentoring. A causal link between individual behavioural change and intensive one-to-one work is more easily subjected to quantification. A deeper analysis of complex social issues that involve young people in an educational process of critical thinking and youth activism is not incentivised. Such approaches defy a straightforward linear relationship between youth work activities and outcomes that can be predetermined and quantified on a funding application. In this way, neoliberal social policy values youth work as a series of interventions to tackle social problems. This perspective is premised on changing behaviours and building the individual capacity of youth to lift themselves out of social need or trouble.

A further critique of youth policy under neoliberalism discerns a depoliticising of practice (Bunyan and Ord, 2012; Taylor et al, 2018). Under this analysis, the political nature of integral concepts including participation, empowerment, citizenship, and informal education are obscured. While the rhetoric of youth participation remains pervasive in policy, it is argued that the assumed mode of participation is an active collaboration in capitalist-oriented structures rather than a critical engagement with notions of power, voice, and influence (Coburn and Gormally, 2017; Taylor et al, 2018; Grasso and Bessant, 2018). Social action and volunteering are stripped of concerns for social justice with notions of empowerment located at the personal rather than collective level. Depoliticising therefore entails positioning young people as recipients of youth work programmes focused primarily on personal and social development to support flourishing within the parameters of their social and cultural contexts. Framing youth as political actors remains absent from this policy discourse (Giugni and Grasso, 2020). Depoliticising policies and practices can be contrasted with those that are intentionally politicising, and not in a pejorative sense. Politicising, in this positive reading, is embraced as the process of involving young people in developing and practising decision-making, distributing resources, holding representatives to account, organising and participating in activities and campaigns that challenge government policy, and thinking critically about concepts such as liberty, equality, equity, power, democracy, peace, solidarity, and justice. Depoliticisation occurs when policy makers and practitioners fail to recognise, foster, and harness young people's political agency. This dilemma is evident in youth work when it 'leans significantly to the preventative, the targeted and individualised conformity' (Davies and Taylor, 2019: 1), rather than being pursued as 'a collective, agitational and politicised practice' (Taylor et al, 2018: 90–91).

Rejuvenating youth work

Youth work practitioners variously accommodate or resist neoliberal trends. De St Croix (2016) captures grassroots stories of resistance demonstrated by practitioners committed to defending features of youth work deemed to be compromised by increasing managerialism and neoliberal ideals. These features include open-access provision rather than targeted programmes; critical perspectives that seek to politicise rather than socialise young people; and anti-oppressive practice that seeks to tackle systemic and structural inequality rather than accepting meritocratic assumptions.

Through practitioner stories de St Croix illuminates complex navigations of neoliberal youth policy, with iterations of accommodation, negotiation, and more explicit resistance (de St Croix, 2016: 183). *Developing counter-discourses* draws on feminist, Black, and anti-colonial theories and practices. It is a strategy reflected in de St Croix's research by practitioners seeking to subvert bureaucratic systems that demand evidence of value through quantitative scales and a funding environment that generates competition. Countering this dominant discourse involves framing practice through the prism of care, empathy, journeying with young people, and cooperating creatively with other youth work agencies. An alternative strategy of *refusing and rebelling* was evidenced in de St Croix's research by practitioners who would not comply with data collection requirements that compromised the anonymity of young people. Further examples included refusing and returning funding due to ethical concerns and resigning from positions where managerialist expectations discredit the practitioner's skills and agency. De St Croix (2016: 186) notes: 'While counter-discourses are widespread among grassroots youth workers, traditional larger-scale resistance such as strikes and demonstrations are less common.' Buchroth and Husband (2015: 119) argue for the necessity of larger scale resistance and the sector to 'collectivise' to resist the imposition of neoliberal ideology within youth work.

Reimagining youth work is the final form of resistance outlined by de St Croix (2016), building on rebelling strategies and creating counter-discourses. Advancing qualitative storytelling forms of evaluation that challenge the sacrosanct place of quantitative outcomes is a strategy adopted by some practitioners. Others began new youth work enterprises that 'reject market-oriented values and supports young people in campaigning' (de St Croix, 2016: 187). Another approach focused on opening youth centres outside of funding-stipulated times to enable the development of practice unconstrained by funder agendas.

Youth sector peacebuilding is doubly subjected to neoliberal policy making from the domains of both youth policy and peace policy. Consequently, tensions are evident in the framing of youth sector peacebuilding as a socialising or politicising practice; reproducing conformity with the status quo or cultivating notions of activism and resistance. In conflict zones, ideas of politicisation, resistance, and dissent have arguably been underutilised due to connotations of dissidence linked to paramilitarism and radicalisation towards violent extremism. However, the concepts of radicalisation and politicisation can be reclaimed as core features of democratic politics that recognise and promote the political agency of young people. This reclamation can help to combat the depoliticising trends of neoliberal advancement in youth sector peacebuilding.

The following section considers the impact of various policies and strategies in the context of the north of Ireland. In keeping with the ideas already explored in this chapter, the policy domain indicates that state priorities consistently tend towards safety and stability. These priorities squeeze out opportunities for a more innovative approach to youth sector peacebuilding, which aims to embed political engagement and youth activism.

More of the same: four decades of mutual understanding policy

The socio-political context of war in the north of Ireland heavily influenced the ideology and direction of youth sector peacebuilding policy. In the 1970s, amid the terror of bomb threats, random shootings, targeted executions, roadblocks, army checkpoints, paramilitary campaigns, and daily news reports of lost lives, peacebuilding initiatives with young people in Northern Ireland came to prominence. Ethnic segregation became more pronounced as people were intimidated out of their homes and forced to relocate to areas of majority Unionist or Nationalist residents. Community leaders and local volunteers worked defiantly to facilitate cross-community contact between the socially, religiously, politically, and educationally divided Nationalist and Unionist communities. In these early years, responding to widespread political violence, the newly formed statutory youth service was focused on 'keeping young people safe' (McCready, 2020: 48). The youth service was 'reactive' and 'needs responsive', conditioning practitioners to engage primarily with young men. Recreation was used to divert them from paramilitary involvement, thus producing a preoccupation with 'keeping young people off the streets' (Jeffs et al, 2019: 38).

Teachers in schools and youth workers in communities supported young people as best they could as a new phase of protracted violence took hold which would persist until the Belfast Good Friday Agreement in 1998. The Department of Education for Northern Ireland (DE) devised the Cross-Community Contact Scheme in 1987, which encouraged schools to actively develop contact between pupils and teachers across the Catholic and de-facto Protestant school divide. While the scheme generated many one-off contact experiences, it failed to foster an ethos of sustained partnership within the segregated education system (Smith and Robinson, 1996). Also in 1987,

DE, the department responsible for the youth service, published *A Policy for the Youth Service*, known as the Blue Book. It noted that cross-community programming should be firmly embedded in youth work. This policy direction was reinforced in the 1989 Education Reform (NI) Order which legislated Education for Mutual Understanding as a statutory cross-curricular theme in schools aimed at increasing respect for difference, interdependence, sharing and understanding cultures, and a commitment to non-violence.

The 1998 Belfast Good Friday Agreement proved to be a crucial political pivot towards peace, with widespread support across civil society and from international actors. The agreement resulted in a dramatic decrease in eruptions and threats of violence. Young people, however, continued to experience legacies of conflict, not least the normalisation of social and educational segregation and sectarianism. Youth work continued to be seen by policy makers as a key mechanism for 'promoting peacebuilding and good community relations' (DE, 2005: 23). In an attempt to clarify the purpose and contribution of the statutory youth service, DE launched *Youth Work: A Model for Effective Practice* (DE, 1997), which emphasised the personal and social development of young people and the role of youth work in 'testing values and beliefs'. Crucially, the notion of political education, which had been part of earlier conversations about the nature of youth work, was dropped from youth work strategy. Almost four decades later, political education is yet to find its way back into youth policy in Northern Ireland as an explicit theme (McCready and Loudon, 2020). In 2003 the newly formed Curriculum Development Unit within DE relaunched *A Model of Effective Practice*, which now included principles of Equity, Diversity, and Interdependence. Critics note that Equity, Diversity, and Interdependence appeared to be an add-on without a thorough development of how these core values could advance a radical youth work curriculum in a contested society (Scott-McKinley, 2020).

At the height of violence, bringing young people together across a political, religious, and cultural ethnic divide constituted radical practice. Arguably, however, the policy machine has remained stuck in this intergroup contact paradigm. Subsequent youth work and education policies such as *Together Building a United Community* (TEO, 2013) and *Sharing Works* (DE, 2015) remained wedded to an emphasis on contact for mutual understanding and building relationships to reduce prejudice across lines of division. This was accompanied by increasing recognition of challenging all forms of xenophobia alongside tackling sectarianism (Hamilton and McArdle, 2020).

Within the formal education sector, tensions exist between proponents of integrated education and those in favour of shared education. The former advocate for radical reform of education structures. As of 2024, approximately 7 per cent of schools were integrated. These integrated schools commit to achieving at least 30 per cent enrolment of pupils from Catholic and

Protestant backgrounds. Shared education, alternatively, adopts a more pragmatic approach to working across existing structures. Emphasis is placed on establishing collaborative partnerships between Catholic Maintained schools which have a large majority of pupils from a Catholic/Nationalist background and schools controlled by the state which tend to have a large majority of pupils from a Protestant/Unionist background. Deemed by some as less ambitious, shared education has been critiqued as 'the least-worst option', while doing 'little to advance reconciliation' (Hansson and Roulston, 2021: 730). Shared education, with a persistent focus on mutual understanding, prioritises social cohesion with the intent of 'fostering social relationships and trust between citizens; and developing shared values and identities' (Hughes and Loader, 2023: 306).

These policy developments in Northern Ireland are not unique. They are demonstrative of policy directions in other conflict societies where formal and informal education is considered a fundamental pathway out of conflict and towards a more harmonious future. While this has led to many examples of creative working and effective practices, too often a deliberate focus on social and structural change with young people has been missing. Acknowledging this reality, the United Nations Youth, Peace, and Security Resolution (UNSC Res 2250, 2015) seeks to embed youth participation in peacebuilding as an inherently political process. The resolution has a radical bent, calling for the unmet political convictions of young people to override a neoliberal peace negotiated by political elites and marketed to the wider population. Similarly, the European Union's PEACE IV programme in Northern Ireland (2014–2020) for the first time incorporated a set of youth work oriented principles for all projects under the Children and Young People funding strand. These included youth-centred practices, youth engagement, voice, partnership, and the centrality of developing relationships (SEUPB, 2018). To transcend tokenism and achieve authenticity, these participatory processes must engage with young people whose voices have traditionally been absent from policy. Such commitments involve embracing risk and discomfort, making space for agitational youth voices whose perspectives can disrupt and challenge broader veneers of peace. By engaging the diverse, competing, and ardent political motivations and aspirations of young people, youth sector peacebuilding can become the site of authentic critical dialogue and activism.

Conclusion

Prewrapped peacebuilding comes with pre-designed targets, indicators, and outcomes. It has become commonplace in an age of widely accepted neoliberal ideas. Large-scale peacebuilding programmes inject cash into conflict zones and expect an expedient positive return on investment. Such logic, however, fails to address the complexities and nuances of context or the needs and interests of differentiated social groups. Neoliberal ideals tend to decontextualise and depoliticise. Subsequently, peacebuilding becomes transactional and positions youth as recipients of short-term programmes.

Youth work as a radical and empowering practice contains the tools and processes to subvert the dominant policy discourse of youth as consumers of ready-made peace programmes. Creative participatory methods can facilitate the inclusion of a broad spectrum of young people as collaborators in actively designing, testing, shaping, and reshaping contextually relevant peacebuilding aims, objectives, and outcomes. The alternative to a one-size-fits-all peacebuilding is young people co-designing locally owned, nationally significant peacebuilding strategies and democratic processes, in partnership with adults.

To avoid recreating the dynamics of top-down neoliberal peacebuilding in which decision-making is controlled by 'political elites', participatory processes ought to be cautious of instituting a group of young people as local youth elites. Simply adding a local dimension does not automatically address the issues with neoliberal peacebuilding (Paffenholz, 2015). Such local approaches require a critical engagement with power dynamics and an intersectional lens which considers the extent to which opportunities to influence the peacebuilding agenda are equitable across multiple demographics including gender, socio-economic status, ethnicity, and ability.

At a policy level, educational initiatives with young people in contested spaces are prone to co-option by the state. In such cases, practitioners are positioned as facilitators of consensus-building and cultivating harmonious citizenship. Northern Ireland is an illustrative case with a long-standing emphasis on mutual understanding as the core peacebuilding priority in the youth sector. Meanwhile, notions of political education and participation have been missing, creating a tension between harmonising versus politicising approaches to youth sector peacebuilding – a key theme further explored in subsequent chapters.

5

A peacebuilding typology

> We are 21 years into a relative peace process, which is actually just the absence of everyday regular violence rather than peace. (YW34)

Introduction

As a contested concept, peacebuilding is fraught with competing political ideas, agendas, and motivations. This chapter hones in on the concepts of peacebuilding and divergent interpretations of these. Based on an extensive review of peacebuilding literature, six interrelated concepts are presented as core in the peacebuilder's lexicon. Many sources cited in this chapter refer to Northern Ireland. However, while situated within this distinctive geopolitical context, the concepts from this literature have many parallels with other contested societies. Furthermore, readers attuned to the complexities of political violence and antagonisms in a context of far-right extremism or post-colonial settings will recognise the relevance of these concepts to such realities. The chapter examines debates, dilemmas, and tensions arising from the following six concepts that consistently feature in discussions on peacebuilding:

- reconciliation
- intergroup contact
- human rights
- justice
- citizenship
- wellbeing

Reconciliation

Reconciliation involves processes that simultaneously seek to transform ruptured relationships while also addressing perpetrators and victims of past hurts (Hughes, 2018). Hamber and Kelly (2005) propose a working definition of reconciliation founded on five key strands:

1. Developing a shared vision of an interdependent and fair society.
2. Acknowledging and dealing with the past.
3. Building positive relationships.

4. Significant cultural and attitudinal change.
5. Substantial social, economic, and political change.

Antagonisms imminently arise when practitioners set out to apply Hamber and Kelly's strands of reconciliation into practice. Distinguishing between victim and perpetrator, for instance, is a highly contentious matter, and subsequently, any approach to addressing the past is problematic. Govier (2009) discusses the notion of 'aversive acknowledgement' as a vital aspect of reconciliation where conflict actors account for the harms they have caused. It is termed *aversive acknowledgement* due to the challenging nature of taking responsibility for actions condemned by others (Lundy and McGovern, 2006). The characterisation of 'evil perpetrator' versus 'righteous victim' sustains the avoidance of acknowledgement (Brewer et al, 2018). Govier (2009) therefore suggests a reframing of aversive acknowledgement that is rooted in restorative justice. Predicated on a belief that guilt is corrosive to the human psyche, aversive acknowledgement is presented as a healing process for both perpetrators and victims, recognising these are not binary positions.

Related to the notion of acknowledgement is the concept of forgiveness, which has been defined as: 'Willingness to abandon one's right to resentment, negative judgement, and indifferent behaviour toward one who unjustly injured us, while fostering the undeserved qualities of compassion, generosity and even love toward him or her' (Enright et al, 1998, cited in McGlynn et al, 2004: 149). Such a conceptualisation of forgiveness encounters the same difficulties of acknowledgement where a victim–perpetrator distinction is not easily defined or is resisted by one or both parties. Despite the challenges presented by the notion of forgiveness and accompanying religious overtones, it is often depicted as a vital component in peacebuilding (Spencer, 2011). The tandem concepts of acknowledgement, forgiveness, and justice mitigate a simplistic conceptualisation of forgiveness characterised by an absence of accountability. This is captured in Lederach's (1995; 1997; 2003) influential work where he emphasises the interdependence of truth, justice, and mercy in his portrayal of conflict transformation.

Thick and thin perspectives of reconciliation

Two competing approaches to reconciliation have been characterised as thick versus thin (Little and Maddison, 2017). The 'thick' or 'maximalist' approach centres on the cultivation of transformed interpersonal relationships. The 'thin' or 'minimalist' approach regards conflict as necessary and imagines how the socio-political landscape may be enriched through a reconciliation that embraces contestation. Writing on the two approaches, Borer (2004: 31) suggests, 'one approach to reconciliation requires people to get along; the other assumes they won't'. The former invests in interpersonal relationship building, while the latter is dedicated to socio-political reform and change. Each invests energy at different levels and is indicative of disparate assumptions about the process of reconciliation. The thick-maximalist approach presupposes the agency of individual actors and creates expectations for individuals to enact reconciliation in their personal relationships. The thin-minimalist approach confers greater emphasis on the structural aspects of reconciliation work and raises critical questions regarding state and institutional accountability for reproducing inequality and oppression in society.

Approaches to reconciliation that give limited attention to structurally embedded legacies of conflict, and instead focus on bringing antagonistic groups together, have been critiqued as 'highly agential' (Little and Maddison, 2017: 147). They tend to 'reify agency over structure' (Hughes, 2018: 637). This agency versus structure dichotomy highlights the complexity of reconciliatory processes that seek to transform relationships and power at personal, social, and structural levels within conflict societies.

Degrees of reconciliation

Some approaches to reconciliation are critiqued as overly idealistic, founded on an aspiration to resolve conflict and establish a harmonious state of peaceful co-existence. Alternative framings of reconciliation reject the normative ideal of a transcendent harmonious state, in favour of a dialogical process that makes space for unresolved issues to be carried forward as part of ongoing political engagement and civil disagreement (Doxtader, 2003; Little, 2011a). Others go further still, using the language of 'narrative reconciliation' which seeks to dispel the myth of a reconciliation consensus. This approach embraces the complexity and reality of opposing irreconcilable narratives, histories, and relationships (Moon, 2006). Little (2011b: 86) explains: 'Talking about reconciliation needs to involve narratives which are not reconciled, which are not forgiving, which do not apologize, which call for punishment. In short, narratives of reconciliation will generate critiques of reconciliatory processes and greater or lesser degrees of non-reconciliation.'

In the context of Northern Ireland, it can be argued that a more optimistic approach to reconciliation has been pursued based on intergroup dialogue and a policy focus on community relations (Hammond, 2008; Harland, 2009; Milliken, 2020). This focus prioritises addressing sectarianism and polarisation between Catholic/Nationalist and Protestant/Unionist communities. However, continued political impasses and the intransigence of ethno-political voting blocs suggest significant degrees of non-reconciliation. Alongside sectarianism, racism has been identified as a core issue, exacerbated by the conditions of parochialism, segregation, and mistrust in Northern Irish society (Brewer, 1992; McVeigh and Rolston, 2007; Knox, 2011a; Gray et al, 2018).

Table 5.1: Dichotomies of reconciliation

Reconciliation as relational	vs	Reconciliation as political
Interpersonal	vs	Structural
Thick/maximalist	vs	Thin/minimalist
Idealist	vs	Sceptical
Platonic	vs	Conflictual
Forgiveness and mercy	vs	Justice and accountability

The narrative and more sceptical approach to reconciliation may extend greater recognition to the experiences of minority groups whose voices have been muted in the dominant dialogue between Unionists and Nationalists (Haydon and Scraton, 2008; Pierson, 2018). The narrative approach further invites identity labels to be problematised and gives voice to multiple memories and experiences of community spaces (McEvoy-Levy, 2012).

Table 5.1 summarises a range of dichotomies contained within the concept of reconciliation. These are divided into orientations towards reconciliation as a relational, interpersonal endeavour or reconciliation as a political process. The following section considers the interpersonal dimension of peacebuilding in more depth, examining the literature on relationships and intergroup contact.

Intergroup contact

In a 1954 publication, *The nature of prejudice*, Gordon Allport introduced his now infamous contact hypothesis. The theory speculates that '[c]ontact between groups would be more likely to reduce prejudice and improve intergroup relations if four "optimal" conditions were met' (Hewstone et al, 2014: 40). These four conditions are:

- equal status among participants;
- working together co-operatively;
- working towards common goals;
- support from institutions, policies or authorities that legitimise contact (Hewstone et al, 2014).

Tajfel's (1982) social identity theory was later attached to the conception of the contact hypothesis. Tajfel observed that individuals belong to certain social groups. Identification with a particular 'in-group' invokes dispositions of trust and rapport. The relationship with 'out-group' members, those that a person does not naturally identify with, is characterised by suspicion and indifference. The prefix of 'intergroup' added to the contact hypothesis reflects the language of social identity theory and calls for mixing in-groups with out-groups (Jones, 2004). Connolly (2000: 170) condenses the premise of the hypothesis to 'intergroup contact reduces prejudice'.

Self-disclosure in contact programmes, as a display of trust, has been evidenced to contribute to breaking down barriers and reducing prejudice (Hughes and Loader, 2015). This process of self-disclosure resonates with Fisher's (1984) Trust Attraction Hypothesis that maintains: 'As A discloses, B perceives this as trust, and is consequently more likely to be attracted to A. This increased liking leads B to disclose more to A ... reciprocity of disclosure may well be based on reciprocity of trust' (Hargie et al, 2003: 87–88). Hargie et al (2003: 88) caution, however, that an emphasis on self-disclosure, attraction, trust, and friendship may generate a 'polite avoidance' of contentious issues and may be counter-productive to peacebuilding.

Single identity work has been advocated as a way of preparing groups for contact (Hammond, 2008). Single identity interventions range from a focus on the celebration of own culture to empathy and respect for other cultures (Jones, 2004). The former places value on single identity work in and of itself as a means of appreciating shared norms and beliefs and building group esteem. The latter is seen as a preparatory phase for participants to identify different viewpoints within their own group identity and consider how intergroup dialogue may provoke a sense of challenge and dissonance. Approaches that employ a critical examination of group identity are considered a useful step in facilitating cross-community dialogue around contentious issues (Hammond, 2008). Others have emphasised the importance of creating 'neutral spaces' for intergroup contact that are not necessarily focused on promoting dialogue around difference but focus on commonalities (Crownover, 2009; McEvoy-Levy, 2012).

Pettigrew and Tropp's (2006) meta-analysis of 515 studies on contact work spanning 1940–2000 and representing over 250,000 participants, found significant support for Allport's hypothesis (Pettigrew and Tropp, 2006; Hewstone et al, 2014). Ninety-four per cent of samples showed an inverse relationship between prejudice and intergroup contact (Pettigrew and Tropp, 2006). The results also indicated that participants typically apply their more favourable attitudes from a contact experience to members of the outgroup in general. This is a crucial point as it suggests a positive encounter with someone from a different social group leads to changes in behaviour and attitudes not just towards those individuals but towards the wider group in general. Pettigrew and Tropp (2006: 766) concluded from their findings that: 'Intergroup contact can contribute meaningfully to reductions in prejudice across a broad range of groups and contexts.' Dixon et al (2005: 700) are, however, more sceptical. They critique the contact hypothesis for misdirecting peacebuilding energies at the individual level, contending: 'These interventions may be successful in creating small islands of integration in a sea of intolerance, but they are unrepresentative of wider processes of contact and desegregation.'

Critiquing contact

Contested perspectives on intergroup contact are indicative of aspirations for change focused primarily at either the personal or societal levels. Critics have argued that a personal prejudice reduction model has generally taken precedence over a collective action and resistance approach (Dixon et al, 2005; Wright and Baray, 2012). Reicher (1986; 2007) prominently advocates the collective resistance model, calling for a transformation of the structures that facilitate ethnic conflict and segregation. He opposes the premise of the contact hypothesis, identifying it as an antithesis to social change and a distraction from deeply rooted inequalities and asymmetrical power relations. Pettigrew (2010: 421) summarises Reicher's argument, writing: 'Negative attitudes, even hatred toward the majority, are necessary for the minority to initiate the conflict necessary for social change.' There is a concern that relationships developed through intergroup contact can placate the minority and oppressed group to inequalities that serve the majority. Pettigrew (2010: 422) designates this as the 'Reicher effect'. While accepting that the Reicher effect may in some instances arise, Pettigrew (2010: 424) contends that a 'counter-Reicher effect' is more strongly evidenced where, as a result of contact, majority group attitudes become more supportive of social change that serves the interests of minority groups.

In the context of contested societies where there is no clear ethnic, cultural, or political majority, identifying a minority or oppressed group is not straightforward. In Northern Ireland, for instance, history and politics are fundamentally contested, and both Nationalist/Republican or Unionist/Loyalist groups may simultaneously identify as the marginalised and victims of structural inequality (Brewer et al, 2018). When applied to such contested societies, the collective resistance model proposed by Reicher could be better understood as intergroup contact that seeks to transform the socio-political situation that is failing all ethnic groups. This stance counterposes an approach to intergroup contact that intends to build friendships across lines of division with minimal concern for effecting wider political and structural change (Wright and Lubensky, 2009).

Common among writers on contact theory, whether proponent or critic, is an agreement that contact alone is insufficient (Dixon et al, 2005; Pettigrew, 2010; Hewstone et al, 2014). While the previous section on 'Reconciliation' identified a duality between interpersonal and structural avenues of peacebuilding, the intergroup contact debate highlights differing orientations towards prejudice-reduction or collective action as the most effective ways to build peace (Wright and Lubensky, 2009). The following section examines the concept of human rights in peacebuilding which have historically been hard-won through collective action on the part of marginalised and oppressed groups.

Human rights

Integrating human rights with peacebuilding requires synthesising different starting points and assumptions. Human rights frameworks are considered more legalistic and outcomes-driven than the process-oriented notions of pursuing reconciliation, relationships, and trust (Beirne and Knox, 2014). Parlevliet (2017) observes three different uses of the concept of human rights. The first is human rights as a *system of law* codified and enforceable by legal institutions and intended to protect citizens and arbitrate human disputes. Second, human rights can be understood as a *set of values* linked to notions of equality and social justice and inspiring action for social change. Third, human rights have been presented as *a vision of good governance* facilitating democratic systems underpinned by transparency, accountability, and participation. A shift from legalistic notions of rights as a system of law to more moral and political conceptions of human rights as values and good governance is a way of bridging the gap between rights activists and reconciliation practitioners (Beirne and Knox, 2014).

Hvidsten and Skarstad (2018) posit that human rights and *positive peace* are conceptually connected. This connection is weakened, however, if a *negative* notion of peace is adopted premised on the absence of violence. Such a restricted view of peace fails to distinguish between oppressive regimes, criminal acts, and actors who instigate protests and rebellions in the pursuit of human rights. Under a negative peace, stability may be prevalent while human rights violations proliferate. Pursuing a positive peace involves building a particular kind of social order, one that many peacebuilders seek to ground in human rights frameworks. Situating peacebuilding within a rights discourse makes space for actions that challenge inequitable social structures. It includes efforts to destabilise a status quo that serves some yet oppresses and marginalises others.

Drawing on national and international charters and legislation, rights activists gravitate towards addressing systemic structural and cultural violence (Galtung, 2000). Describing structural and cultural violence as 'invisible' compared with the overt actions of direct violence, Galtung invites a deeper analysis of violence. Structural violence is intertwined in the everyday interactions between people and institutions, in the systems that govern the lives of individuals and groups. It can be uncovered by identifying dynamics of privilege and disadvantage (Del Felice, 2008). Cultural violence is an even more subtle form of oppression where norms and dominant discourses about right and wrong, good and bad, sacred and profane, legitimise particular instances of direct and structural violence while delegitimising others

(Galtung, 1990; 2000). For instance, direct action by student-led anti-war movements which cause disruption on university campuses are often framed by administrators, security forces, mainstream media, and the government as illegitimate. Such framing serves to justify the heavy-handed policing of these protests. The actions of students and others involved are determined by those in power as harmful while the forceful response of policing is depicted as proportionate and necessary. Appealing to rights-based frameworks establishes an onus on state and non-state actors to recognise and protect rights and offers a way of redressing structural and cultural violence as well as direct violence.

A rights realisation gap

Rights feature prominently in United Nations Security Council Resolution 2250, Youth, Peace and Security (UNSC Res 2250, 2015). The emphasis of the resolution is on recognising the contribution of young people to peacebuilding. While the *protection* of rights is presented as a key platform, there is also a focus on young people standing up for their rights and the rights of others (Simpson, 2018). In conflict and post-conflict settings, the resolution advocates there is a need to address a 'rights realization gap' to ensure 'full socioeconomic, cultural and political rights for young people' (Simpson, 2018: 101). Structural and cultural violence experienced by young people associated with unfulfilled socio-economic rights is an ongoing concern that tends not to be adequately addressed in societies transitioning from conflict (Evans, 2016). The violence of exclusion is one aspect of such structural violence. UNSCR 2250 urges that young people should be fully engaged in political processes, have access to inclusive education that fosters critical thinking, have access to non-exploitative employment, and have their gender identities recognised and valued (Simpson, 2018). This final point is developed in the broader literature that emphasises the cognisance of gendered experiences of peacebuilding.

Gender, rights, and peacebuilding

Ashe (2012; 2019) and Pierson (2018) determine that a critical analysis of gender is decidedly absent from research into the dynamics of conflict and peacebuilding in Northern Ireland. Ashe (2012) pursues an examination of masculinities and conflict in Northern Ireland, noting that men as combatants, politicians, and community leaders has been widely studied, however, the significance of gender identities has not been sufficiently explored. She proceeds to argue that militarised masculinities and the potency of a protection-of-communities narrative has perpetuated male dominance over women. Such male dominance persisted through the peace process and is reflected in the celebrated notion of former combatants transformed into builders of peace.

The power-sharing style of politics established in the 1998 Belfast Good Friday Agreement has normalised appeals to traditional ethno-nationalist allegiances. This predominantly two-community approach to politics and peacebuilding processes has negated and silenced other perspectives and issues, including gender, class, and race (Pierson, 2018). From a human rights perspective, Pierson points to United Nations Resolution 1325 on Women, Peace, and Security (UNSC Res 1325, 2000). For some feminists, the resolution is esteemed as progress, redressing how the role of women in peacebuilding has been perpetually overlooked and dismissed. Others critique the resolution as anti-feminist, claiming that it maintains normative gender roles and assumes traditional militarist assumptions of conflict. As such, the resolution is seen as feminising women, viewing them as in need of protection. Pierson (2018) perceives that the resolution has the potential to put gender issues firmly on the agenda and disrupt traditional gendered peacebuilding dynamics when accompanied by feminist critiques. Increased inclusion and recognition of feminist perspectives would help to develop policy and research on conflict and peacebuilding in Northern Ireland.

Questions of inclusion and meaningful participation are crucial considerations in a peacebuilding process underpinned by rights frameworks (Hvidsten and Skarstad, 2018). The violence of exclusion continues to be experienced by young people living in areas of multiple deprivation. In Northern Ireland, as with other conflict settings, it is these areas that tend to bear the brunt of the most pervasive conflict legacies, including social segregation, sectarianism, intergenerational trauma, and residual paramilitarism. Within a human rights framework, such violations of exclusion require redress. These issues are developed further by examining the allied concept of justice.

Justice

Constructions of justice are a crucial component of peacebuilding. Multiple qualifiers are used to distinguish approaches to justice such as retributive, restorative, social, transitional, and transformative. Retributive justice is concerned with just deserts for conflict actors who orchestrated or inflicted violence. Social justice, in contrast, takes a broader view of systemic injustices which are at risk of being overlooked in legal proceedings, tribunals, and truth recovery processes. It is concerned with addressing disparities across diverse groups in relation to rights, opportunities, and wealth, and redressing the unequal distribution of resources (Thompson, 2016; Ledwith, 2020). Transitional justice, while critiqued as too focused on retribution, aspires to meet demands for penal action while also responding to calls for amnesty, restorative processes, and implementing frameworks to achieve greater social justice (Li et al, 2018). This section considers the interplay of transitional, restorative, social, and transformative justice in societies emerging from protracted violence.

Transitional justice

Transitional justice encompasses the theory and practice of how societies deal with a legacy of past mass abuses, an enterprise that has become increasingly established in conflict societies since the 1990s (Dudai, 2018). Societies transitioning from violent conflict are confronted with questions of truth recovery, redressing impunity, policing and legal reform, dealing with injustice, and instituting reparations. In implementing mechanisms to address these issues, transitional justice faces dilemmas of balancing justice as accountability with notions of amnesty and impunity. This has been framed as the 'peace versus justice' problem (Tolbert, 2009). Societies in transition from conflict are tasked with holding violent state and non-state actors to account in a way which provides victims with a sense of justice, while also incentivising truth recovery and establishing mechanisms that encourage former combatants to embrace non-violence.

In practice, transitional justice has been critiqued as too focused on outcomes and addressing symptoms of conflict through legal routes rather than valuing processes that seek to address root causes and underlying tensions (Gready and Robins, 2014; Baker and Obradovic-Wochnik, 2016). It has also tended to focus on high-level actors such as political and (para)military leaders as well as international interventionist bodies such as the United Nations (Akhavan, 2009). While strategically and symbolically important, these approaches to transitional justice can further marginalise the voices and experiences of local communities. Transitional justice, therefore, can be critiqued as an attempt to objectify the conflict, appealing to outside parties to make rulings about right and wrong. Such sub-contracting of peace and justice processes risks neglecting the subjective and deeply interpersonal dynamics of conflict that need to be confronted and grappled with through relational and dialogical encounters between opposing groups. To this end, calls have been made for more localised participatory processes that bring politically and culturally opposed groups into direct contact with each other, situating community-led initiatives as central to the transition process (Lundy and McGovern, 2008).

Restorative justice

A key aspect of transitional justice in Northern Ireland has been youth justice reform underpinned by the ideas of restorative justice (Chapman et al, 2018). This has been guided by restorative principles including:

- provide space for people to meet and communicate;
- enhance a culture of respect;
- strengthen just social relations; and
- address directly harmful behaviour. (Chapman et al, 2018: 135)

Restorative justice is explicitly relational as opposed to a retributive approach. The emphasis is not on assigning blame and scapegoating, which leads to isolation; rather, it is a perspective of justice oriented towards human connection. Chapman et al (2018) link the fields of community relations, peacebuilding, and restorative justice by identifying the common thread of dialogue to build and heal relationships. The distinctive aspect of restorative justice relates to the circumstances by which individuals come together in this dialogical process centred around specific acts of harm. The approach seeks to engage victims, perpetrators, and the wider community (O'Mahony et al, 2012). It is argued that restorative justice is a valuable alternative to criminal justice, facilitating restorative and relational processes in situations that can be resolved without criminal proceedings. In Northern Ireland, such approaches rely on the state to fund and legitimise the work of restorative justice organisations.

Lohmeyer (2017a) proposes a critical scepticism when analysing youth restorative justice by considering issues of power. Perceiving that restorative practices conducted through institutions are an extension of state power, there is an overarching orientation towards social control. In a post-conflict context where disaffection and social exclusion of young people act as drivers for engagement in behaviours deemed by the state to be problematic and anti-social, restorative justice is used to modify individual behaviours rather than underlying inequalities. Once again, Galtung's (1990) notion of cultural violence is relevant in considering how social inequalities are legitimised through social norms and power hierarchies.

Transformative justice

In response to the limitations of transitional justice and critiques of restorative justice, the concept of *transformative* justice has been proposed as a more holistic approach (Lambourne, 2009). This conceptualisation of justice seeks to instil a greater focus on socio-political relations and power dynamics alongside participation from grassroots actors, incorporating notions of social justice more explicitly. Transformative justice seeks not only retributive justice for past wrongs but also to reconstitute political, social, and institutional systems and processes to promote greater social equality in a renewed social landscape (Lambourne, 2009). It aspires to move beyond arbitrating claims of injustice at the individual level towards effecting wider institutional and structural change, from the bottom up. Rather than 'moving on from the past' the emphasis shifts towards ongoing activism for change and creating a platform for competing notions of peace, justice, and reconciliation to be debated alongside the notion of transitional justice itself (Gready and Robins, 2014). To achieve this, a radical notion of citizenship is proposed that refers not to legal rights and responsibilities but agency and activism at various levels with an emphasis on challenging dominant discourses. Such radical notions of citizenship are not always evident in policy or practice. The next section considers citizenship literature in relation to peacebuilding, spanning from conformist understandings to more radical and emancipatory interpretations.

Citizenship

Citizenship invokes notions of identity, status, rights, responsibilities, contribution, decision-making, voice, and belonging. In contested societies, prominence is placed on citizenship as a marker of ethno-nationalist and cultural identities (Smith 2003; Stevenson and Sagherian-Dickey, 2018). Writing in the context of Northern Ireland, where national loyalties are polarised and antagonistic, Smith (2003) highlights that a patriotic sense of citizenship is destined to exacerbate tensions. The language of multiculturalism has been used in policy discourse in an attempt to manage the existence of distinctive cultural communities. Two approaches to embedding cohesion in Northern Ireland are characteristic of contested approaches to multiculturalism – separatist and pluralist. The former concedes that diverse groups in society cannot be integrated and will remain separate. In this situation, government institutions comply with this assumption and work to separatist expectations (Knox, 2011b). In the latter, it is assumed that unity and diversity co-exist and communal identities interact within a pluralist environment. Developing upon a dichotomy of separatist versus pluralist approaches to pursuing social cohesion in divided societies, Smith (2003) outlines four distinct conceptions of multiculturalism, summarised in Table 5.2.

Linked to the various interpretations of multiculturalism is the notion of superordinate identities, which downplay distinct group identities in favour of an existing or new shared overarching identity (Hughes and Loader, 2015). *Global citizenship* is an exemplary superordinate identity. It involves awareness of global issues, embracing cultural diversity, empathy towards others, promoting social justice and sustainability, and a sense of responsibility to act for the betterment of the world (Reysen et al, 2012). Reysen and Katzarska-Miller (2017) found that young people who identified with a global citizenship identity were more likely to support values related to peace, including notions of forgiveness, social justice, and a concern for human rights. Those who were more inclined to adopt an alternative superordinate identity such as 'human' or 'American' were less likely to embrace such peace-related ideals. The researchers concluded that the *global citizen* superordinate identity tends to be more clearly defined and connected with humanitarian principles than a nationalistic identity (American) or the more nominal notion of *human* as a shared identity.

Table 5.2: Distinctions of multiculturalism

Monoculturalism	A single dominant identity is promoted, and minorities are expected to fit in and certainly not stand out. 'Diversity is perceived as a threat' (Smith, 2003: 28).
Liberal multiculturalism	'Emphasises similarity by drawing attention to what is in common by members of diverse groups' (Smith, 2003: 29). Tends to assume there is equality of opportunity and a merit-based system. Invokes ideas of creating neutral spaces. However, this can lead to ignorance and downplaying of inequality and avoids confrontation.
Pluralist multiculturalism	Seeks to celebrate diversity and emphasise the differences between groups. It can lead to tokenistic sharing and partaking in cultural traditions. 'Diversity may be seen as an intrinsic virtue' (Smith, 2003: 29).
Critical multiculturalism	Distinguished by 'a willingness to acknowledge inequalities between different groups in society' (Smith, 2003: 29). It recognises similarities and differences, but the critical point is addressing unequal access to power and resources. Heightens awareness and challenges prejudices and discrimination that are ingrained in society.

Source: Based on Smith (2003: 28–29)

In a context where ethnic nationality is fundamentally contested, sub-group identities may tend to feel threatened and thus advocate maintaining group salience instead of assuming a superordinate identity (Reysen and Katzarska-Miller, 2017). In Northern Ireland, for instance, despite the identifier 'Northern Irish' growing in popularity among some young people (ARK, 2023b), the extent to which this is an inclusive identity for all citizens remains controversial and tends to be embraced more so by those from a Protestant rather than Catholic community background. More broadly, for those who perceive that their national identity is threatened or at risk of dilution, societal shifts to the rhetoric of post-nationalistic conceptions of *global citizenship* may be resisted.

The education system is a powerful arbiter of how citizenship is understood and indicates the extent to which young people are positioned as political actors or a disengaged and problematic population (Shultz, 2009). Critical approaches to citizenship education draw on pedagogies inspired by educationalists such as Paulo Freire (1921–1997). Freire's (1970) critical pedagogy begins by questioning why things are the way they are, forming the basis for collective action to challenge social exclusion, inequality, and systems which reproduce power, privilege, and disadvantage (Ledwith, 2016). In contested societies, a critical approach to citizenship education includes an emphasis on democratic participation and political literacy (Carter, 2004; Smith et al, 2019).

Political literacy was a term 'invented to mean that someone should have the knowledge, skills and values to be effective in public life' and its inventor emphasised the radical implications of the concept (Crick, 2007: 245). It is focused on fostering agency where citizens not only understand how institutions in society work but are active in tackling social problems, equipped to effect change, and, where necessary, hold institutions to account (Henderson, 2006; Crick, 2007). Tensions exist regarding the extent to which educationalists are enabled or have an appetite for engaging young people in this radical notion of citizenship that tackles complex and contentious socio-political and cultural issues in a divided society (McMullan, 2018; Smith et al, 2019). Consequently, citizenship education occurs on a continuum from conservative and conformist to radical and emancipatory (Shaull, 1996), where the state tends to be invested in the former (Shultz, 2009). The final concept discussed in this chapter is that of wellbeing in relation to peacebuilding with young people.

Wellbeing

Increasingly, public attention is focused on the wellbeing not only of those who have endured direct experience of living in a society embroiled in violent conflict but also the next generations (McAlister et al, 2021; Kagoyire et al, 2023). While not as explicit as other concepts explored in this chapter, notions of addressing transgenerational trauma and mental health repeatedly appear in literature as part of a wider discussion on peacebuilding. More explicit is a burgeoning literature on epigenetics examining how trauma is held in the body and transmitted biologically, creating a predisposition towards stress-induced negative impacts on wellbeing. Reviewing the literature, O'Neill (2015: 9) notes: 'If a pregnant mother is affected by chronic stress, epigenetic modifications in the child may act as a molecular or cellular memory that tune the offspring for one or several generations for survival in a hostile environment, making generations more vulnerable for mental illnesses, including suicide.'

Similar to other regions marked by protracted violence, the longevity of conflict in Northern Ireland, along with ongoing political tensions, poverty, and residual paramilitarism, continue to adversely impact young people's mental health and wellbeing (McLafferty et al, 2016). There is a growing consensus on the need for trauma-informed practice across various disciplines working directly with children and young people (Bunting et al, 2019). This framework has led some to re-emphasise the value of therapeutic interventions with young people within the youth sector (Carr, 2022).

Mental health and psychosocial programming

Disparate notions of addressing trauma and mental health concerns related to post-conflict environments are brought together in the framework of Mental

Health and Psychosocial Support (MHPSS) (Hamber et al, 2014). MHPSS recognises the contribution of clinical interventions through psychiatry, psychotherapy, and counselling, as well as community-based initiatives that generate therapeutic effects through building positive relationships, developing resiliency, and exploring self-help strategies (Anderson et al, 2022). This psychosocial approach to addressing the impacts of conflict and accompanying legacies focuses on individual and subjective experiences. It situates these within the context of family and community, linking the psychological with the social. While identifying opportunities for synergy between psychosocial and peacebuilding initiatives, Hamber and Gallagher (2014: 43) criticise the tendency of psychosocial interventions to orient towards a 'personal transformation model'. Practitioners immersed in a policy framework and logic that espouses personal transformation are disinclined to frame their work as contributing to more expansive notions of social change and positive peace.

Common to both the psychosocial and peacebuilding approach is a tendency to consider trauma and mental health as an individualised concern, separate from broader peacebuilding goals of societal transformation and structural change. This medical model may involve practitioners adopting roles as 'paraprofessionals' in addressing mental health (Hamber et al, 2014: 8). Such instances involve practitioners drawing on their professional training to inform interventions while not being fully equipped as qualified mental health professionals. In this regard, youth workers are better placed to complement rather than replicate interventions delivered by mental health practitioners (Schubotz and McArdle, 2014). While this brings many benefits it also is limited to the extent that the personal transformation model of mental health and psychosocial support tends to be fragmented and reactionary (Hamber et al, 2014). Furthermore, it can too quickly pathologise individuals and groups by presuming certain young people require psychological and personal development support before they can participate in peacebuilding processes. Opportunities to build a more coherent and integrated approach where psychosocial programming is aligned with notions of capacity building for social transformation would benefit from more empirical and theoretical work in both the fields of MHPSS and peacebuilding.

Conclusion

This chapter has explored integral peacebuilding concepts that are continuously debated, interpreted, and applied in distinctive ways. This array of ideas and perspectives gives rise to a complex tapestry of peacebuilding that can only partially be captured in single definitions. Each concept that feeds into the theory, policy, and practice of peacebuilding does not stand alone; rather, it rubs against other ideas. Reconciliation relies on notions of intergroup contact and justice, which draw on human rights frameworks, which inform notions of citizenship, and which account for wellbeing concerns. Whichever concept is taken as the entry point, soon enough the other concepts will be encountered.

While each concept constitutes an entire field of study replete with scholarly insights and deliberations as well as practical applications, several common fault lines can be observed. A key distinction is a disposition towards harmonious interpersonal relationships or democratic, dialogical, and potentially agitational politics. This tension is most evident in the literature on reconciliation, intergroup contact, and citizenship, where some call for platonic social relations built on friendship, commonalities, shared identities, and civic engagement as a form of contributing to the flourishing of social cohesion. Others, however, regard this as an idealistic 'transformative fiction' (Moon, 2006: 272) and instead propose such concepts should emphasise the need for critical and sceptical engagement at the political level. This results in degrees of reconciliation including actors who do not embrace dominant reconciliation narratives; who continue to critique forms of structural and cultural violence that are less visible and embedded in the social fabric; who call for a citizenship that is unashamedly political and does not recoil from confrontation and contentious issues.

Another distinction is the positioning of young people in contested societies. The interpretations of core peacebuilding concepts reveal dispositions towards youth variously as deviant, vulnerable, impressionable, or enlightened. Youth are not a homogeneous group and the imposition of labels from adults will often be resisted. Yet within the literature, certain notions of wellbeing and mental health support risk pathologising young people when not grounded in strengths-based capacity-building approaches. When young people's rights are presupposed and not engaged with critically, forms of disenfranchisement and rights abuses can be overlooked. This can be observed in the often-elusive economic dividend from peacebuilding for young people from disadvantaged communities who rarely benefit from the promise of better employment and education opportunities. Policing and justice practices that put young people under surveillance and use them to gather intelligence on others in their communities serve a state social control agenda (Lohmeyer, 2017b). Stories of young people making positive contributions to their communities are often cited in evaluation reports, yet these forms of civic engagement are partial when disconnected from a concept of citizenship that promotes political literacy and engagement in political processes at various levels from local to national and international.

A final fault line inscribed in the concepts of peacebuilding is personal versus social change. This age-old debate in the social sciences is also expressed as agency versus structure (Bourdieu and Wacquant, 1992). Those who orient towards agency and personal change focus on the individual level of peacebuilding processes that seek to reduce prejudice, restore relationships, and maximise personal development, decision-making, and wellbeing within the parameters of wider social, political, and cultural forces. Conversely, those who gravitate towards social and structural change aspire to radically reorganise social, political, and institutional systems premised on values of social justice, equity, and egalitarianism. From this perspective, improving individual and group wellbeing in a post-conflict context involves campaigning for increased resources and wider access to quality preventative and crisis healthcare services. The enactment of justice is not merely to avenge the pain of victims but necessitates the redistribution of wealth and power away from elites who are largely buttressed against the impacts and legacies of conflict.

These distinctive interpretations present challenges for those working with young people. Should the focus be on structure or agency, social control or social change, personal development or social transformation? Of course, these constructions are in many ways 'false dichotomies' that might better be presented as continuums or spectrums of interpretation. Whether understood as dichotomies or degrees of difference, how these concepts are interpreted and applied in policy generates different focal points of practice. The next chapter presents a framework for mapping how individuals and groups construct their understanding of peacebuilding based on how they prioritise the ideas and concepts outlined in this chapter from core through to peripheral components. The proceeding chapter also outlines the conceptual and methodological process whereby the literature reviewed in this chapter formed the basis of our study into different youth workers' perspectives on peacebuilding with young people.

6

Morphology: an analytical tool for peacebuilding

The noise of thoughts being churned up and ideas being challenged. (YW40)

Introduction

Diverse interpretations, combinations, and applications of peacebuilding concepts result in different approaches to practice. This chapter lays out a way of mapping these distinctive perspectives. A novel approach is outlined which connects morphological analysis with Q methodology. While these terms may initially appear obscure, a step-by-step approach is taken to explaining these ideas. They merit some unpacking as, combined, the conceptual lens of morphological analysis and the practical approach of Q methodology underpin the new ideas discussed in the proceeding chapters. Earlier chapters have provided a foundation for understanding morphological analysis by examining the context and concepts of youth sector peacebuilding. Q methodology provides a way of operationalising a morphological analysis of peacebuilding, which is the crux of new insights presented and discussed in the remaining chapters. The appeal of Q methodology is not just as a research method but as a technique that is tactile, experiential, and deliberative. It can be applied in creative ways with young people, students, youth workers, policy makers, and wider communities of practice.

Peacebuilding and morphological analysis

Peacebuilding fits the mould of what Gallie (1956) termed 'essentially contested concepts'. Engaging with such concepts 'inevitably involves endless disputes about their proper uses' (Gallie, 1956: 169). There is no single depiction of peacebuilding that captures all the ways in which peacebuilding is thought about in distinctive geopolitical and socio-cultural contexts. This was evidenced in previous chapters where critical peace scholars have advocated for a 'local turn' away from the homogenising and top-down approaches of liberal peacebuilding. Furthermore, the concepts of peacebuilding including reconciliation, intergroup contact, human rights, justice, citizenship, and wellbeing are themselves contested, shaping how peacebuilding is understood and practised. While peacebuilders all share the same concepts from the peacebuilding lexicon, they interpret and prioritise these in different ways, generating different trajectories of practice. Freeden's (1996; 2013a) framework of morphological analysis is a way of mapping how individuals and groups prioritise concepts and gather around distinctive interpretations that orient them to the social and political world.

Freeden (1996) developed morphological analysis as a way of studying political ideologies. This section details his approach by making explicit applications to peacebuilding. Connections are also made between Freeden's work and the theoretical premises of Lave and Wenger's *communities of practice* and Bourdieu's sociological lens that was outlined in Chapter 3. The starting point for morphological analysis is the all-encompassing nature of political thinking which involves 'the thought-practices that accompany, foreshadow, and trail material and physical collective actions' (Freeden, 2013b: 2). Such thought-practices are similar to Bourdieu's notion of 'schemes of perception' generating dispositions and patterns in human thinking and action which over time take on an instinctive quality.

Freeden (2013b: 24) determines that 'politics and political thinking revolve around the struggles that occur on the never-ending and deceptive road to conclusiveness'. Acting within the social world necessarily involves ordering and selecting certain definitions over others, adopting specific ways of making sense of the world while negating other possibilities. Freeden names this process 'decontestation' and defines it as 'the attempt to control equivocal and contingent meaning by holding it constant', responding to 'the essential contestability of concepts and their complex morphology' (Freeden, 2013b: 23). This complex morphology arises from the ways in which language changes over time, taking on new meanings. It reflects cultural shifts and the interplay of reconstruction and resistance to changing common-sense understandings of concepts. Lave and Wenger's (1991) explanation of communities of practice resonates strongly with this premise of morphological analysis, where meanings defy a universal fixed position but are constantly negotiated and evolving in relation to specific contexts. Freeden's use of the term 'decontestation' parallels the more explicit phrase used by Lave and Wenger – the negotiation of meaning.

Through a morphological analysis of political ideologies, Freeden highlights how ideologies such as liberalism shift and morph over time yet maintain a certain coherence that distinguishes them from other ideologies. He uses Wittgenstein's notion of 'familial resemblance' where attention is redirected from rigid boundaries towards an appreciation of regularities among patterns of thought and behaviour that share enough in common to be grouped together. Bourdieu, making the same point, invokes the notion of an *overall resemblance* (Nicod, 1961: 43, cited in Bourdieu, 1990: 88). Rather than conceiving of a hard border between conservativism, liberalism, socialism, anarchism, and so on, it is more beneficial to think of a 'border zone' where 'one pattern permeates and mutates into another and where we move from one sphere of family resemblances into another' (Freeden, 2013a: 116). It is in this border zone where ideas are most open to change, to a process of coming and going.

Which room are we in?

Morphological analysis is a way of identifying patterns in political thinking that are indicative of distinctive modes of thought and action. To help convey this process of morphological analysis, Freeden (2013a) uses the metaphor of rooms in a house that contain distinctive configurations of furniture. A room occupied by a desk on which sits a computer, and behind which is situated a chair on wheels is likely to be a home office. A room with a sink, fridge, and cooker will likely be a kitchen. Remove the sink and the cooker from the kitchen, and it becomes less 'kitchen-like' (depicted in Figure 6.1). At some point, it may cease to be acknowledged as a kitchen at all if the characteristic features of kitchens continue to be removed.

If the home office also contains a fridge and a sink, it may make deciphering the type of room more difficult. In such a case, particular attention is given to how the furniture is arranged. If the desk and computer are arranged as the focal point of the room, and a bookshelf filled with academic books is prominent, then it is likely to be a home office that also has a fridge and a sink, rather than a kitchen (depicted in Figure 6.2).

Figure 6.1: Features of a kitchen

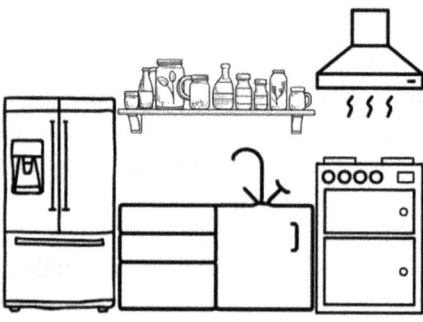

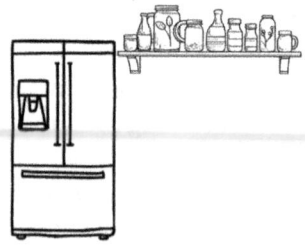

Figure 6.2: A multipurpose home office

Applied to the field of youth sector peacebuilding, we can expect to observe multiple peacebuilding concepts and ideas (discussed in the previous chapter) appearing across a range of policies and practices. Distinctions can, however, be made. For instance, if intergroup contact between young people from opposing communities is front and centre, with the aim of reducing prejudice and finding common ground, while exposing and critiquing differences is tucked away in the corner, then we can distinguish this as an approach to peacebuilding premised on mutual understanding rather than critical dialogue. Similarly, if tackling paramilitarism through restorative justice is presented as a flagship idea, while supporting young people to become engaged in politics and to develop their political agency is simply incidental, then we can conclude this is a restorative lens on peacebuilding rather than one of political activism. Some peacebuilding approaches claim to be radical. Remove from these a willingness to use strategies of activism and resistance and, like the stripped-back kitchen purged of its sink and cooker, these 'radical' approaches lose something of their full essence.

Where Freeden (1996) deploys the rooms in a house analogy to introduce a macro analysis of political ideologies, we focus on the shared and divergent perspectives that exist in relation to youth sector peacebuilding. Rather than ideologies, we think of *ideational structures*. These ideational structures are the thought-patterns and mental maps that practitioners draw upon and develop as they engage in the work of peacebuilding with young people. Morphological analysis is a way of identifying these ideational structures by examining how ideas and concepts are prioritised and valued relative to other ideas and concepts.

Core, adjacent, and peripheral concepts

The process of morphological analysis involves identifying core, adjacent, and peripheral concepts that make up an ideological structure, or in our case an *ideational* structure. Freeden (2013a) depicts the model of morphological analysis as concentric circles with core at the centre, followed by adjacent, and then periphery as the outer circle.

Core components

The core components of an ideology or ideational structure are those 'ineliminable features' (Freeden, 1996: 61). These are concepts that, if removed, would render the ideology essentially meaningless and unintelligible. This ineliminable feature is clearly illustrated by example; if liberty is removed from the core of liberalism, it appears suspiciously unlike liberalism. Similarly, an activist orientation to peacebuilding which did not include political participation as a core concept would call into question the credibility of this 'activist' peacebuilding. In morphological analysis, the first step in identifying the formation of an ideological or ideational structure involves determining how concepts are arranged in the core and the meaning and importance attached to them in relation to each other. If notions of resistance and civil disobedience appear as more central to the core than political participation, it suggests there is a tendency for this activist approach to peacebuilding to advocate for public protests and non-institutional forms of political engagement rather than working within formal political mechanisms sanctioned by the state. To further decipher the nature of the ideational structure we move from the core to logical and cultural adjacencies.

Adjacent components

Freeden insists that an ideology cannot be reduced to its ineliminable core. It relies on other concepts arranged adjacent to the core. The first of these adjacencies is termed 'logical adjacency'. Logical adjacent concepts permit what on the surface may appear as competing political concepts to co-exist, each giving meaning to one another. Extending the illustrative case of liberalism, Freeden (1996) places self-development as a logical adjacent concept along with self-determination, autonomy, and power. As such, these adjacent concepts of self-development and self-determination encourage a form of liberalism that promotes flourishing as opposed to self-destructive tendencies. The combination of logical adjacent concepts add directionality and parameters in how they interrelate with the core concepts.

Within an activist conception of peacebuilding, aligning the concepts of equality, equity, and social justice as logically adjacent to the core concepts of political participation, activism, and resistance starts to determine the orientation of peacebuilding as activism. It is an activism focused on issues such as rebalancing the distribution of wealth and resources and the protection of rights for minority groups rather than activism towards economic growth or the preservation of existing capitalist structures and ideas of meritocracy.

The morphological approach continually seeks to narrow down the universe of contested meanings that a cluster of concepts may represent. Alongside the mechanism of logical adjacency, the notion of cultural adjacency is a further way of achieving this goal. Cultural adjacency anchors the morphological approach to specific social, cultural, environmental, and historical contexts, referring to 'temporally and spatially bounded social practices, institutional patterns, ethical systems, technologies, influential theories, discourses, and beliefs (to include reactions to external events and to unintentional or non-human occurrences)' (Freeden, 1996: 69–70).

Cultural adjacency is vital to understanding how ideologies, or in our case the ideational structures of peacebuilding, reflect and are attached to everyday lives. Two modes of cultural adjacency are identified. The first employs the analogy of a brake, stopping certain logical adjacent concepts from being pursued. In the example of activist orientations to peacebuilding, the core concepts of resistance and activism could give rise to adjacent concepts of either violence or non-violence. Depending on cultural context, it is likely that one will appear as more dominant than others. Peacebuilders tend to reject physical violence and seek alternative methods for competing aspirations and needs to be expressed and won. Therefore, non-violence as a cultural adjacent concept shapes the nature of activism and resistance strategies.

The second mode of cultural adjacency is *legitimising the illogical*. It reflects the sense whereby adjacent concepts do not always follow logically from the core but are culturally accepted. A stark manifestation of this is in ideological systems where equality has been espoused as a core concept and equality of opportunity exhorted while simultaneously denying rights to certain minority groups (Freeden, 1996). This is similarly observed in conceptions of peacebuilding where inclusion and participation are core concepts yet are rarely translated into ensuring the role and voices of women and LGBTQIA+ individuals and groups are brought to the fore (Pierson, 2018). It is the facet of cultural adjacency that integrates such contradictions. This quality of morphological analysis recognises all ideational structures contain contradictions and parallels Bourdieu's (1977) position that social practices defy rational logic and generate common-sense ideas that pave over the cracks of contradiction. The final part of morphological analysis involves identifying peripheral concepts.

Peripheral components

Peripheral components of morphological analysis are categorised by Freeden as *margin* and *perimeter* concepts. The margin represents political concepts that have little influence over the core and adjacent concepts. They may come and go with relative ease and little to no disruption to the overarching orientation of the ideological or ideational structure. In peacebuilding, 'single-identity work', where groups with a shared identity marker meet together before engaging with those from a different social group, has moved from a more central position towards the periphery of peace policy in Northern Ireland. Despite featuring strongly in early peacebuilding practice, the more marginal place of single-identity work has little effect on the broader distinctions in how practitioners conceptualise peacebuilding, for instance, as activism or as social cohesion.

Perimeter components act as an interface with current affairs and are often 'specific ideas or policy-proposals rather than fully fledged concepts' (Freeden, 1996: 80). This function of the perimeter is indicative of cases where a political idea may be promptly adopted by an ideational structure to help explain or facilitate responses to a current issue. Concepts of co-creation and co-production have become hot topics in the policy arena and as such certain perspectives on peacebuilding may start to integrate this language. In practice, however, those serious about co-creation with young people will likely already have this deeply embedded in their understanding of peacebuilding, prioritising notions of participation through core and adjacent ideas. Those only just picking up the term will struggle to incorporate this meaningfully if it has not already featured significantly in their practice.

By identifying how people arrange and prioritise the concepts of peacebuilding from core through to peripheral, distinctive thought structures can be revealed. While Freeden does not offer a detailed method for undertaking morphological analysis, we have identified Q methodology as an effective way of achieving this.

Operationalising a morphological analysis of youth sector peacebuilding

Q methodology sets out to identify distinctive perspectives that exist on a topic under investigation, combining statistical inference with researcher-led judgements. While not directly employing Freeden's (2013a) language of core, adjacent, and peripheral concepts to map ideational structures, the sorting procedure integral to Q methodology implicitly generates a similar structure to that of morphological analysis. Furthermore, underpinning Freeden's morphological analysis is the intent of capturing political thinking, revealed when agents 'distribute significance by ranking social aims, demands, processes, and structures in order of importance or urgency' (Freeden, 2013b: 35). Q methodology implores participants to display this type of political thinking as they are tasked with ranking the relative importance of ideas in relation to one another.

Avoiding an overly technical discussion, the remainder of this chapter outlines how the authors undertook this Q methodology study with 43 youth work practitioners, facilitating a unique morphological analysis of youth sector peacebuilding. The origins of Q methodology are traced to 1935, with founder William Stephenson's concise letter to the journal *Nature*. There are many useful primers on Q methodology (for example, Brown, 1980; Watts and Stenner, 2012). Here we will keep the specialised language of Q methodology to a minimum and instead describe the process. In brief, the first step undertaken by the authors was an extensive review of peacebuilding literature (see previous chapter) and developing statements capturing a full range of ideas about peacebuilding. Initially, 170 statements were constructed and reduced to 48 based on interviews, focus groups and a pilot with practitioners and academics (Hamilton and Hammond, 2023). Individually each practitioner sorted the same set of 48 statements on a grid from most agree to least agree in response to the question 'What should be the main focus of peacebuilding with young people in Northern Ireland today?' The full list of statements is provided in the Appendix. Figure 6.3 depicts a participant halfway through the process of sorting the 48 statements on the sorting grid. The numbers underneath each column of the grid indicate how many statements can be ranked there; two statements can be placed at +5 (most agree) and two at -5 (least agree), three statements can be placed at +4 and three at -4 and so on working into the middle of the grid where eight statements can be placed at 0.

The statement cards outside of the sorting grid in Figure 6.3 are yet to be placed by the participant, who may continually move cards around until they are satisfied with their final arrangement. It is this Q sorting process which reflects the core–peripheral structure of morphological analysis and therefore lends itself to the operationalisation of a morphological analysis of peacebuilding.

Research participants

The 43 youth workers who participated in the study were tasked with arranging the 48 statements on the sorting grid (resulting in their individual

Figure 6.3: The sorting process in action

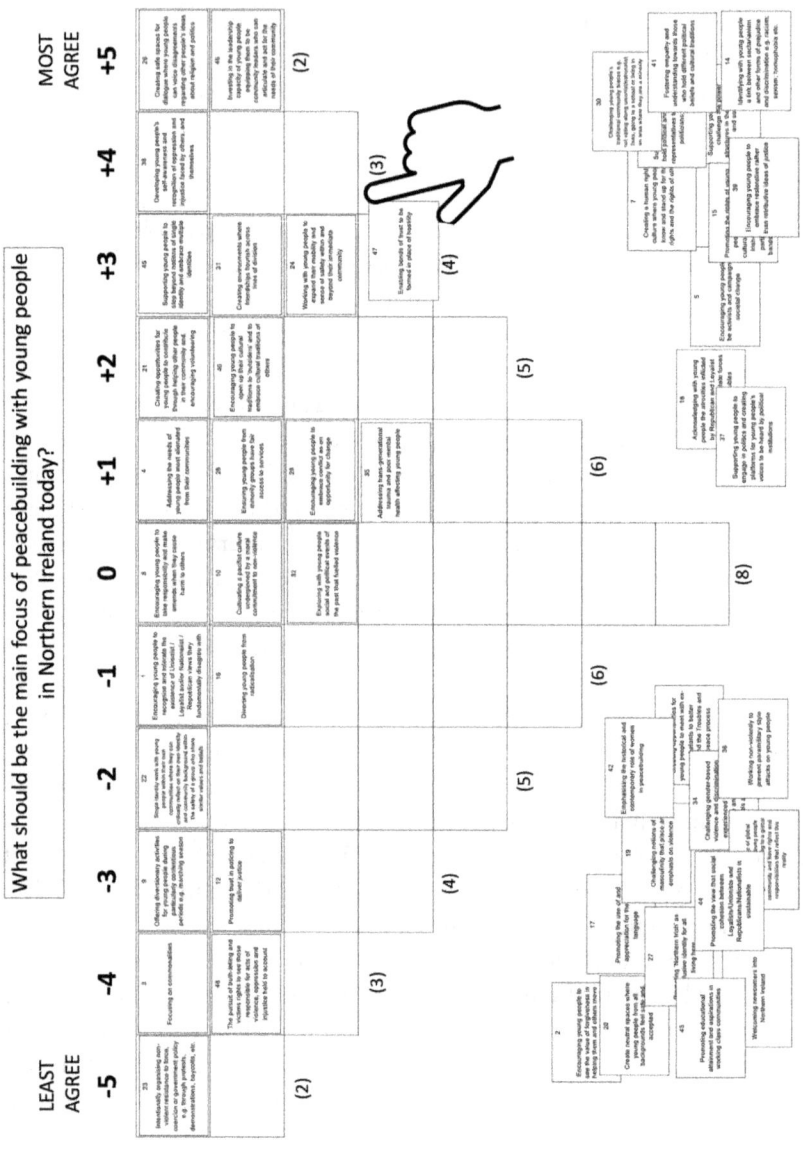

'*Q sort*') to depict their perspective on peacebuilding. Later these were analysed and grouped to identify shared perspectives. Demographics of participants are outlined here as they hold significance in later chapters which present an analysis of the perspectives found through the study. The central concern for deciding on the total number of participants was to ensure a wide enough group to establish a range of viewpoints (Brown, 1980). Consideration was given to identifying participants who would bring a range of perspectives including Nationalist and Unionist backgrounds, Protestant and Catholic religious traditions, male and female, and varying lengths of post-qualifying experience as a youth worker.

All practitioners had completed a degree level qualification in youth work and self-identified as having had some experience in facilitating peacebuilding work with young people, however minimal or extensive. An opportune pool of practitioners was evident in the European Union (EU) PEACE IV funded programme. The 'Peace4Youth' (P4Y) strand funded over 200 youth work staff across 11 projects, delivering their programmes from 2017 to 2021 across Northern Ireland and the border counties of Ireland (Government of Ireland, 2020). Thirty-one of these P4Y practitioners took part in the study. Another cohort of practitioners was identified to mitigate any intrinsic bias towards an EU version of peacebuilding, indicative of the P4Y funding stream. Twelve non-P4Y practitioners took part. Finally, following an initial analysis, the lead researcher (Hamilton) also participated in sorting the statements. This proved beneficial for applying a reflexive lens and better understanding this researcher's positionality as they interpreted the findings. Table 6.1 provides an overview of participant demographics outlining specific attributes for the final 44 study participants (which includes one of the authors, Hamilton, as the lead researcher).

Table 6.1 shows more practitioners identifying as Protestant (24) took part in the study than Catholic (15). Traditionally there has been a tendency to conflate religious affiliation with national and political identity in Northern Ireland. While patterns have been observed, these identities tend to shift in contested societies and many reject simplistic identity markers. To acknowledge this complexity and avoid making assumptions or providing only binary options, participants were presented with a six-point continuum for both national and political identity. Figure 6.4 shows responses for national identity where 1 represented most strongly Irish and 6 most strongly British.

Table 6.1: Practitioner demographics

Sex		Religious affiliation			Cohort		
Male	Female	Catholic	Protestant	Other	P4Y	Non-P4Y	Researcher
24	20	15	24	5	31	12	1

Figure 6.4: Continuum of national identity

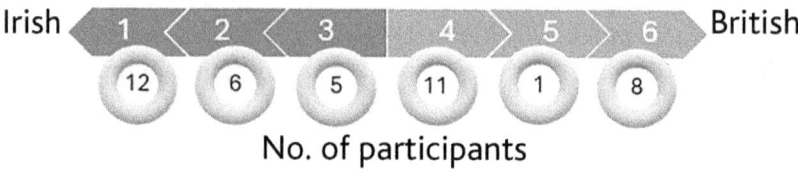

No. of participants

Figure 6.5: Continuum of political identity

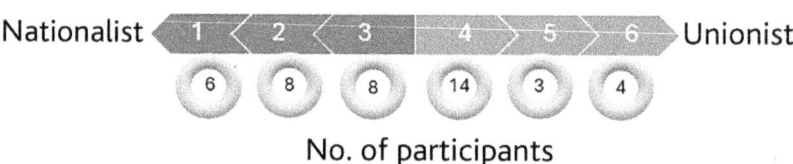

No. of participants

Figure 6.5 shows responses for political identity where 1 represented most strongly Nationalist and 6 most strongly Unionist.

Twenty-three practitioners identified more with an Irish identity (those aligned with points 1–3 on the scale, Figure 6.4) and 20 more so with a British identity (those aligned with points 4–6, Figure 6.4). A similar picture is portrayed concerning political affiliation where 22 practitioners oriented towards a Nationalist affiliation (points 1–3, Figure 6.5) and 21 towards Unionist (points 4–6, Figure 6.5). This problematises any reductive tendencies to conflate Unionism, Britishness, and Protestantism, or Nationalism, Irishness, and Catholicism. One participant chose not to respond to national identity or political affiliation questions, describing themselves as a 'foreign national', and therefore found the scale inapplicable.

Data on length of experience as a practitioner was gathered to allow an analysis of experience against orientation to peacebuilding. Figure 6.6 shows 20 practitioners had over 16 years' experience, bringing perspectives to the study (conducted in 2019) stretching back to the early years of a post-1998 Belfast Good Friday Agreement landscape. Seven practitioners were relatively early in their professional career having less than six years' experience. This range from less than two to over 16 years of experience was not intended to be representative of the entire population of practitioners. It did, however, mean perspectives derived from early to established career practitioners were included.

From individual sorts to shared perspectives

Having collated all the completed sorting grids (*Q sorts*) and recorded each practitioner's positioning of statements from +5 to -5, the next step was

Figure 6.6: Post-qualifying experience

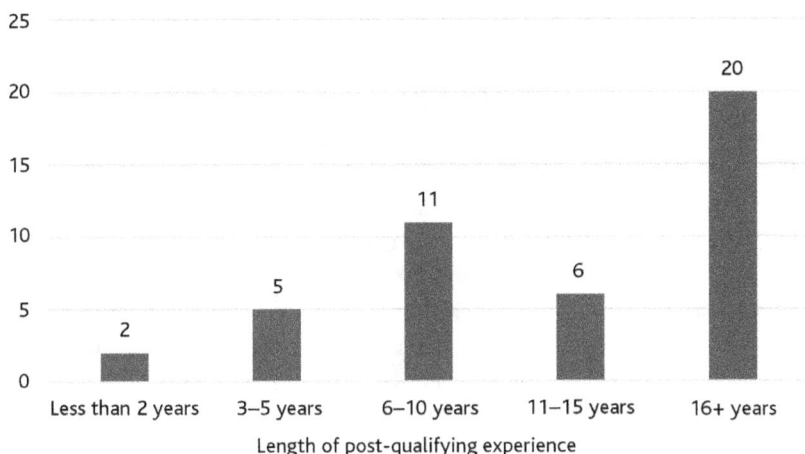

Q factor analysis. Traditional factor analysis is a data reductive technique employing correlation statistics to simplify large data sets into meaningful configurations. It enables studies with many variables to be reduced to a smaller number of explanatory or latent variables. In Q factor analysis, correlations are made among completed Q sorts, identifying participants who have sorted the statements in statistically similar ways. For those that are grouped together, an exemplifying Q sort is generated, representing that perspective. Subsequently, in Q methodology, a factor can be simply understood as a shared viewpoint within the data. These shared viewpoints can equally be understood as a shared ideational structure. Four viewpoints were identified in our study.

The next chapter presents and examines these four distinctive viewpoints on peacebuilding with young people. During the sorting process, practitioners were also interviewed to ascertain their rationale for ranking some statements higher than others, exploring why certain statements were core and others more peripheral. This dialogical, qualitative data offered rich insights aiding the interpretation of the four perspectives. The voices of practitioners are integrated with the presentation of the four viewpoints in Chapter 7.

Practical applications of Q methodology

The sorting technique at the heart of Q methodology is brimming with possibilities for creative application in a diverse range of settings. The 48 statements developed for this study, known as the *Q-set* (listed in the Appendix), provide stimulus material for an array of activities. The authors have tried and tested various applications which do not require the more technical step of Q factor analysis (although we would encourage using the term 'Q technique' or an alternative name rather than Q methodology when developing activities which do not go as far as conducting the methodological procedure of Q factor analysis). The statements, along with the sorting grid, offer a ready-made group work or training exercise based on extant literature. The set of statements can be adapted, reduced, or added to by educators and trainers to suit the context and needs of learners. For instance, with undergraduate community youth work students, we have taken 12 of the 48 statements, laminated them on small cards, and tasked students in small groups to arrange them on a +3 to -3 sorting grid to represent their priorities for peacebuilding with young people. Students then compared grids, and this has been a highly effective way of sparking dialogue. This process can be useful within and across a range of sectors where there is a remit for peacebuilding, including within the police service, education authorities, funding bodies, and policy departments.

Conclusion

Peacebuilding is not a fixed or static concept; it evolves and morphs across time and context. Yet, amidst such morphing, there are broad patterns of thought and practice that share a familial resemblance. Freeden's conceptual approach of morphological analysis, operationalised through William Stephenson's Q methodology, offers a unique way of distinguishing various families of thought that guide different approaches to youth sector peacebuilding. In our study, this mapping was conducted by analysing how practitioners arranged statements, constructed from an extensive literature review, from most agree to least agree on a sorting grid in response to the question 'What should be the main focus of peacebuilding with young people in Northern Ireland today?'

While the study is grounded in the context of Northern Ireland, the four perspectives are indicative of dispositions that resonate with peacebuilding approaches in other contested societies. It is valuable both for clarifying the competing priorities within youth sector peacebuilding and locating self amid the multiple perspectives and approaches written into policy and carried out through practice. Utilising Q methodology with youth workers in a contested society has enabled the first morphological analysis of youth sector peacebuilding. The remainder of this book presents and discusses the findings of this morphological analysis.

7

Four viewpoints on youth sector peacebuilding

> Core to my value has always been around promoting the place of equality and a human rights approach and young people being able to take the opportunities to take their own power and being filled full of information and being let loose. (YW18)

Introduction

Identifying, interpreting, and analysing distinctive and shared orientations towards youth sector peacebuilding is a pivotal contribution of this book. This chapter delineates four viewpoints that have been generated from our Q methodology study with youth work practitioners and discusses how these perspectives have resonance not just in the north of Ireland but other contested societies worldwide. By viewpoint, we mean more than mere opinion. The four viewpoints are indicative of the thinking vectors and mental models that practitioners have available and draw upon as they engage in the practice of peacebuilding. As Q methodology researchers our starting point was to understand the viewpoints as *ideational structures* – thought-patterns shaped by past experiences, socialisation processes, and political ideations situated within contemporary policy and practice contexts. We project this understanding onto the terms *viewpoint* and *perspective* throughout the remainder of the book to reduce constant references to the more unwieldy terminology of ideational structures or the technical language of 'factor arrays' used in Q methodology. While some readers may be eager for more detail on the technicalities of Q methodology,[1] we have kept such details to a minimum. The chapter is dedicated to a rich qualitative description and interpretation of each viewpoint, drawing on direct quotations from practitioners as they sorted and discussed their peacebuilding priorities in work with young people.

Four viewpoints on youth sector peacebuilding

Our study found four distinctive viewpoints on youth sector peacebuilding:

- viewpoint 1: critical thinking and dialogue (7 practitioners + 1 researcher[2]);
- viewpoint 2: mutual understanding (15 practitioners);

- viewpoint 3: social cohesion and restoration (6 practitioners);
- viewpoint 4: political engagement and social justice (6 practitioners).

Each viewpoint represents a group of youth work practitioners who have arranged a heterogeneous set of 48 statements about peacebuilding (see previous chapter) in a statistically similar way and, in doing so, have applied order and meaning to the items. It can be inferred that those grouped on each viewpoint hold in common shared patterns of thought in their approach to peacebuilding within the youth sector. The bracketed numbers beside each viewpoint indicate how many of the 44 participants make up that viewpoint. Four practitioners were split between two viewpoints and, therefore, are not included in the final count of the four viewpoints. A further five practitioners did not meet the statistical threshold to be included in the make-up of any of the viewpoints (Hamilton and Hammond, 2023). The primary focus of interpretation and analysis is on the four viewpoints. A brief note on the practitioners who did not align with any of the viewpoints is presented towards the end of this chapter.

Each viewpoint is discussed in turn, with reference to core concepts and more peripheral ideas. Several tables are included comparing how key statements were ranked differently across the four viewpoints, from +5 to -5.[3] Direct practitioner quotations are presented in italics and referenced with the abbreviation YW (for youth worker) followed by a number from 01 to 44, for example, YW01. Salient demographic features of the practitioners are also noted as key points of interest.

Viewpoint 1: Critical thinking and dialogue

The job of the youth worker is that kind of critical consciousness. (YW28)

Dialogue is a core feature of viewpoint 1, along with notions of critical pedagogy. Emphasis is placed on challenging taken-for-granted assumptions about the social world and raising awareness of inequalities and unequal power relations. For viewpoint 1, peacebuilding begins when young people recognise themselves as interdependent agents capable of critical insights within inequitable and unjust social structures. One practitioner explained, *'one of our gifts as youth work practitioners is questioning and asking questions to get people to think and reflect – it's a real skill'* (YW22). While this work involves introspection, it is primarily a process facilitated through relationship with others. This relational approach emphasises cultivating friendship with those from different socio-political and cultural backgrounds. These relationships are understood as complementing rather than circumventing engagement on contentious social issues and competing political rights. It is this bridging of interpersonal relationships alongside dialogue on rights that YW28 sees as distinctive, where relational and rights-based approaches are '*completely reliant on each other*'.

Practitioners distanced themselves from notions of neutrality and, in doing so, conveyed their view that peacebuilding is an educative process that builds political consciousness. One commented, '*neutral for me suggests you're trying to suppress the very things that make young people who they are and their identities*' (YW39). Another critiqued the notion of '*neutral spaces*' as a place where '*you're just reassured that everything is ok*' rather than creating opportunities for '*people to have difficult conversations in a way that is good for them and others*' (YW28). Similarly, notions of 'focusing on commonalities' and diversionary work are ranked negatively in this viewpoint and are disregarded as strategies for avoiding meaningful engagement and difficult conversations. Rather than a polite avoidance of contested issues, the role of the youth worker is perceived as facilitating '*robust spaces*' that elicit '*cognitive dissonance*' and '*the noise of thoughts being churned up and ideas being challenged*' (YW40).

Table 7.1 shows five statements that have been ranked significantly differently in viewpoint 1 compared with the other three viewpoints. Statement 20, regarding neutral spaces, is ranked -3 in viewpoint 1, the lowest ranking across all four viewpoints. This positioning reflects how viewpoint 1 practitioners distance themselves from notions of neutrality. Safe spaces for dialogue and disagreement are instead given the highest ranking of +5 (statement 26 in Table 7.1). Statement 38 similarly receives the highest ranking of +5 in viewpoint 1, reflecting a commitment to a critical pedagogy of self-awareness leading to an aptitude for recognising social and political inequalities. Statement 32, 'Exploring with young people social and political events of the past that fuelled violence', is ranked at +2 in viewpoint 1, which is in marked contrast to the negative rankings

Table 7.1: Selection of distinguishing statements for viewpoint 1

Statement	Viewpoint			
	1	2	3	4
20. Create neutral spaces where young people from all backgrounds feel safe and accepted	-3	5	0	2
26. Creating safe spaces for dialogue where young people can voice disagreements regarding other people's ideas about religion and politics	5	4	0	0
32. Exploring with young people social and political events of the past that fuelled violence	2	-3	-5	-2
38. Developing young people's self-awareness and recognition of oppression and injustice faced by others, and themselves	5	0	0	2
42. Emphasising the historical and contemporary role of women in peacebuilding	0	-4	-3	-3

assigned to this statement across the three other viewpoints. YW35 affirms that a core purpose of peacebuilding work with young people is supporting them to be '*a critical thinker about the past*'. In line with a propensity to bring contentious issues to the fore, YW23 criticises a tendency to avoid the live issue of sectarianism, noting, '*there is an avoidance, a polite avoidance if you want to say, but there's definitely an avoidance*'. YW39 agrees, highlighting the dangers of an avoidance culture within peacebuilding work with young people, leading to '*an avoidance of looking at sectarianism and the things that have been most divisive in Northern Ireland*'.

For YW28, an engagement with history is '*not just learning about the past but trying to deconstruct it and give young people a kind of critical consciousness to be able to make different choices in the present*'. Appreciating multiple histories and narratives is key to acknowledging our '*multiple and complex and sometimes contradictory identities*' (YW40). It is noteworthy that statement 42, 'Emphasising the historical and contemporary role of women in peacebuilding', is ranked highest in viewpoint 1, suggesting a level of critical awareness of the gendered nature of peace work. However, it is only ranked at '0' here and is placed at -4 and -3 in the other viewpoints, which is indicative of a persistent tendency to sideline and overlook young women in peacebuilding.

While dialogue on contentious issues is emphasised, promoting *the expression* of particular cultural identities is not a significant feature of this viewpoint. The Irish language, marching bands, and bonfire building are perceived as politically and culturally divisive issues, and dialogue is needed around these themes rather than an unequivocal endorsement. YW28 illustrates this dialogical approach by reflecting on the cultural and politically infused practices of bonfire building which have periodically been the focus of peacebuilding funding streams:

> *There are agencies that have bonfire building programmes, and I understand that they're trying to work with the young people to keep them a bit safer, but I think it's problematic. If there's no real challenge function, I think, as to why you're doing this in the first place, what's behind it, why does it give you meaning, could other things give you meaning too? Without the kind of critical understanding that comes out of exploring the past, self-awareness, empathy, it could just promote the idea of separate and parallel communities.*

The notion of inviting others to experience and share in cultural events and traditions that would ordinarily be unfamiliar to them is considered more favourably from this perspective. Such activities fit within a broader framework of facilitating dialogue, empathy, and a critical engagement with difference.

By raising critical consciousness, young people develop a critical self and social awareness that acts as a catalyst for emancipatory thought and action. Equipped with an expanding critical consciousness, peacebuilding work from this perspective also seeks to address power imbalances between adults and youth by supporting young people to have their voices heard. Emphasis is placed on youth participation in political arenas where they have opportunities to advocate for their rights and the rights of others. To this end, peacebuilding is framed as a radical endeavour. Practitioners aligned with viewpoint 1 relegated notions of diverting young people from radicalisation and challenged pejorative conceptions of radicalisation. YW22 concluded, *'peacebuilding could be a form of radicalisation because you're radical, you're fuelled by a mission to do something'*. Notions of promoting trust in policing and restorative approaches through state-endorsed initiatives were secondary concerns for this viewpoint. For some practitioners in viewpoint 1, collaborating with the police was seen as antithetical to critical thinking. YW40 declared, *'youth work is not an apologist for the British state; youth work is not there to rubber-stamp everything that the reformed police force does'*. His statement provokes controversies surrounding the historical and contemporary role of policing in Northern Ireland, a theme this viewpoint would certainly not shy away from discussing with young people.

Despite intimations towards peacebuilding as a revolutionary practice, this viewpoint stops short of advocating for civil and political resistance. Purposeful political organisation to subvert oppressive structures is deemed unnecessary and perceived as a counterproductive approach. Instead, emphasis is placed on engaging young people in existing political mechanisms to challenge institutions as part of a youth-led developmental process. Finally, the notion of addressing mental health, wellbeing, and trauma experienced by young people is recognised as a need that cannot be ignored in peacebuilding work. However, as discussed by YW39, practitioners ought to be aware of the limitations of their profession and acknowledge when health professionals should be involved; *'you do have a responsibility to meet young people's immediate needs – in a way that fits within your role'*.

Demographics of viewpoint 1

The viewpoints generated through Q methodology reveal particular modes and predominant patterns of thinking. The small number of practitioners that make up each viewpoint in our study, and in Q methodology studies in general, are indicative of an approach which seeks to identify perspectives rather than quantify them. In other words, the viewpoint is significant in that from a relatively small cross-section of people, there are statistically significant patterns by which individuals arrange statements which depict a shared viewpoint. We cannot, however, make statistical inferences about how widespread this perspective is in the wider population. While generalisable conclusions cannot be drawn from the demographic composition of

Figure 7.1: Demographics of viewpoint 1

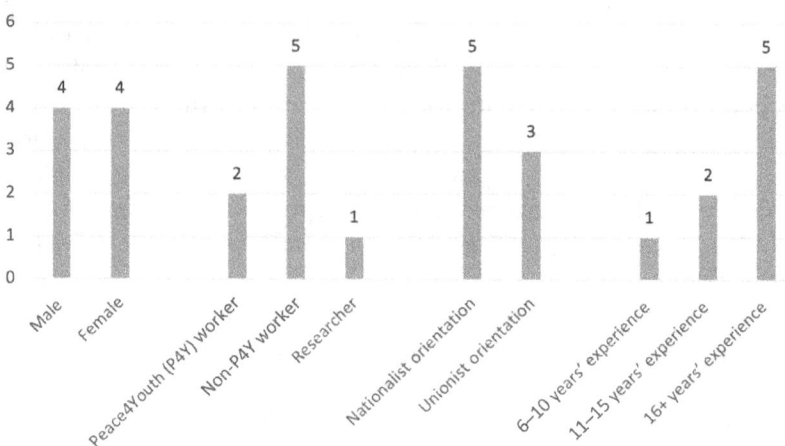

each viewpoint, several demographic features, as outlined in Figure 7.1, merit consideration.

It is noteworthy that only two practitioners that make up viewpoint 1 were employed through the European Union (EU) Peace4Youth (P4Y) programme compared with five practitioners who were unaffiliated with the P4Y programme. As the majority of practitioners in the study were employed through the P4Y programme (31) compared with a control group of 13 practitioners unaffiliated with P4Y, viewpoint 1 accounts for more than a third of the non-P4Y practitioners in the study overall. Therefore, those practitioners not working to EU targets disproportionately align with viewpoint 1. This limited appetite from the P4Y practitioners for the critical thinking and dialogue orientation of viewpoint 1 may be indicative of alternative themes and orientations prioritised within the EU PEACE IV programme or how these have been interpreted at the implementation stage by practitioners and youth organisations.

Viewpoint 1, *critical thinking and dialogue*, is made up of relatively experienced practitioners. Seven of the eight practitioners that make up this viewpoint have at least 11 years of experience as qualified practitioners (the researcher accounted for the 6–10 years of experience category). It may be the case that experienced practitioners feel best equipped to facilitate the sensitive work of critical dialogue in the context of a polarised and contested society. The emphasis on exploring the past may also be a salient point for older practitioners who had greater exposure to the Troubles and the ensuing peace process. While this is not the case for all practitioners who experienced the latter part of the 20th century in Northern Ireland, it is interesting that younger practitioners in our study did not align with this viewpoint. The average age of practitioners aligned with viewpoint 1 was 43.6, with the lowest age 30 and the highest 52.

A last point of interest regarding demographics for this viewpoint is that those with a strong Unionist identity in our study did not orient towards this perspective. On a scale where 1 represented the strongest alignment with a Nationalist identity, and 6 represented the strongest alignment with a Unionist identity, the range of scores for this viewpoint was 1 to 4.

Viewpoint 2: Mutual understanding

Creating new friendships, not just for cross-community relationships, just almost like a cross-community country. (YW31)

The mutual understanding viewpoint was the largest in our study. It reflects many assumptions of early community relations work with young people during the height of the Troubles in Northern Ireland from the 1970s onwards. This includes an emphasis on downplaying difference, seeking to create neutral and safe spaces for young people from different communities to come together, promoting harmonious relations, and avoiding anything considered as a contentious or divisive issue. Ultimately, learning to live harmoniously with difference is a guiding principle of viewpoint 2. This is exemplified by the statements in Table 7.2 and their high rankings in viewpoint 2.

Practitioners aligned with the mutual understanding viewpoint prioritised cultivating friendships across lines of division, as evidenced by the high ranking of statement 31 (shown in Table 7.2). YW15 reflects on the supremacy of friendship in peacebuilding work:

Table 7.2: Selection of distinguishing statements for viewpoint 2

Statement	Viewpoint			
	1	2	3	4
3. Focusing on commonalities	-4	2	-2	-2
20. Create neutral spaces where young people from all backgrounds feel safe and accepted	-3	5	0	2
22. Single identity work with young people within their own communities where they can critically reflect on their own identity and community background within the safety of a group who share similar values and beliefs	-2	3	-3	-4
27. Promoting 'Northern Irish' as an inclusive identity for all living here	-5	0	-4	-5
31. Creating environments where friendships flourish across lines of division	3	5	-1	2

> *The big thing came down to whether they like each other as a person and a friend, and they got to know them as people before they found out the cultural and community stuff about them, and then it really didn't have that much of an impact on the relationship because it had been built and sustained.* (YW15)

The nature of these relationships is founded upon establishing common ground and mutual understanding. As such, this was the only viewpoint to give a positive ranking to statement 3, 'Focusing on commonalities'. YW42 explained, '*I've always wanted to focus on those common themes.*' Similarly, YW21 felt, '*if we focus on commonalities, we can create more space, environments for friendships to flourish. If you've more to agree on, you've less to disagree on*'.

Connected with the notion of common ground is the idea of neutrality which positions this viewpoint as one concerned with placating and avoiding potentially divisive issues in peacebuilding work with young people. Neutrality appears as a salient idea in both the arrangement of statement 20 at +5 (shown in Table 7.2) and comments from practitioners. YW05 advocates for '*creating a neutral space where young people can feel safe and accepted, we need to do it more*'. YW12 envisages neutral spaces as facilitating co-existence, commenting, '*neutral space as well ... I just think there's something in creating a picture of places where people can be together and can exist together*'. While conversations on disagreements and differences are relevant aspects of peacebuilding for this viewpoint, caution is taken to avoid controversy. YW41 articulates their approach to dialogue where, '*it's not shouting at each other, it's not stepping on each other's toes, it's more talking to each other, getting a solution because you understand where each other's coming from*'. Implicit is a desire to resolve and temper disagreements and incompatible world views. YW10 adopts a similar stance to facilitating conversations around difference – '*it's not in your face, it's not confrontational, it's about exploring things*'. YW29 deems neutrality as optimal in reference to the youth work practitioner's role in facilitating peacebuilding work with young people. He states: '*Everybody's got a bias, and everybody's got an agenda of some sort, so you know what I mean, you need to sort of go in with a clear head on it and not be tempted by it*' (YW29).

It is noteworthy that statement 27, 'Promoting Northern Irish as an inclusive identity for all living here', is ranked at 0 for viewpoint 2 compared with -5 or -4 in the other viewpoints. While not actively endorsing Northern Irish as a communal identity marker, this viewpoint is most open to the idea of establishing a shared, superordinate identity for all. YW41 reflected: '*If it came to like a mutual agreement to identify as sort of one big thing, I think it would be easier to push forward, do you know, because then every other thing that distracts would be sort of pushed away for the meantime and come together as one.*'

Viewpoint 2 prioritises personal development that focuses on the needs and flourishing of young people. YW11 determines that through addressing the needs of individuals, peacebuilding happens: '*You think of a youth worker, you're thinking about the needs of young people, and you're thinking about giving them safe space and a sense of belonging, and I think then that becomes where peacebuilding happens.*' YW10 points to a dichotomy between the needs of young people and the work of peacebuilding stating, '*I would put the needs of a young person first and not the needs of like peacebuilding.*' YW12 expresses a similar commitment, noting: '*The kind of phrase "starting points of young people" is in my head, you know, every session are we focused on peacebuilding? I wouldn't put it into that box. You know we're about informally educating young people, and their personal development is massive in that*' (YW12).

This distancing from the 'needs of peacebuilding' reflects a commitment by workers to first meet the most acute pressing needs of young people. For many practitioners within viewpoint 2, the immediate welfare and wellbeing issues take precedence over wider peacebuilding ambitions for social and structural change. To this end, YW14 explains:

> *I understand what all like the peacebuilding goals are, I understand all that, but I think currently at the stage we're at, it's become outdated, and it's more about the process of getting them ready to the point where they are ready to go on to what they want to do. So, it's a process of their confidence, their self-esteem, their skills, all of these, their insecurities, self-denial.* (YW14)

Addressing mental health features prominently as part of the personal development focus. YW05 observed: '*Mental health is coming out as one of the biggest issues affecting young people, and it's one of the things that most of our staff team are having to deal with because it's just such a huge thing in society at the moment.*' YW31, noting the personal situations of the young people they work with, expressed, '*they're struggling, and mental health issues are huge in Northern Ireland*'.

Once the immediate personal and psychosocial needs of young people are met and they are at a stage where they can engage in more focused peacebuilding, single identity work is viewed as a useful starting point for successful engagement with groups from different community backgrounds. Such work enables young people to develop self-awareness and appreciation of their cultural traditions, building confidence for engaging with others. This viewpoint was the only one to give a positive ranking to statement 22 on single-identity work (as shown in Table 7.2). YW42 elaborates on the role of such work in the process of building mutual understanding: '*There's no point trying to move forward with these communities if the people in those communities don't understand themselves ... if you can understand yourself, you can understand others.*' YW26 agrees with the significance of single identity approaches, noting: '*Without a deep sense of understanding of your own culture, your own experience, your own, your own biases, without understanding those things, I think it's really difficult to engage with the other.'*

Aligned with an emphasis on the level of personal change and development, viewpoint 2 steers away from notions of peacebuilding as engaging young people in transforming political structures or activism for societal change. Many practitioners aligned with this viewpoint were disillusioned with politics. YW11 contends, '*I think it's very idealistic to say that peacebuilding should aim towards young people being social changers and to be active*'. YW37 shares this concern, noting the precarious political infrastructure, arguing, '*if young people don't have an adult population supporting them, again we're setting them up for a fall*'. YW41 agrees with this analysis. Discussing the statement 'Encouraging young people to be activists and campaign for societal change' (ranked at -2 in this viewpoint) he questions, '*what's the point in saying, encouraging young people to do this whenever you know they're going to get knocked back?*' He continued: '*There are big head people high up, the likes of PEACE IV who's already doing it, they're already doing it for young people ... it's already being done, so why put the responsibility on young people again?*' This top-down approach, where funders and policy makers assume the role of driving social change, is accepted in a common-sense way. Youth sector peacebuilding is thus not understood as an agitational practice that seeks to generate social change from the ground up and in ways that might conflict with the logic of institutions entrusted with determining peacebuilding indicators and outcomes.

YW11 explicitly states the subtext cutting across viewpoint 2 – '*in terms of youth work practice, I don't feel as if it's our role to promote anything to do with politics*'. YW14 perceives an alternative track of peacebuilding work that moves away from political issues and instead towards issues of personal development and individual economic security. He ruminates:

Young people just despise politics; they have no interest in it, don't want to learn about it, don't want to speak about it, and I think it's at the point there's other alternatives in peacebuilding ... there are other ways to peace build such as, my view is focus on commonalities between people so they see they all have their own issues, they all choose to be here for the same reasons, they all want to get to move on to further education, employment and training, that's why they are here to get themselves ready, it's a process to get them ready, a stepping stone to move on. (YW14)

Viewpoint 2, mutual understanding, gravitates towards ameliorating tensions and divisions with an emphasis on friendships, commonality, neutrality, and the depoliticisation of issues within the context of a contested society. It is noteworthy that within our study, this viewpoint accounted for the largest

Figure 7.2: Demographics of viewpoint 2

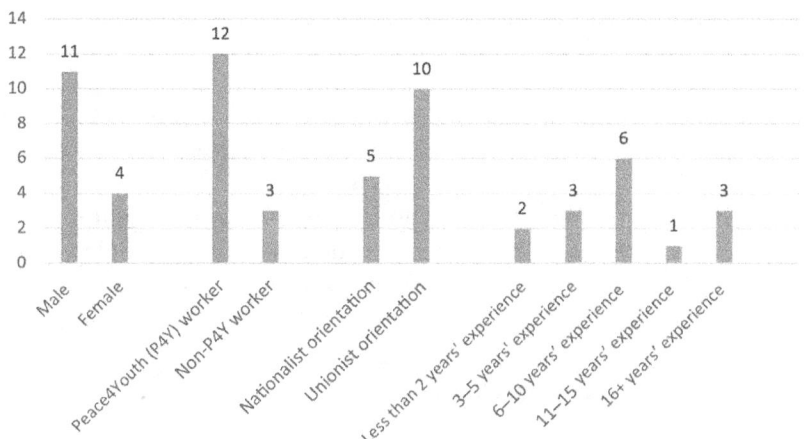

number of practitioners. The demographics of viewpoint 2 are outlined in Figure 7.2.

The EU-funded P4Y practitioners dominate viewpoint 2. Twelve P4Y practitioners are joined by only three non-P4Y practitioners. It is also a male-dominated viewpoint with 11 males and four females. There is a tendency for those most recently qualified to gravitate towards this viewpoint. Five practitioners have less than six years of post-qualifying experience, while six are in the category of 6–10 years' experience. More experienced practitioners are less likely to align with this mutual understanding viewpoint. Only four of the 15 practitioners have more than 11 years of experience as qualified workers. The demographics also suggest that those with a Unionist orientation are more likely to align with this viewpoint. Ten of the 15 practitioners within this viewpoint were Unionist-leaning, scoring themselves from 4 (moderate alignment with unionism) to 6 (strong alignment with unionism) on the continuum of political identity (see Figure 6.5 in the previous chapter). Only five practitioners in this viewpoint self-selected as Nationalist. No one selected 1 on the scale, which equates to the strongest alignment with Nationalism. Two practitioners selected 2, and three selected 3 on the six-point scale.

More than twice the number of practitioners make up viewpoint 2 as make up viewpoints 3 and 4, and almost twice as many as viewpoint 1. The disproportionate number of EU P4Y funded workers associated with this viewpoint indicates an alignment between this view of peacebuilding and the objectives of the EU P4Y programme.

Viewpoint 3: Social cohesion and restoration

Peace requires forgiveness. (YW34)

Viewpoint 3 is a firmly restorative approach to youth sector peacebuilding. Current issues emanating from conflict legacies, particularly community dysfunctionality and residual paramilitarism, are the primary lens through which this viewpoint orients practitioners towards peacebuilding. Within this context, emphasis is placed on encouraging young people to adopt restorative principles of forgiveness, non-violence, 'pro-social' behaviours, and support for policing. This is accompanied by an emphasis on personal responsibility to act as respectable and productive citizens and to challenge cultures of blame and denial. YW33 explains:

> *People are very quick to point the finger at everybody; it's the way things have been done here forever, it takes the limelight off yourself and points it at somebody else. Whereas if everybody took that wee bit more responsibility for themselves and that self-awareness, then those positive vibes and energy would be out there in the community.* (YW33)

Similarly, YW17 raises frustrations at embedded cycles of retaliation, stating:

> *There's a culture, particularly in these communities, where if someone does something to you, you need to get them for it. For young people, it's about taking a bit of responsibility for their actions and not blaming other people or blaming their culture or blaming just the way things are.* (YW17)

The ideas of personal responsibility and forgiveness are coupled together and receive the highest ranking of +5 (as depicted by statements 2 and 8 in Table 7.3). YW07 explains, '*you can't move forward if you don't accept some responsibility for something that's went wrong*', and YW08 affirms, '*if young people can learn to forgive, then they can move on*'.

YW34 points to the enduring nature of animosity and suspicion embedded as a result of the 'Troubles' in Northern Ireland and the crucial role of forgiveness that must accompany any notion of 'moving on'. He invokes Galtung's (1964) distinction of negative and positive peace, suggesting the former is achievable in the absence of forgiveness while the latter is dependent upon it: '*I think encouraging young people to see the absolute value of forgiveness is ... it's what the adults around them can't do. We are 21 years into a relative peace process, which is actually just the absence of everyday regular violence rather than peace because peace requires forgiveness*' (YW34).

Ongoing levels of paramilitary activity that ripple through this contested society are a persistent source of child exploitation. Young people, particularly

Table 7.3: Selection of distinguishing statements for viewpoint 3

Statement	Viewpoint			
	1	2	3	4
2. Encouraging young people to see the value of forgiveness in helping them and others move forward	-1	1	5	-1
8. Encouraging young people to take responsibility and make amends when they cause harm to others	0	2	5	0
12. Promoting trust in policing to deliver justice	-3	-2	1	-4
16. Diverting young people from radicalisation	-2	-1	4	-3
36. Working non-violently to prevent paramilitary style attacks on young people	-2	-1	4	-3
39. Encouraging young people to embrace restorative rather than retributive ideas of justice	1	-2	3	-1

young men from disadvantaged communities, are exposed to paramilitary-style violence and threats or recruitment into paramilitary groups to carry out attacks and facilitate an illicit drug trade. Practitioners aligned with viewpoint 3, therefore, are committed to countering violent extremism and dismantling the allure and influence of paramilitary actors who prey upon young people.

YW34 highlights the necessity for the youth sector to address unchecked paramilitarism and its impacts on young people. He reflects: '*There's been quite a chunk of my work has been around paramilitary-style attacks on young people – because it was an issue that nobody else was tackling and nobody else was kind of dealing with*' (YW34). Practitioners pointed to the manipulative recruitment tactics of paramilitary organisations with young men in '*at-risk communities*' where '*they use fear to coerce them and groom them into joining*' (YW34). Similarly, YW08 observed: '*They target these young guys, so they've got like a sense of security, you know, the whole thing with being in a gang because that's really what it is.*' Interrupting such cycles of criminality and violence is, for viewpoint 3, '*the big thing in peacebuilding*' (YW08).

In tackling paramilitarism and building towards social cohesion and restoration, this perspective prioritises notions of diverting young people from radicalisation (see statement 16 in Table 7.3). This diversionary work ensures young people are '*able to be themselves and not being influenced or brainwashed about other people and the atrocities that have happened here*' (YW33). Furthermore, trust in policing and justice mechanisms are valued in this viewpoint; indeed, this was the only viewpoint to give a positive ranking to statement 12, 'Promoting trust in policing to deliver justice'. YW08 reflects: '*I have lived in societies where policing works, and to me, it's a game-changer. I think that's really what it comes down to, the whole trust issue. There's only one way that you are going to get rid of them [paramilitaries], and that's with policing.'* Restorative approaches that work in partnership with the institutions of the state are championed as ways to emancipate young men and women from paramilitary influence and community ostracisation.

Linked to the violence both past and present, this viewpoint is concerned with addressing transgenerational trauma and mental health issues experienced by young people. YW33 explains: *'Trauma then, through the epigenetics, will be passed down through generations, that stuff hasn't been dealt with and has sort of just been swept under the carpet.'* YW34 further elaborates on the *'emerging research on adverse childhood experiences'* as a growing area of concern in conflict societies exacerbated by paramilitary-style retribution and community control. Consequently, for viewpoint 3, mental health and wellbeing is a peacebuilding imperative.

While residual violence is to be tackled head on from this viewpoint, political and social issues of the past are considered with caution, concerned that exploring these will result in *'reopening old wounds'* (YW08). It is deemed more judicious to take the approach of *'letting dogs lie'* (YW34). Furthermore, history has been used as a weapon where *'you can see them [young people] almost being radicalised back again into levels of mistrust and pushed towards violence by revisiting stuff of the past'* (YW34). As such, *'some stuff in the past just needs to be consigned to the past'* (YW34).

Conflict legacies have embedded a sense of territoriality that excludes those who deviate from the dominant identities. In response, this viewpoint prioritises the notion of 'welcoming newcomers'. Peacebuilding is considered a way of equipping young people to challenge sectarianism and xenophobia by fostering a sense of shared communities. Efforts are channelled into empowering young people to take ownership of community spaces and enabling them to feel safe within them. Encouraging young people to be active contributors to their communities is a significant way in which they can establish themselves as 'trustworthy' actors. This kind of responsible citizenship is required for the cultivation of cohesive and well-functioning communities.

Figure 7.3 outlines the demographic features of the six practitioners who make up viewpoint 3. There is an equal ratio of female to male practitioners. Three identify on the Nationalist end of the scale, and two practitioners identify moderately as Unionist. One practitioner does not identify themselves on the Nationalist–Unionist continuum, stating their positionality as a 'foreign national'.

It is interesting to note that no one with less than six years of experience as a qualified practitioner is undertaking the work of tackling paramilitarism and promoting social cohesion. The lack of any practitioner who identifies most strongly as Nationalist or Unionist aligning with this viewpoint is also of interest. However, with a relatively small grouping and an absence

Figure 7.3: Demographics of viewpoint 3

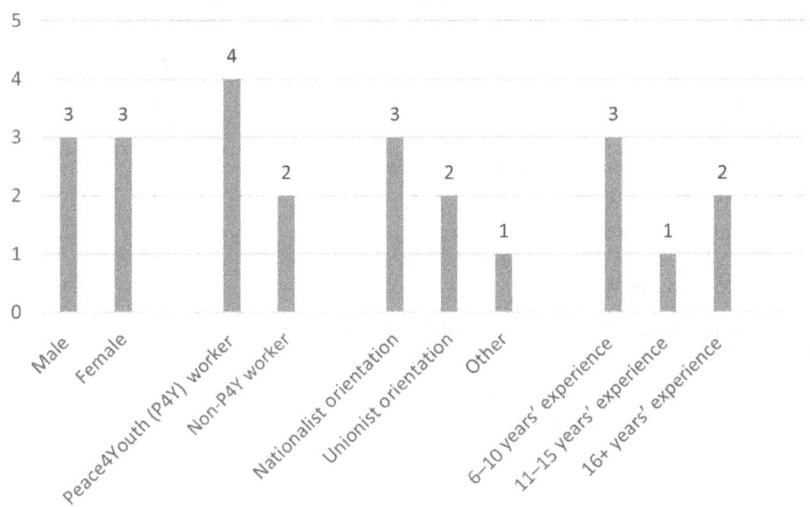

of starkly disproportionate attributes, limited insights can be extrapolated from the demographics of this viewpoint.

Viewpoint 4: Political engagement and social justice

It's all about young people coming together collectively to fight common causes. (YW03)

Viewpoint 4 is the most politicised approach to peacebuilding with young people, focused on supporting youth to engage in political issues and act as agents of social change. A critical notion of empowerment is advocated that insists on youth participation in political processes, with a particular focus on the interplay of rights and responsibilities. Young people are positioned as having a key role in challenging those in positions of power and influence, as well as disrupting traditional ethnocentric voting patterns. Practitioners who make up this viewpoint articulated concerns for social justice and support the targeting of resources towards working-class areas that have been disproportionately impacted by violence and conflict legacies. YW20 reflected, '*I think in any country in the world when there's trouble, it's always those less fortunate are those most affected*'. The selection of distinguishing statements for this viewpoint depicted in Table 7.4 evidence an action-oriented disposition towards youth sector peacebuilding that supports young people to take and use their power. For YW38, this is a response to their sense that '*for years, young people have been sidelined, it's been too easy for them to be ignored*'.

Table 7.4: Selection of distinguishing statements for viewpoint 4

Statement	Viewpoint			
	1	2	3	4
5. Encouraging young people to be activists and campaign for societal change	1	-2	-1	3
6. Supporting young people to challenge the power structures in their community and society	1	1	2	5
23. Intentionally organising non-violent resistance to force, coercion, or government policy, for example, through protests, demonstrations, or boycotts	-4	-5	-2	-1
25. Supporting young people to hold political and institutional representatives to account (for example, politicians, police)	0	-1	-2	3
37. Supporting young people to engage in politics and creating platforms for young people's voices to be heard by political institutions	3	0	-1	4
43. Promoting educational attainment and aspirations in working-class communities	-1	3	1	5

Each of the six practitioners who make up viewpoint 4 expressed personal experiences of becoming politicised as they reflected on their peacebuilding priorities. YW20, for instance, contemplated:

> *I don't think I ever realised, even growing up, how important politics is. But it's only as I get further up the ladder I start to understand more how important politics is. Me, just as one youth worker on the ground, I don't have the power to change laws or whatever else. So, I think that's where politics comes into it, and that's why it's important to engage young people in politics.* (YW20)

Similarly, YW24 recounted:

> *I'm more politically minded over the past couple of years because I have another role where I support the Northern Ireland Youth Parliament, and I can see the benefits of supporting young people to be active within their community and make decisions and to try and give them space so they can learn about their rights. I have seen how young people can lobby and get involved in democracy to make things happen.* (YW24)

While it was through their work that these two practitioners went through a process of what Freire would call *conscientisation*, others were socialised in a family environment of political activism and hence from an early age were learning to think critically about power and oppression. YW18 explained:

My family are majority strong women who have all been involved in peacebuilding; my aunt started part of the civil rights campaign in the late 60s. Core to my value has always been around promoting the place of equality and a human rights approach and young people being able to take the opportunities to take their own power and being filled full of information and being let loose, go for it! (YW18)

YW03, reflecting on her *'proud working-class roots'*, emphasised the importance of *'understanding a lot of the political aspects of being working-class'* and how working-class young people *'can be voices for their communities if only people give them the adequate support that they need in order to do so'*. While YW03 observes that these young people are *'really let down by government'*, she highlights that *'youth workers have a unique opportunity to work with these young people and develop their educational attainment'*. YW18, who works with young people who have disengaged from mainstream education, noted that the emphasis is *'not necessarily just education in terms of English and Maths or those type of academic qualifications'* but it's *'looking at politics with a small p'*.

The notion of 'small-p politics' is evoked by several practitioners from viewpoint 4. This perspective distances itself from politics and politicisation that is intentionally divisive or seeks to maintain traditional voting blocs. Instead, it seeks to reclaim the language of politicisation as one of critical thinking and collective action to address cross-cutting social issues and problematise binary identity politics. YW24 noted:

It's not just the Unionist-Nationalist lines; it's not just voting for what your mummy or daddy or your granny and grandad or your community tells you to vote for. So, I would encourage young people to vote and to support the parties who are going to do what they say they're going to do in their best interests and for their needs, to maybe help move society along. (YW24)

YW20 holds a similar vision of:

[Y]oung people coming together from different communities to tackle politicians and supporting young people to challenge the power structures in their society and community on a dual background approach so Catholics and Protestants or whoever it may be, newcomers, LGBT like a coming together as one like just one big group of young people's voices. (YW20)

Young people occupy a position to challenge the legacy of sectarian politics and call such practices to account. Colloquially this division has been referred to as Green versus Orange, derived from the symbolic significance of the respective colours for Nationalists and Unionists. YW38 argues:

> *We're being failed by politicians and have been for a long time, and the voting across party political lines, you know, the Green and Orange stuff, if we're able to give young people more of an opportunity and to hold politicians to account, then things mightn't be so Green and Orange.* (YW38)

For viewpoint 4, peacebuilding involves fostering opportunities for young people to be creators and innovators of change within their communities. It's an approach that champions the grassroots where '*the people on the ground need to be pushing for change*' rather than '*having one or two per cent of the population at the top dictating everything down for the majority*' (YW20). It engenders a '*political understanding of rights and trying to tackle injustice*' that seeks to '*give young people the tools to empower themselves and their communities*' (YW03). For YW24, this is best encapsulated by the notion of active citizenship, '*where young people are getting involved in politics and having their voice heard, they are learning about their rights; it is about participation and asking questions*' (YW24). Active citizenship involves young people having a role in addressing '*structural changes that are needed*' (YW30). The practitioners aligned with viewpoint 4 see their approach to peacebuilding as a radical one that seeks to challenge the status quo. YW38 reflects on the notion of speaking truth to power and perceives this as '*a radical step where there are risks involved*'.

Within this perspective, practitioners were also keen to note a developmental approach that works with young people from their starting points. YW24 noted that in their work with young people labelled as NEET (not in education, employment, or training), it was difficult to persuade them to get an ID card so they could vote. Therefore, they took the approach of '*selling it to them*', explaining that an ID card is required to open a bank account or fly and '*once they have it, it's about planting a seed and maybe encouraging them to register to vote*' (YW24). Similarly, YW20 speaks to the first steps in developing political consciousness whereby '*youth workers engage with young people regarding politics, just even opening their eyes to politics and how important politics is in society and how connected it is to everything*'.

Despite being the most politicised of the four viewpoints, it is noteworthy that the findings indicate a limited place for notions of resistance as a political strategy in viewpoint 4. While statement 23, 'Intentionally organising non-violent resistance to force, coercion or government policy, for example, through protests, demonstrations, or boycotts', is valued higher here than in any other perspective (at -1), at best, it can be understood as an adjacent concept, moving towards the periphery. This finding suggests that for all the radical leanings of viewpoint 4 towards activism for social change, limits have been internalised within the perspective on acceptable notions of resistance. A cautious disposition towards the politics of resistance in the youth sector renders the viewpoint less radical than it might have been. This critique is explored further in the proceeding chapters.

Figure 7.4: Demographics of viewpoint 4

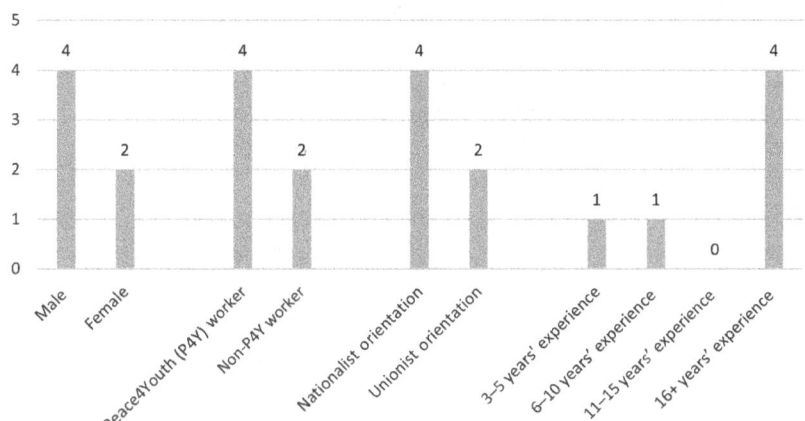

Figure 7.4 shows that six practitioners make up the political engagement and social justice viewpoint, four male and two female. Four are EU P4Y funded workers, and two are non-P4Y. The majority have over 16 years of experience as qualified practitioners, although one practitioner has 3–5 years of experience. Like viewpoint 3 participant demographics, there are limits on what can be inferred from the small cohort aligned with viewpoint 4.

A final point on viewpoint 4 pertains to YW03's reflection on her arrangement of statements, where she was encouraged that *'it's very anti-injustice stuff like fighting power, which is nice to see'*. She continued, *'I haven't lost a lot of my fiery roots, for a long time I've been conflicting with myself that maybe I'd dulled myself down a little bit, but it's still there, so I'm happy to see that.'* This reflection is pertinent to our analysis of the four viewpoints. YW03 was employed through the EU P4Y programme, which in our study is best represented by viewpoint 2, mutual understanding. A key feature of the mutual understanding viewpoint is a tendency to depoliticise and promote harmonious relations at all levels with a much lower inclination to critique and challenge institutional power. It may be that the tension YW03 describes is exacerbated by working within the context of a peace programme that prioritises harmonisation while their personal value base is one of politicisation. This analysis is developed in the next chapter.

Outliers

In Q methodology, a statistical process called 'Q factor analysis' is used to determine the number of viewpoints to be extracted from a data set of completed Q sorts.[4] Those participants whose Q sort does not neatly fit into one viewpoint but is aligned significantly across multiple viewpoints are known as a confounded Q sort. It is standard practice to exclude these confounded Q sorts rather than include them on multiple viewpoints. Four participants in our study were split across two viewpoints and, therefore, were not included. A further five Q sorts did not meet the threshold criteria to be aligned with any of our four viewpoints. Notably, four of the five practitioners who did not reach the level of significance to be associated with any of the four viewpoints had over 16 years of experience as qualified practitioners, while the remaining practitioner had 11–15 years of experience. It may be inferred that this group is most likely to have developed, through experience, more nuanced perspectives on peacebuilding work with young people, not fitting neatly within the categories identified in the study. While these outliers point to areas of interest for future research and the identification of additional perspectives, the primary focus of Q methodology, and by extension our study, is on the identification of salient viewpoints with statistically significant properties that participants are aligned with.

Negotiating neoliberal policy

The final section of this chapter gives voice to practitioners' experiences of peacebuilding within a neoliberally oriented policy and practice climate. None of our 48 statements included explicit reference to the neoliberalisation of youth sector peacebuilding. Practitioners, however, were keen to point out how they negotiated top-down targets, short-term programmes, and surveillance of prescribed outputs and outcomes. Only one practitioner suggested collectivising and resisting neoliberal trends but ultimately concluded with a pessimistic tone that changing the policy and funding environment was unlikely and creative ways had to be devised to navigate the existing structures. YW40 most clearly articulated the concern that:

> *There's a neoliberal agenda, it has to be measurable, it has to be quantifiable, and the way we quantify it is by producing to the lowest common denominator – courses where we can say that '41 young people from deprived community A managed to obtain qualification C which is equivalent to two-thirds of a GCSE' and that's how it's measured. Where the real measurement is actually in the hearts and the minds of the young people and that stuff ... that's beyond measuring.* (YW40)

Frustration over who sets, monitors, and evaluates targets and outcomes was consistently reported. YW36 reflected, '*I remember we used to set out our own programmes, we used to set our own targets and objectives and stuff, and it moved.*' This shift in policy making, where '*government departments are becoming outcome dependent*' (YW33) and there is a '*top-down approach*' (YW06), creates a dilemma for practitioners who are:

> *Trained as youth workers to work on a needs-led basis, to work with what's in front of us in a room, to work to what groups or communities need and then we are being asked by, and this isn't just [EU] PEACE funding it's all funding you know if you're having to work to a funder's agenda then that can have an impact on your impact with the group.* (YW18)

As a result, practitioners '*have to target a certain number, so then it's not about the young people, it becomes about your numbers*' (YW15). This requires more time to be spent on evidencing outcomes, which in turn shapes the nature of practice. YW22 stated there needs to be '*less form filling for those who receive the funding, less bureaucracy*'. Within the EU P4Y funding stream there was a perception among some practitioners that: '*We've had some "suit" sit and predetermine that for young people to conform, for there to be a real positive change in them, they need to complete at least 249 hours over a six-month period, they need to meet set outcomes of each target area*' (YW06). From this perspective, policy makers are regarded as out of touch with a sense that '*nobody asks the workers on the ground what do you think the needs are or what do you think is the best way to do this?*' (YW15). Agreeing with this perception, YW35 asserted, '*there is very little youth worker input. There's a lot of civil servants put them things together, but it's not really coming from the ground and coming back up again*'. For YW38, despite policy makers' claims to be taking account of young people's needs within local communities, they felt '*as a grassroots sort of approach, it's not working*'.

The inconsistency of funding and unrealistic expected outcomes within a project's life cycle was noted as problematic. Contemplating barriers to successful peacebuilding initiatives with young people, YW11 commented: '*It needs to be the continuity with funding. It seems to be it funds, it stops, then it comes back up again. If the sector knew that it was being continuously funded to do this work, then it doesn't become tokenistic.*' An objection was voiced about the expectation that youth work produces linear and easily identifiable outcomes. YW33 argues:

> *Funders sometimes want things to be very fast fixing; they want to see some kind of change, some kind of learning right away. But sometimes it's not until you've had a couple of different experiences and you can piece all that together, and you can go, that's what that is.* (YW33)

In the Northern Ireland context, targeted and outcome-driven funding and policy are increasingly perceived as the dominant logic of youth sector peacebuilding. Value for money must be demonstrated through efficient and effective programmes that have quantifiable inputs and outputs. Funding bodies dictate prescribed outcomes, and measurement of personal change is a constant imperative. Financial penalties are applied where outputs are not met. It is within this context that the four viewpoints exist and compete for recognition as legitimate ways of developing peacebuilding work with young people.

Conclusion

While not an exhaustive presentation of all existing viewpoints on youth sector peacebuilding, our Q methodology study with youth work practitioners has led to the identification and naming of distinctive perspectives with differentiated priorities:

1. critical thinking and dialogue;
2. mutual understanding;
3. social cohesion and restoration;
4. political engagement and social justice.

Adaptations and gradations of interpretation can be applied to each viewpoint. However, the Q methodology procedure, which groups together those who have sorted statements in a statistically significant similar way, is the basis from which we present each viewpoint as having a distinctive character. Although generated within the specific context of Northern Ireland, the four viewpoints provide a basis for conceptualising different approaches to peacebuilding in various international contexts. The perspectives pertain not only to peacebuilding work with young people but also to peace and reconciliation work across wider civil and political society. The next chapter discusses similarities and differences across the viewpoints and critiques the prioritisation of perspectives that tend towards harmonisation at the expense of more politicising approaches to peacebuilding. The discussion moves to formulate a new model of youth sector peacebuilding that houses each of the four viewpoints.

8

A new model of youth sector peacebuilding

> There's other alternatives in peacebuilding ... there are other ways to peace build. (YW14)

Introduction

This chapter presents the Hamardle model of youth sector peacebuilding constructed from our analysis of the four viewpoints presented in the previous chapter. Implicit in the preceding presentation of viewpoints are propensities towards either *politicisation* or *harmonisation* alongside a primary emphasis on either *dialogue* or *action*. This chapter makes these positions explicit, with each of the four viewpoints making up one of the quadrants in the model, as shown in Figure 8.1. The person icons in each quadrant depict how many of those who took part in the research made up each viewpoint.

The Hamardle model draws upon the philosophy of morphological analysis, as discussed in Chapter 6, particularly the notion of family resemblances, whereby patterns are recognised and grouped (Freeden, 2013a). Despite idiosyncrasies in individual thinking and action, each viewpoint has a particular structure and pattern with distinguishing features that merits designation as a distinctive approach to peacebuilding that wider populations will be able to situate themselves within. In this way, individual practitioners' thought structures on peacebuilding share a familial resemblance with others and subsequently are grouped into an overarching viewpoint.

While each quadrant of the model represents a distinctive perspective, we seek to avoid hard borders that box individuals and groups into a fixed way of thinking. Rather, the axis lines are dashed to represent the morphing of perspectives at the borders. Through time and space, ideas, concepts, language, and thought structures borrow and blend from one another and are refashioned and infused with new meanings. Similarly, through reflexivity, individuals go through shifts, ruptures, and transitions in their thinking as they participate in practices and experience their social, political, and cultural surroundings in new ways. As such, youth sector peacebuilding is a praxis perpetually in the process of becoming (Freire, 1970).

Employing the logic of family resemblances, the viewpoints we have uncovered are sufficiently broad to encapsulate a diverse range of thinking patterns and thought structures that share affinity with one of the four

Figure 8.1: Hamardle model of youth sector peacebuilding

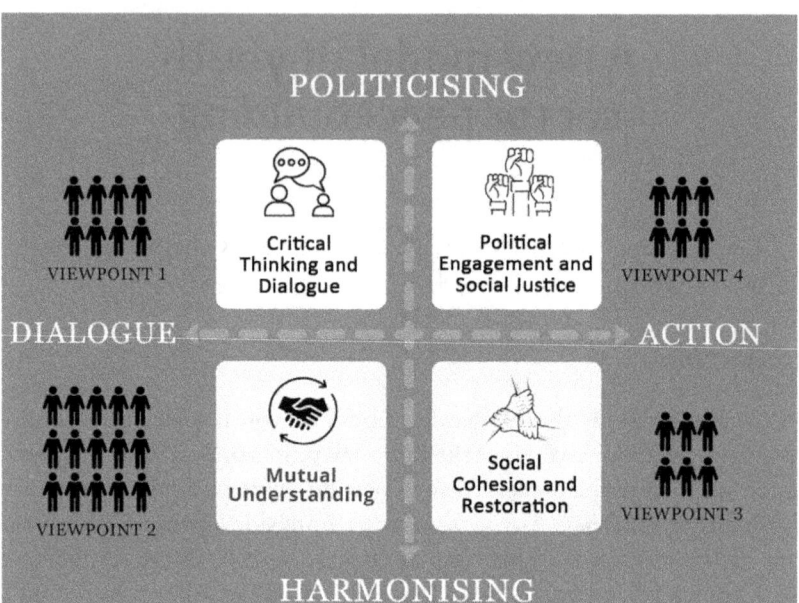

viewpoints. This argument does not negate the value of further studies identifying additional significant viewpoints that supplement or challenge those generated through this study. In other countries, regions, and time points, alternative viewpoints and patterns will be observed. That stated, we propose our Hamardle model, with its four quadrants discussed in this chapter, is a useful heuristic that additional viewpoints on peacebuilding, within the youth sector and beyond, can be positioned and mapped within.

Viewpoint 1 as politicising dialogue: high on politicising, high on dialogue

Viewpoint 1, critical thinking and dialogue, cultivates an approach to youth sector peacebuilding premised on what we term 'politicising dialogue', as presented in Figure 8.2.

This perspective draws heavily on a Freirean notion of critical pedagogy involving dialogical processes of critical reflection and conscientisation 'in order to recognise oppression as a political injustice rather than a personal failing' (Ledwith, 2016: xi). As inequitable and oppressive power structures are analysed and the dehumanising aspects of these are exposed through critical thinking and dialogue, the personal becomes fundamentally political. Conscientisation can be viewed as a process that necessarily politicises young people.

Figure 8.2: Viewpoint 1 as politicising dialogue

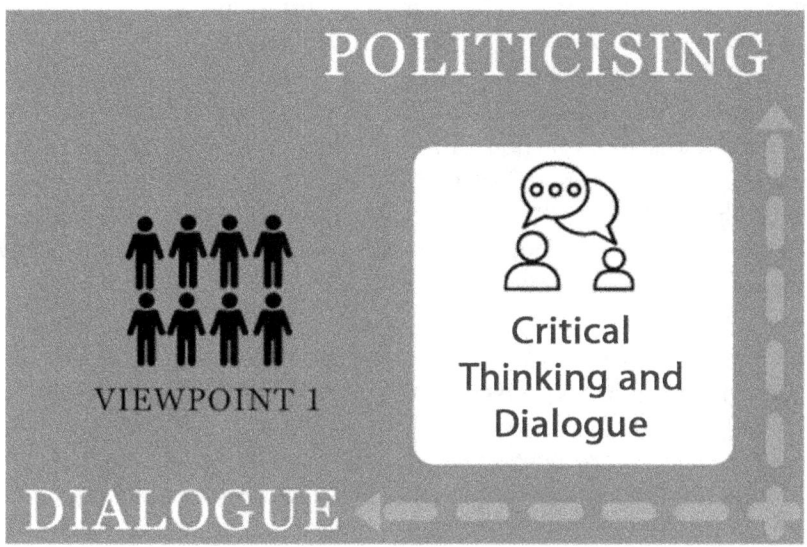

The term politicisation risks pejorative connotations. For viewpoint 1, politicisation communicates a conviction that education is not neutral and will have both implicit and explicit agendas. The educationalist, therefore, either facilitates 'the integration of the younger generation into the logic of the present system and bring about conformity to it', or they facilitate an emancipatory practice where 'men and women deal critically and creatively with reality and discover how to participate in the transformation of their world' (Shaull, 1996: 16).

Concepts of reconciliation and intergroup contact are politicised within viewpoint 1. This approach to peacebuilding invites difficult conversations and recognition of disputed narratives while maintaining the need for those with oppositional ideas to cooperate in dialogue with one another. The approach to reconciliation can be understood as a dialogical process that sets aside ambitions of reaching a harmonious state between conflicted parties (Doxtader, 2003). Similarly, the notion of pursuing intergroup contact is advocated as a vehicle for facilitating critical dialogue rather than primarily for prejudice reduction (Allport, 1954; Pettigrew and Tropp, 2006). The focus instead is on pursuing intergroup contact to stimulate critical thinking and engagements that can shed light on individual or group cognitive dissonance. In a state of cognitive dissonance, inconsistent thoughts, beliefs, values, and behaviours can co-exist, causing discomfort and unease for the individual. Such cognitive dissonance can be exposed when traditional and partisan ways of understanding the world are challenged through encounters with others who express alternative worldviews.

A more contested term could be used in the Hamardle model (Figure 8.1), replacing *politicisation* with *radicalisation*. Far from diverting young people from radicalisation, viewpoint 1 seeks to cultivate 'the radical, committed to human liberation' (Freire, 1996: 21). This notion of radicalisation is set against 'sectarianism, fed by fanaticism' (Freire, 1996: 19). Freire explains: 'Radicalization, nourished by a critical spirit, is always creative. Sectarianism mythicizes and thereby alienates; radicalization criticizes and thereby liberates' (Freire, 1996: 19). Viewpoint 1 orients towards a politicised form of citizenship education that seeks to foster a radical and critical analysis of the socio-political, cultural, and economic context. Young people learn to link their analysis of societal power with their individual position and agency. This educational process originates in the immediate circumstances of young people's everyday lives and develops as an organic unfolding of the systems and structures that dehumanise, exclude, and deceive. As the extent of oppression becomes increasingly understood, it becomes more difficult to dismiss experiences of discrimination and prejudice as individuated.

Viewpoint 1 builds on an understanding of youth work grounded in education (Cooper, 2018; Hammond, 2018). It is an education that is participatory, emancipatory, politicised, and radical. Dialogue is evident in this viewpoint as a fundamental catalyst and vehicle for driving a peacebuilding process with young people that unsettles sectarianised social relationships and disrupts the common sense of segregation. This viewpoint also seeks to continually rethink the logic of peacebuilding interventions and the ways in which they require practitioners to act as 'the foot soldiers of oppressive policy and regimes' (Shultz, 2009: 10), not least through the reproduction of meritocracy, individual self-interest, and an obsession with outputs and outcomes.

Some practitioners considered this viewpoint as a radical approach to peacebuilding. However, the agitational potency of this viewpoint is dampened by the tendency towards sustaining positive relationships and operating within existing political frameworks. Organising collective action and resistance are peripheral concepts within this perspective. The tendency to prioritise dialogue at the expense of action further curtails Freire's (1970) vision of a radical praxis that integrates both these dimensions. While there is evidence of emancipatory and radical forms of critical thinking espoused by this viewpoint, it is not accompanied by a similar propensity for radical and emancipatory action.

Seven practitioners, plus the researcher, made up this viewpoint in our study. Including one of the authors, Hamilton, in the Q methodology process has aided our reflexivity. Such reflexivity is focused on exploring dispositions and propensities to both mitigate bias in our analysis as well as better understand our frame of reference. Through many conversations and probing encounters, the three authors engaged in a Bourdieusian notion of reflexivity as 'a common and shared effort, aiming at making explicit the "unthought" categories, perceptions, theories and structures that underpin any pre-reflexive grasp of the social environment' (Deer, 2014: 198). As a result of this reflexive process, it became clear that all three authors were drawn to the critical thinking and dialogue perspective. While advocating for a more politicised peacebuilding practice with young people embedded throughout the policy-making process, we appreciate the contributions of harmonising viewpoints for specific contexts in the initial stages of peacebuilding.

Viewpoint 2 as harmonising dialogue: high on harmonising, high on dialogue

Viewpoint 2, mutual understanding, is the most favoured viewpoint of all four, with 15 practitioners from the study aligned to it, as shown in Figure 8.3.

Supreme value is attributed to cultivating harmonious relationships, and this perspective seeks to de-escalate conflict and division through building empathy and understanding of difference. It is an approach to peacebuilding guided by the pursuit of harmonising dialogue. The presumed logic is that greater understanding leads to increased acceptance of others and reduces the gulf between in-groups and out-groups (Tajfel, 1982; Jones, 2004). From this perspective, practitioners highlight contact work and exposure to difference as the key to peacebuilding processes. Connolly's (2000: 170)

Figure 8.3: Viewpoint 2 as harmonising dialogue

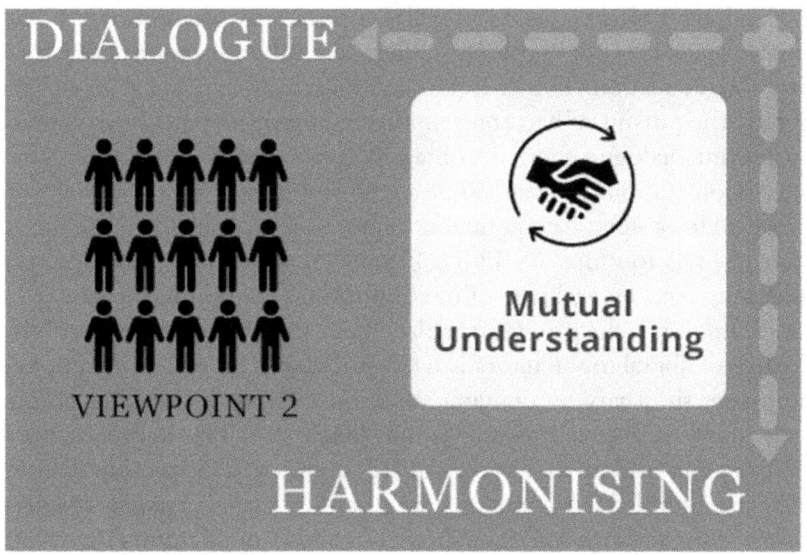

succinct maxim 'intergroup contact reduces prejudice' is the driving principle of this perspective. While contact between distinctive communities is encouraged, caution is taken in not equating this with a dilution of cultural identity. In this regard, the emphasis on single identity work can be used as a framework for addressing anxieties and concerns about meeting with those from different backgrounds. These approaches enable 'own culture validation' as well as building 'respect for diversity' (Jones, 2004: 22–23).

Complementing the contact hypothesis (Allport, 1954), this perspective is implicitly informed by Fisher's (1984) Trust Attraction Hypothesis that maintains: 'As A discloses, B perceives this as trust, and is consequently more likely to be attracted to A. This increased liking leads B to disclose more to A ... reciprocity of disclosure may well be based on reciprocity of trust' (Hargie et al, 2003: 87–88). This reciprocal relationship contributes not only to the accommodation of difference but an affinity that facilitates the building of friendships. Dialogue is a consistent feature of this harmonising perspective whereby preparing for and engaging in contact with the distanced other is premised on conversational and relational approaches involving the discovery of commonalities.

In the Northern Ireland context, viewpoint 2 can be understood as a contemporary manifestation of the Education for Mutual Understanding (EMU) policy established as a compulsory addition to the education curriculum from 1992 onwards (Richardson, 1997). The policy was underpinned by principles of respect for self and others, understanding, interdependence, and diversity (Smith and Robinson, 1996). It was argued through the EMU policy, using Giroux's (1988) language, that 'schools will need to become "sites of contestation"' (Whitehouse, 1990: 498) or places for difficult discussions. Smith et al (2019) suggest this did not occur and that the Northern Ireland school sector has continuously demonstrated limited appetite, or success, for engaging with the radical implications of EMU and citizenship education. This critique can similarly be directed at viewpoint 2, whereby the pursuit of harmonising dialogue renders practitioners reticent to forefront dialogue around contested issues, much less create 'sites of contestation' (Giroux, 1988). While aligned with the EMU policy view that 'education has a significant contribution to make in dispelling prejudice and improving relationships' (NIECD, 1988: 11), viewpoint 2 steers a course that circumvents an embrace of discomfort and contentious issues.

In viewpoint 2, the importance placed on 'focusing on commonalities' is reflective of liberal multiculturalism (Smith, 2003). Liberal multiculturalism 'emphasises similarity by drawing attention to what is shared in common by members of diverse groups' (Smith, 2003: 29). This approach mirrors Stevenson and Sagherian-Dickey's (2018) concept of citizenship discourses which are founded on *constructing unity* rather than *integrating difference or accommodating diversity*. Smith's appraisal of liberal multiculturalism is an apt critique of the mutual understanding perspective, where he writes: 'One of the criticisms of such approaches is that they generate a superficial politeness that avoids controversy at all costs' (Smith, 2003: 29). Hargie et al (2003: 88) similarly caution that an emphasis on trust and friendship, as evident in the findings for viewpoint 2, may result in a 'polite avoidance' of deeply embedded differences with sectarian undertones.

Viewpoint 2 can be understood as harmonising across multiple dimensions. Most explicitly, it advocates a harmonisation of conflictual relationships as core to the peacebuilding process. It seeks to de-contest contested spaces by practitioners building a culture of neutrality and reciprocity in physically and psychologically 'safe' spaces (Hargie et al, 2003). Another dimension of harmonisation indicative of viewpoint 2 is the accommodation of outcomes and targets that are driven by policy makers and funders. While the findings show practitioners within this quadrant may express some frustrations at increasingly outcomes-driven funding, they tend to reconcile this with notions of excellence and accountability, striving to deliver and communicate impact through quantitative outputs and outcomes (Bunyan and Ord, 2012).

Viewpoint 3 as harmonising action: high on harmonising, high on action

Viewpoint 3, depicted in Figure 8.4, conveys an approach to peacebuilding characterised by harmonised action. Restorative principles are the quantum materials of this perspective, intended to promote reconciliation of relationships at the interpersonal and inter- and intra-community levels (Chapman et al, 2018). While dialogue is a key restorative process, greater emphasis is placed on 'action and doing' – taking responsibility, moving forward, preventing violence, and diverting from radicalisation. At the interpersonal level, individual and community harm reduction is prioritised by engaging with those young people most alienated from their communities and perceived to be 'at risk' of becoming victims and perpetrators of violence (Magnuson, 2007).

Unique to this viewpoint is an emphasis on tackling paramilitarism. This is indicative of a commitment to work with young people who are invisible to wider society and exploited by coercive paramilitary control and violence (Byrne et al, 2016; Smyth, 2017). The viewpoint is attuned to the experiences of adolescent boys and young men who, in contested societies, are confronted with culturally engrained militarised masculinities. Paramilitarism reinforces narratives of territorialism and ever-present expectations and threats of violence (Harland and McCready, 2014; Murray, 2023). Practitioners within this viewpoint are eager to emphasise that 'Our young people act out of the dynamics that we have created and recreate through our segregated and divided society' (Smyth, 2011,

Figure 8.4: Viewpoint 3 as harmonising action

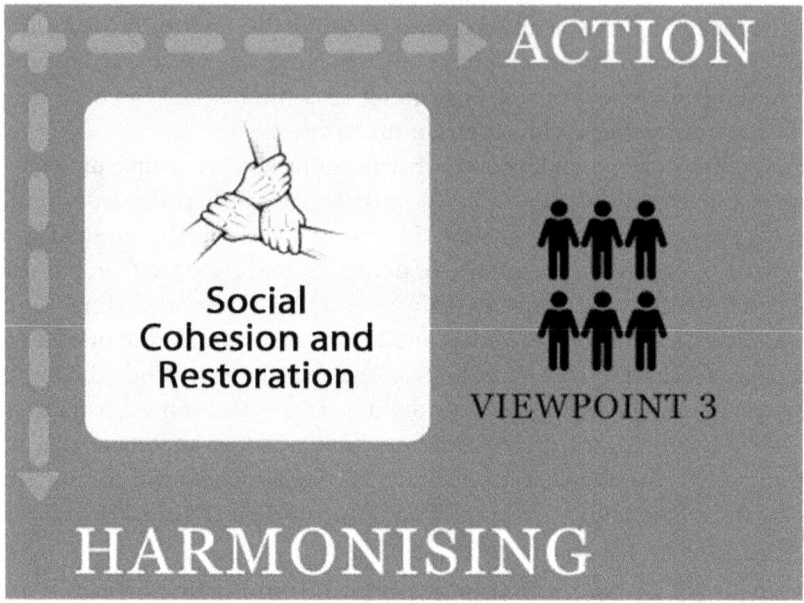

cited in Haydon et al, 2012: 507). In response, the primary peacebuilding priority is to engage these young people in restorative processes involving victims, perpetrators, and the wider community (O'Mahony et al, 2012). While Lohmeyer (2017a) casts a sceptical eye on restorative justice as an extension of state authority concerned with social control, this perspective is unperturbed by such an analysis. Although unlikely to view their approach as a social control function, practitioners aligned with this perspective advocate cooperation with policing to establish law, order, and stability in communities. Building community cohesion is prioritised through the re-socialisation of young people supported by a network of adults exerting a positive influence on their lives.

Viewpoint 3 draws attention to an inescapable past of terror and trauma that resides in the everyday lives of those who inhabit the post-conflict environment (Brewer et al, 2018). In this context, forgiveness is considered an imperative. Viewpoint 3 steers the youth sector away from the complex field of truth recovery and victims' rights for justice regarding past abuses. The focus is firmly on addressing contemporary harms, particularly the manifestation of transgenerational trauma in children and young people, as well as the impacts of adverse childhood experiences (O'Neill, 2015). The harmonising action orientation of the social cohesion and restoration viewpoint is particularly attuned to these realities. Several practitioners were cognisant of research highlighting the 'correlation between a high number of adverse childhood experiences and future violence, and entry into the criminal justice system' (Grant, 2019).

Viewpoint 3 aligns with the United Network of Youth Peacebuilders' proclamation that 'youth centres can play significant roles in fostering social cohesion and inclusivity by reaching out to marginalized youth' (Rogan, 2016: 33). Such outreach is a strategy to counter 'exploitation, including recruitment of organized social groups often aligned around a destructive goal' (Rogan, 2016: 33). The emphasis on tackling paramilitarism and diverting young people from radicalisation evidenced in the findings for viewpoint 3 suggests it tends towards a masculine perspective on peacebuilding. These concerns prioritise work with young men who are statistically more likely to be involved in the violent aspects of conflict (Harland, 2011).

The role and case of young women in peacebuilding was not emphasised in the findings by any of the four viewpoints. This focalises an under-recognised and often under-resourced area of practice that mirrors early policy developments in the Northern Ireland youth service (McArdle and Morgan, 2020; McCready, 2020). It appears that young women's contribution to peacebuilding has not been fully appreciated and the evidence of their exposure to paramilitary violence has not been duly acknowledged (McAlister et al, 2022). Practitioners have been more likely to note the significant contributions of the youth sector in working with young men in the contested space of Northern Ireland. A critical gender lens is required to redress the disregard and omission of a clear focus on young women in the youth service more broadly and in peacebuilding specifically.

Viewpoint 3 mirrors a positive youth development model of youth work that emphasises building youth resiliency (Cooper, 2018). The harmonising orientation of this perspective is evident in the impetus for employing restorative processes to reconcile wrongdoing and heal social fractures resulting from harm. It is also harmonising in a functionalist sense (Hurley and Treacy, 1993), seeking to restore confidence in policing and advocating the importance of supporting institutions that order social life.

Viewpoint 4 as politicising action: high on politicising, high on action

Viewpoint 4, political engagement and social justice, exhibits an approach to peacebuilding underpinned by politicised action, indicated in Figure 8.5. This perspective shares with viewpoint 1 a commitment to fostering political thinking. The impetus, however, shifts from dialogue to action. It is concerned with political engagement in the public sphere, where 'public opinion is formed and translated into political action' (Verkoren and van Leeuwen, 2013: 160). A vision for social justice animates this viewpoint where peacebuilding requires more than the prejudice reduction formula of Allport's

Figure 8.5: Viewpoint 4 as politicising action

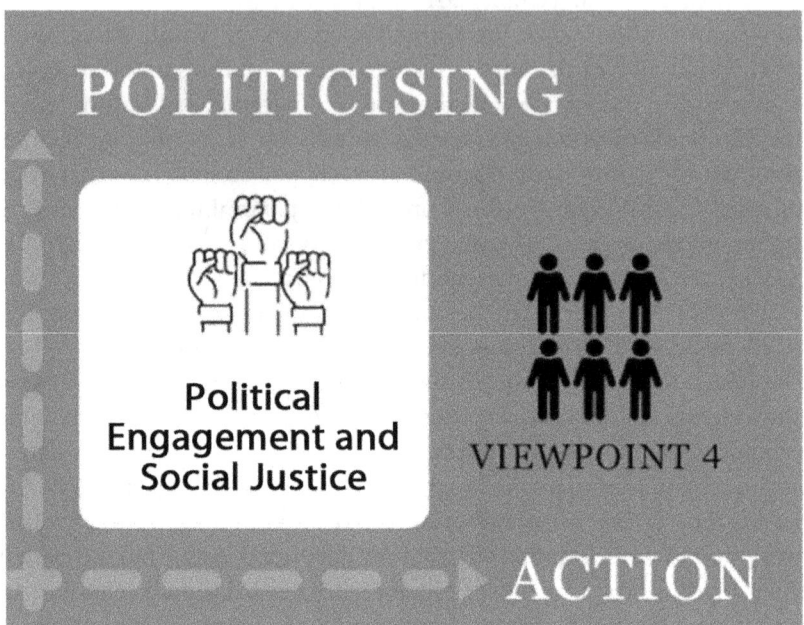

(1954) contact hypothesis. Rather, collective approaches are necessitated that invoke active resistance and social change (Reicher, 1986; 2007).

This viewpoint sets out to tackle issues of social stratification and unequal distribution of resources as fundamental concerns in peacebuilding. Social justice requires collective rather than individual action, advocating a social-political approach to global citizenship education (Veugelers, 2011). This accentuates the need to challenge inequalities and for critical reflection on social and political relations. Evident in this perspective is Crick's (2007) notion of a citizenship education that equips young people for democratic participation and generates competency in navigating political institutions and systems. Proponents of viewpoint 4 advocate for an *experiential* citizenship education that equips young people not only to be politically active and navigate existing structures but also to hold those in power to account and campaign for social change. As such it is not enough for political education to be *studied* through a didactic school system. Rather, fostering activism for societal change is anchored to concerns for structural justice, universal human rights, and fairness in the distribution of resources (Coburn and Gormally, 2017). Addressing the 'rights-realisation gap' (Simpson, 2018) for young people in contested societies is most prominent in viewpoint 4 with an emphasis on enacting young people's socio-economic and political rights, particularly for those from minority groups.

This perspective begins with a conviction that young people are a crucial and overlooked demographic in the political realm. Therefore, emphasis is placed on young people exercising their voice and influence through active engagement in political arenas and supporting creative contributions of young people to effecting political and social change. Viewpoint 4 is founded on an understanding of youth work as a form of radical democratic practice (Beck and Purcell, 2010; Batsleer, 2013). It is a perspective that advocates: 'A level of collective empowerment [that] seeks to problematise the world, and to activate individuals into challenging existing social policies and political decisions' (Forrest, 2010: 68). Furthermore, viewpoint 4 is the most attuned of all the viewpoints to tackling enactments of symbolic and cultural violence as a primary feature of peacebuilding (Galtung, 1990; Bourdieu and Wacquant, 1992; Del Felice, 2008; Lohmeyer, 2018). Structural violence arises from the violations and infringements imposed through inequitable state policies and practices. Cultural violence supports such structural violence by embedding these ideas and practices as cultural norms accepted as common sense. From flags and emblems that celebrate war and instil territorialism, to supremacy narratives that stoke divisive nationalism or patriotism, cultural violence lives in the taken-for-granted ideas that are in the very air we breathe. In opposition to these structural and cultural forces, viewpoint 4 orients towards supporting young people to be politically active and counter these manifestations of violence within the social system they are part of. These aspects of the political engagement and social justice viewpoint highlight its politicising disposition.

Conclusion: locating self in the Hamardle model

The Hamardle model of youth sector peacebuilding allows students, practitioners, policy makers, and researchers to locate their primary dispositions and the priorities that guide their practice. The harmonisation–politicisation vertical axis of the model draws upon sociological themes of personal versus political, and agency versus structure. Harmonising approaches to peacebuilding tend to focus on interpersonal relationships, individual agency, personal responsibility, and connections between people to replace hostility, mistrust, and separation. Politicising approaches gravitate towards structural issues and concerns with power and powerlessness in peacebuilding. These politicising approaches tend to be more agitational and at ease with facilitating discomfort and challenge to the status quo. Rather than seeing peacebuilding as a way of enabling everyone to get along, emphasis is placed on cultivating young people's political consciousness. The dialogue–action horizontal axis of the model speaks to process. Two of the viewpoints are more inclined to forefront conversation and dialogical encounters, whereas the other two are geared towards young people and practitioners taking action; doing something that will redress harm or oppression and be visible to others in their communities.

The internal boundaries of the model blur at the edges, indicating how viewpoints are never fixed. Alongside points of divergence, there are also many aspects of convergence. The Hamardle model is morphic rather than categoric. We contend, however, that unearthing, reflecting upon, and critiquing individual and collective dispositions towards harmonising or politicising, and dialogue or action, is a liberating process that enables biases to be named and new possibilities to be explored.

The model acts as a reflexive tool adding layers of analysis that have often remained hidden and below the level of consciousness for practitioners, academics, and policy makers. It invites critical awareness of distinctive trajectories of practice and consideration of how these are influenced by external stimuli and political agendas. With these explorations, actors can adjudicate whether their conceptual position on the model is congruent with their practice, their context, and their philosophical intentions. The next chapter makes the case that harmonising approaches to peacebuilding are consistently incentivised by state actors at the expense of politicising practices and overlays the Hamardle model with a critique of power hierarchies in the field of youth sector peacebuilding.

9

Radicalising youth sector peacebuilding

> Neutral for me suggests you're trying to suppress the very things that make young people who they are and their identities. (YW39)

Introduction

Substantial and pervasive power dynamics are at play in the field of youth sector peacebuilding. Policy makers and inter-state funders, equipped with economic resources and the authority to set peacebuilding aims and targets, are well placed to determine dominant and common-sense ideas in the domain of peacebuilding. While many youth work organisations and practitioners buy into and reproduce the policy-funding status quo, others seek to resist and mount counter-offensives to combat hegemonic and deeply ingrained ideas. This chapter returns to the ideas of Bourdieu and Lave and Wenger to notice and name these powerful forces which bear down on practitioners and shape the regimes of competence across youth sector peacebuilding communities of practice. The antidote to a state-sanctioned sanitised and depoliticised approach to peacebuilding lies in a critical engagement with the Hamardle model of youth sector peacebuilding. This chapter proposes that youth sector peace practitioners can use the model to reveal insights into their positionality, stance, and directions they pursue in practice. Such a reflexive critical analysis is presented as an emancipatory process, revealing socio-political and economic biases and commonly accepted ideas that shape the practitioner and the practice. This approach will lead to 'questioning everyday life's taken-for-grantedness to see the contradictions we live by more clearly in order to act for change' (Ledwith, 2016: xi).

Harmonising versus politicising

As delineated in the previous chapter, the four viewpoints that practitioners embody in relation to youth sector peacebuilding have been mapped within the Hamardle model that identifies propensities towards politicisation or harmonisation. Viewpoints 1, critical thinking and dialogue, and 4, political engagement and social justice, orient towards a politicising approach to peacebuilding. These politicising viewpoints centre on conflicting perspectives and agitational politics to pursue the transformation of political and social structures deemed to be oppressive. Viewpoints 2, mutual understanding, and 3, social cohesion and restoration, gravitate towards a harmonising agenda, seeking to expel conflict, reduce prejudice, cultivate amicable relations, and build cross-community cohesion.

Viewpoints 2 and 3 generally expect positive intergroup relations, the former being most emphatic about focusing on commonalities and cultivating friendship. Viewpoint 3 is less concerned with notions of friendship but emphasises the restorative approach as a way of maintaining harmonious relations, particularly where harm has been caused. Viewpoint 3 is also most overt in expressing support for policing, while viewpoint 2 attributes limited value to notions of holding politicians and institutions to account. In short, the harmonising viewpoints seek to generate intergroup harmony among young people from different backgrounds as well as embed propensities towards harmonious relations between young people, the youth sector, wider social institutions, and the state.

Viewpoints 1 and 4 are more inclined to be at ease with conflictual social relations and resist reconciling strategies founded on notions of neutrality or common ground. In contrast, these viewpoints invite critical and competing perspectives to be surfaced and explored. Viewpoint 1 focuses on generating increasingly open, honest, and critical dialogue. Viewpoint 4 seeks to harness conflict to generate collective will for emancipatory action.

Another way of expressing the distinction between these politicising and harmonising viewpoints is to present the politicising orientations of viewpoints 1 and 4 as concerned with cultivating young people's political consciousness. In contrast, the harmonising nature of viewpoints 2 and 3 concentrates on generating a civic consciousness. Political consciousness-raising involves advocating a sceptical disposition where agents employ critical reflection to 'become aware of contradictions and inconsistencies' (Cooper, 2012: 107). This political consciousness prompts youth workers and young people to think about tackling structural segregation, inequality, and social injustice. Civic consciousness, on the other hand, suggests a more conformist disposition. Practitioners and young people disposed to harmonising tend to think about making positive contributions to society without fundamentally challenging the assumptions on which the social order is built. While the politicising perspectives are inclined to question the legitimacy of power relations and differentials inherent within the social system, the harmonising perspectives are more likely to take these for granted. This analysis adds to existing studies and literature that identify distinctive trajectories of youth work as geared towards regulatory social control or more radical notions of social change (Hurley and Treacy, 1993; Cooper, 2018).

Distinctive orientations towards harmonising versus politicising approaches to peacebuilding are not incidental or value neutral. They are, rather, indicative of how youth sector peacebuilding communities of practice exist and evolve, connected to the historical, cultural, economic, political, and symbolic power of the state. Drawing upon Bourdieu's concepts of state meta-capital and symbolic power, the following sections critique how mainstream peacebuilding policy incentivises harmonising approaches to practice at the expense of more politicising orientations.

The influence of meta-capital and symbolic power

The four viewpoints within the Hamardle model of youth sector peacebuilding are not equally regarded or embedded across the field of youth sector peacebuilding. Bourdieu's commentary on capital and symbolic power provides an insight into how some practice ideations are elevated while others remain more peripheral. As discussed in Chapter 3, Bourdieu identifies four primary archetypes of capital (and the term capital can be substituted with the term power) – economic, cultural, social, and symbolic. Once stocks of one type of capital are accumulated, these can be converted into other types of capital and a fluid metamorphosis is enacted.

Bourdieu describes the state as a purveyor of 'meta-capital' endowed with the power to convert capitals at will and set an index of values on which specific types of capital are most valued within and across fields of practice. This monopoly of capital and accompanying symbolic power positions the state as a hugely significant player in the world of youth sector peacebuilding. Economic capital, in the form of funding for organisations and programmes, interacts with cultural and social capitals that serve to generate and reproduce dominant practices and philosophies or regimes of competence within the field. The skills, knowledge, expertise, and social networks that practitioners develop through their experience can be understood as specific types of cultural and social capital. Economic capital can be used to pay for practitioner training and resources, increasing their knowledge and further enhancing their cultural capital. Symbolic capital refers to levels of recognition and significance that is accompanied by increasing levels of economic, cultural, and social capital. The merits of this symbolic capital are bestowed on organisations and practitioners through economic or symbolic endorsement – with the funding of specific projects being perceived as a stamp of approval. This stamp of approval is an operation of state power.

The meta-capital of the state is bestowed on policy makers, funders, and auditors of peacebuilding programmes whose criteria, prescriptions, contractual stipulations, target monitoring, and financial regulations create a system in which resources and practice trajectories reinforce and reproduce statutory priorities and state interests. This ultimately impacts the direction of youth sector peacebuilding, with the most dominant ideas attracting funding and, in return, practice strengthening the dominant ideas. Through our research and policy analysis in the context of Northern Ireland, *mutual understanding* as a harmonising dialogue approach to peacebuilding has consistently been most credited in policy and embedded in practice.

Incentivising compliance

Mutual understanding is a hegemonic perspective. As such, this approach to peacebuilding garners a broad consensus and becomes a reference point in which all other ideas and actions are situated. It was the largest viewpoint in our study with more than twice as many practitioners aligned to it compared with the other three. This perspective appears to dominate the field and represents the interests of those with symbolic, economic, and political power. The concentration of capitals held by state-sanctioned funders confers a symbolic power, that is, power 'based on the possession of symbolic capital' (Bourdieu, 1989: 23) to authorise an 'official discourse' or 'legitimate point of view' (Bourdieu, 1989: 22). This official point of view is bound to how such funders define what counts as peacebuilding. They do this by setting objectives, measurable outcomes, targeting stipulations, and auditing procedures for funded projects.

Bourdieu's notion of doxa points to how an official discourse and taken-for-granted ideas become accepted norms. Similar to 'orthodoxy', Bourdieu uses doxa to refer to a 'set of shared opinions and unquestioned beliefs' that permeate a field of practice (Wacquant, 2008: 270). There are parallels between Bourdieu's concept of doxa and Gramsci's (1971) conceptualisation of hegemony. For Gramsci, hegemony explains conformity and social control achieved by consent rather than coercion. It is 'an order in which a common social-moral language is spoken, in which one concept of reality is dominant, informing with its spirit all modes of thought and behaviour' (Femia, 1981: 24).

Extrapolating from Gramsci's theorisation of hegemony, the significant number of practitioners embodying viewpoint 2 can be analysed as consent towards a dominant perspective that those in power have established. It is hegemonic in the sense that 'one discourse is elevated above others, not because it is superior but because the most powerful group put it there' (Laclau and Mouffe, 2014: xii). The hegemonic perspective of viewpoint 2 is symbolically violent to the extent that those who have internalised it are unaware of how it reproduces practices that serve a global neoliberal discourse and suppresses inclinations towards a more radical democratic and emancipatory politics (Laclau and Mouffe, 2014). The field of youth sector peacebuilding has witnessed the inculcation of a hegemonic perspective that values harmonisation and depoliticisation over agitation and politicisation.

Also noteworthy is that viewpoint 2, mutual understanding, disproportionately accounted for practitioners with less than six years of post-qualifying experience. Only four of the 15 practitioners aligned with this perspective had more than 11 years' experience. The harmonising propensity of this perspective appears to orient practitioners towards accommodating and assimilating the technocratic logic of targeted and outcomes-based practice directed by funders and further reinforced by the precariousness of the youth sector (de St Croix, 2016; Buchroth and Connolly, 2019). Widespread compliance with the policy-funding framework arises in a context of fixed-term contracts where practitioners are concerned with establishing their value by excelling in the form of practice most celebrated within the field. Funders and policy makers monopolise positions of influence within the field and invest their economic and symbolic capital in authorising what counts as excellence in practice. Enhancing position within the field requires playing by the rules of the game as set by those with the economic and symbolic capital, and thus symbolic power, to guide the dominant discourse of youth sector peacebuilding. Femia's commentary on hegemony is insightful here where he writes:

> An individual consents, then, because he perceives no realistic alternative; i.e. no other alternative which does not run the risk of diminishing or eliminating his satisfactions … in a condition of scarcity and interdependence, it is simply imprudent not to behave in certain socially accepted ways; conformity arises out of the existential conditions that make social units interdependent. (Femia, 1981: 40)

Individual practitioners, youth work organisations, funders, and policy makers are interdependent. It is not, however, an interdependence of equity. In a field where permanent youth work posts are rare, competition is generated for available jobs, thus disincentivising counter-discourses or resistance strategies to subvert the status quo. Neoliberal logic, of course, considers this competition healthy and desirable in a meritocratic society. To increase standing and security within the sector, practitioners and the organisations they work for are incentivised to adapt to funders' stipulations on the prescribed content of programmes and the prescribed target group. Those with power prescribe, and those with less power follow such decrees.

It is furthermore instructive that no practitioners identifying most strongly as Nationalist were aligned to the mutual understanding viewpoint. The conciliatory and harmonising emphasis that seeks to move beyond the intractable and divisive issues of the past and present is perhaps unappealing to those whose experience is that of enduring British colonial control. However, it would be erroneous to deduce essentialist claims that those who define themselves as strongly Nationalist are predisposed to dismiss the mutual understanding viewpoint. A more robust claim that transcends signifiers of national identity is that those inclined to support agitation and contestation as part of the peacebuilding process are unlikely to align with the mutual understanding perspective.

State appropriation of restorative practices

Viewpoint 3, social cohesion and restoration, while not as dominant a perspective as that of mutual understanding, can be seen to similarly assimilate state priorities. It is the centrality of the restorative approach within the harmonising propensity of this viewpoint that evidences overt linkages with the neoliberal state. Woolford and Ratner (2003: 188) suggest that the restorative approach contains the potential to radically transform how justice is understood in society and instigate a 'counter-hegemonic discourse' to the long-standing logic of criminal justice. However, within a neoliberal political economy, there is a tendency for the restorative approach to be co-opted and 'colonized' by the state (Woolford and Ratner, 2003: 189). This colonising enables the state to 'socialize citizens to the non-conflictual standards … of hegemonic consent to an overarching neoliberalism' (Woolford and Ratner, 2003: 189). As such, the radical propensities of restorative approaches are tamed and redirected to legitimise the socio-political status quo. The result is a practice less concerned with tackling structural injustice and more focused on methods of self-responsibilising.

Predisposed to embed law, order, and social stability, viewpoint 3 advocates positive and proactive relationships between young people and police. Restorative justice is perceived from this perspective as a fundamental framework within the peacebuilding process. Practitioners encourage and facilitate the participation of young people in restorative approaches, particularly when they have been perpetrators of harm. This application of participation may be critiqued as 'a participatory policy rooted in maintaining social control over the disenfranchised, who are historically and persistently viewed as either problematic or in need' (Podd, 2010). Restorative youth justice has further been critiqued as an extension of state power and a sophisticated form of social control, replacing more overt but antiquated coercive measures (Lohmeyer, 2017a).

In the north of Ireland, Community Restorative Justice Ireland emerged in 1998 to provide 'a radical alternative to capitalist justice' (Auld et al, 1997: 12) within a context where 'the legitimacy of the police and courts [was], at least, questioned' (Auld et al, 1997: 35) in many Nationalist communities. Aspirations are evident towards the radical potential of restorative justice. In addressing issues of paramilitary control, these community-based organisations negotiated with paramilitary groups. In their formative years, such organisations may have circumvented what Lohmeyer (2017a) critiques as an extension of state control. However, it is conceivable that in another way, they implemented social control by adopting a policing role of communities by less violent means than had been implemented by paramilitary groups. In a more contemporary context, the two major restorative justice agencies in Northern Ireland (Community Restorative Justice Ireland and NI Alternatives) are characterised by arm's-length state control. Not officially connected to the formal policing and justice system, these organisations have been 'accredited' under the Justice and Security Northern Ireland Act, 2007 (DoJ, ca. 2024). Furthermore, both agencies emphasise their collaborative working relationship with the state police service (CRJI, 2020; Alternatives, ca. 2024). This move to accredit community-based restorative justice is an overt example of the meta-capital of the state being used to align the cultural and symbolic capital of these agencies with the expectations and priorities of governmental institutions.

The harmonising orientations of viewpoints 2 and 3, mutual understanding and social cohesion & restoration, are most imprinted with neoliberal and state-compliant propensities. Subsequently, these viewpoints carry greater credit in terms of symbolic capital as authorised by the symbolic power and meta-capital held by state-sanctioned funding bodies. This analysis claims that the drivers of peacebuilding in the youth sector, imbued with state meta-capital, incentivise the most neoliberally aligned ideations. Practitioners internalise common-sense ideas of the field, reflecting back to the architects of policy and funding a consensus with state priorities. Consensus is thus generated for a pragmatism associated with neoliberal ambitions to fix what is broken, focus on the individual, depoliticise social and political issues, and target specific demographics deemed 'at risk' with the aim of socialising them into a prevailing social order.

The influence of regimes of competence on youth sector peacebuilding

It would be erroneous to conclude that state meta-capital and the symbolic power of funders and policy makers have a unilateral and explicitly oppressive grip on youth sector peacebuilding. This is an oversimplification of the forces at play. To a large extent practitioners are complicit in reproducing the conditions that give rise to particular forms and discourses of practice. The field is structured not only from the outside in but also from the inside out. Lave and Wenger's (1991) notion of *regimes of competence* illuminates this reality.

A community of practice such as youth sector peacebuilding is always in the process of negotiating meaning and establishing credibility both to insiders and outsiders. Through this process, certain regimes of competence come to the fore, some of which are prescribed but many of which are unwritten assumptions about how to operate in a way that fosters legitimacy. Whereas Bourdieu's notion of a field is broad and includes many actors across different sub-disciplines, communities of practice can be viewed as more discrete groups. Rather than youth sector peacebuilding policy makers and practitioners being viewed as actors within the same field, at the level of communities of practice, we can better distinguish between a practitioner community of practice that interacts with a policy community of practice. Policy makers generate a plethora of boundary objects designed to facilitate communication and implementation of policy in the domain of practice. These inevitably impact the nature of practice. However, practitioners rarely simply implement policy exactly how it was intended. Rather, a process of interpretation, re-negotiation, and testing limits occurs. Practitioners mould policy to their philosophies and convictions of how practice should be pursued. The processes involved in belonging to a specific community of practice mediate professional behaviours and choices.

Chapter 3 identified how members of a community of practice gain professional legitimacy by using a shared repertoire of skills, ideas, approaches, and practices. The development and use of these competencies becomes a marker of mastery. If practitioner communities of practice collectively and consistently resisted the harmonising propensities of state-sanctioned peace policies and funding programmes, this would eventually reshape the policy domain. However, in the absence of a sustained critique and analysis of trajectories of practice, dominant discourses become woven into the fabric of youth sector peacebuilding and practitioners internalise regimes of competence grounded in harmonising rather than politicising practices.

These regimes of competence value different skill sets and motivations, cultivating divergent types of capital. Broadly these can be characterised as harmonising compared to politicising symbolic capitals. At a more granular level, harmonising practices might include restorative processes and trust building with individuals and groups; conflict mediation work; partnerships with policing; single-identity work; supporting young people to access employment and training opportunities; promoting personal development and interpersonal skills; encouraging volunteering; responding to young people in crisis. Politicising practices are more likely to focus on supporting the development of critical and political consciousness; engaging young people in politics at local, regional, national, and international levels; connecting young people with campaigns for social and political change; harnessing conflict for social change; incorporating human rights discourses into practice; developing campaigning strategies; eliciting the attention of those in power to listen to young people.

It is helpful, following Bourdieu, to think of the power dynamics and regimes of competence that constitute fields and communities of practice as a game so immersive that players forget they are gaming (Grenfell, 2014). Practitioners go about their practice, pursuing their particular approach to peacebuilding which reflects their motivations and interests. From their point of view, their approach best serves the young people with whom they are working. Similarly, those representing funding bodies and developing policy are immersed in their particular fields and communities of practice where neoliberal and technocratic rationality is the common-sense approach. They are guided by notions of delivering results and setting targets that can be quantitatively measured to evidence value for money. As such our analysis is not one of good and bad actors or honest and deceitful players. Rather, the case we are making is that common-sense ideas and practices which are uncritically accepted and pursued conceal how, over time, a radical and politicised approach to youth sector peacebuilding is displaced without a deliberate or concerted effort.

Radical peacebuilding – within limits

Viewpoints 1 and 2, critical thinking and dialogue and political engagement and social justice, are predisposed towards what could be termed a radical and agitational approach to peacebuilding. The Freirean critical orientation of viewpoint 1 is indicative of experienced practitioners who had secured positions of influence in the sector by demonstrating a commitment to visionary principles of youth work as independent from state agendas for social control. An emancipatory approach to practice is evident, focusing on enabling young people to grasp institutional forms of discrimination, sectarianism, and oppression. This perspective resonates with the campaign group In Defence of Youth Work's assertion that youth work is based on a 'commitment to critical dialogue ... [and] a self-conscious democratic practice, tipping balances of power in young people's favour' (IDYW, 2014).

The core emphasis attributed to critical dialogue in viewpoint 1 was not accompanied by a similarly significant place for political activism. Viewpoint 4, in contrast, can be seen to diminish the importance of critical dialogue in favour of activism. It is noteworthy that despite viewpoint 4's more radical orientation, active resistance to government policy was not prioritised. This points to a radical politicising practice constrained within parameters.

The politicising perspectives can be viewed as a potential threat, more inclined to destabilise rather than reinforce state agendas and a neoliberal consensus. To maintain a stake in the field, practitioners and organisations must accrue enough capital (economic, social, cultural, and symbolic) to be recognised as credible actors. This credibility can be measured by the extent to which practitioners contribute to the aims and objectives set by policy makers and funders. It can be inferred that even the most radical of practitioners must comply to some extent with the game's rules. Accepting funding from the state or funders involves a trade-off. The freedom and legitimacy in challenging and opposing neoliberal policy is replaced by becoming complicit in that very system of rewards and sanctions. This is a feature and outcome of hegemony that curtails radical criticism by integrating open challenge in the form of making space for mild resistance and critique. Symbolic power is used to referee the limits of politicising perspectives, taming the more radical propensities. This approach acts as a subtle form of social control.

A critical approach

The critical approach to youth sector peacebuilding requires the practitioner to consider not only their positionality within the four viewpoints on the Hamardle model but also an analysis of power. This is particularly pertinent in understanding and unravelling the effects of state-centric meta-capital on the field and on dominant directions for practice. The notion of reflexivity is a crucial aspect of agency where actors can work towards challenging, resisting, and transforming the regimes of competence and rules of the game that constitute the field.

'Returning to people the meaning of their actions' and 'learning to know oneself, to situate oneself, to reflect upon one's position' is the emphasis of Bourdieusian reflexivity imbued with emancipatory potential (De Saint Martin, 2003: 331, cited in Susen, 2016: 22). Through this reflexive approach, agents can consider how more critical and politically active approaches to peacebuilding work can be fostered with a focus on swinging the pendulum back the other way from the long-standing gravitation towards harmonising approaches that uncritically align with state priorities. This rebalancing would involve practitioners, policy makers, funders, academics, and young people naming and noticing their positionality and ultimately redressing the dearth of support for youth sector peacebuilding as a politicising practice by attributing more recognition and value to such approaches.

Through a collective appraisal of power relations and working through the viewpoints that make up the Hamardle model, youth sector peacebuilding communities of practice can pursue new strategies to consider unexplored possibilities in how peacebuilding work with young people is done. In this way, as Costa et al (2019: 21) explain, reflexivity 'extends beyond concepts of self-reference and self-awareness to deal with the systematic exploration of the "unthought categories of thought which delimit the thinkable and predetermine the thought"' (Bourdieu and Wacquant, 1992: 40). The following paragraphs apply a critical reflexive lens to each of the four viewpoints to identify and transcend the limits imposed within each approach.

Within viewpoint 2, mutual understanding, a reflexive approach might inspire alternative manifestations of personal development. Responses to individual needs could coalesce in the collective power of groups to demand more of institutions. The meritocracy consensus could be critiqued, exposing flaws in assumptions that individuals are responsible for personal success despite the impacts of poverty and social exclusion. Politics might also be considered more holistically within viewpoint 2, recognising the ubiquity of political thinking and a commitment to exploring how the political realm is personal and the personal is political.

A reflexive engagement with viewpoint 3, social cohesion and restoration, might begin by challenging the presumption that restorative approaches equate to instilling compliance with law and order aligned with the status quo. An alternative manifestation of a restorative concept may include working with young people to harness and redirect anger, disillusionment, frustration, and confrontation into non-violent means of combating oppressive systems of power and domination that exploit these young people.

Regarding the politicising perspectives, a reflexive engagement with viewpoint 1, critical thinking and dialogue, may examine the apparent disconnect between critical thinking and critical action. Viewpoint 1 could adopt a more action-oriented lens where dialogical encounters are more intentionally focused on becoming a catalyst to act for social change. Conversely, viewpoint 4, political engagement and social justice, could bring more focus on dialogical approaches as complementary to action. Viewpoint 4 is primarily concerned with the pursuit of social justice through a collective action approach to peacebuilding. In contrast with viewpoint 1, it is less likely to focus on discussing the past and the impacts of sectarianism on young people today. There is a challenge for this viewpoint to not simply seek to transcend but to engage with and tackle the polarisation of constitutional politics in Northern Ireland. While viewpoint 4 is the most radical in terms of facilitating political engagement and activism, it is reluctant to prioritise direct action and resistance. There is scope to further consider the role that civil resistance might play in youth sector peacebuilding, thus unlocking new categories of thought. This focus could advance the creative, agitational, and transformative dimensions of practice.

Challenging orthodoxy

A more sustained and collective reflexivity is required to advance youth sector peacebuilding. This calls for constructive engagement, challenge, and co-creation between practitioners, young people, and those endowed with the meta-capital of the state, namely funders and policy makers. Transforming the common-sense orthodoxy or, in its more concealed form of unquestioned shared beliefs, doxa, is a difficult task. It gets to the heart of struggles within and between fields and communities of practice. The particular challenge posited here is modifying the type of practice capital most valued in the domain of youth sector peacebuilding. It requires questioning the status quo and championing a practitioner and youth-led rather than funding-led paradigm. The goal is to induce a counter-hegemony so that politicised rather than harmonising orientations become more favourable. The struggle involved and persistence required to counter the dominant norms is encapsulated by Bourdieu where he writes: 'The dominated classes have an interest in pushing back the limits of doxa and exposing the arbitrariness of the taken for granted; the dominant classes have an interest in defending the integrity of doxa or, short of this, of establishing in its place the necessarily imperfect substitute, orthodoxy' (Bourdieu, 1977: 169).

In the context of youth sector peacebuilding, the struggle is better presented not as dominated and dominant classes but as grassroots practitioners and policy actors. This reflexive approach requires more than criticism directed towards funders as being detached and indifferent to the realities of practice. Equally, it goes beyond an introspective self-reflection on practice. It calls for holistic reflexivity of structures, systems, and the personal and professional. Fundamentally, this reflexive process necessitates self-examination of complicity in reproducing a dominant logic of practice. Uncovering such complicity reveals how individual and collective interests are served in playing by the rules of the powerholders. This is especially evident where those rules invite a measure of criticism, creating a veneer of radical challenge.

Pursuing this challenge is the task of the sector and requires wider research to elaborate further. Importantly, Bourdieu notes that the sociologist does not assume 'the role of the liberating hero' (Bourdieu, 1984, cited in Susen, 2016: 16). Instead, sociology should provide the conceptual and methodological tools to 'uncover and to challenge mechanisms of domination but also to allude to the possibility of creating social conditions allowing for processes of both individual and collective emancipation' (Susen, 2016: 22). The ideas presented in this book, including the methodological tool of Q methodology, the Hamardle model of youth sector peacebuilding, Bourdieu's arsenal of thinking tools, and Lave and Wenger's depiction of communities of practice, have been integrated to advance a critical analysis of approaches to peacebuilding with young people which takes account of the social, cultural, and political conditions which shape practice. The sector is encouraged to utilise these tools and build on the new knowledge derived from the research to pursue a more reflexive and emancipatory practice which stimulates 'the awakening of political consciousness' (Bourdieu, 1977: 169).

Conclusion

In contested spaces, educational initiatives with young people are prone to co-option by the state. In such cases, practitioners are positioned as facilitators of consensus-building and the cultivation of harmonious citizenship. This approach to youth sector peacebuilding risks excluding agitational youth voices whose perspectives hold crucial insights in supporting the 'non-recurrence of past conflict and prevention of new or emerging sources of conflict' (Henao-Izquierdo, 2021: 11). Alternatively, holding firm to values of social change and grassroots participation, the youth sector can progress peacebuilding approaches that harness the diverse, competing, and ardent political motivations and aspirations of young people as the site of authentic critical dialogue and activism, thereby 'according them recognition and legitimacy as (political) agents of change' (Henao-Izquierdo, 2021: 12). This tension between harmonising versus politicising approaches to youth sector peacebuilding is illuminated through Bourdieu's critical analysis of state power, the unequal distributions of capital, and the common-sense ideas that reproduce state priorities and depoliticised practices. Restructuring the field to bring a greater sense of value to politicising approaches requires cultivating new regimes of competence based on the political engagement of both practitioners and youth. The next chapter makes the case that radicalising the youth sector towards peacebuilding necessitates involving young people in the co-creation of peacebuilding strategies and programmes where youth are active in the process of designing, implementing, and evaluating peacebuilding in partnership with funders and policy makers. As such, politicisation depends on creative participation methodologies where young people are positioned as architects rather than passive objects of peacebuilding.

10

Peace activism with and by young people

> For years young people have been sidelined ... it's been too easy for them to be ignored. (YW38)

Introduction

Politicising youth sector peacebuilding is an important philosophical, theoretical, and conceptual idea that has largely been absent from discussions on peacebuilding with young people. Ideas, however, are only part of what makes a practice. Participating in the interpretation and application of ideas, theories, concepts, and models is what brings a practice to life (Wenger, 1998). In this penultimate chapter, we propose that developing a peacebuilding approach that politicises young people must begin by practising youth participation. Politicisation, then, is not simply a goal to aim towards as part of a peacebuilding programme that young people are recruited into. Rather, the very process of debating and deciding what counts as peacebuilding, what peace looks like, what the aims and objectives are, how to monitor and evaluate, how to designate resources, and so on, is not isolated to policy makers, researchers, and administrators. Engaging young people in these processes becomes a central way of engendering democratic participation and dialogue, thus disrupting traditional top-down power dynamics and the predominance of state-centred priorities.

While institutional commitments towards co-creation and co-design have become in vogue across many democratic states, in reality, lots of young people experience limited involvement rather than legitimate political agency (Conner et al, 2016; Corney et al, 2020). Underpinned by the foregoing analysis and critique, brought together in the Hamardle model of youth sector peacebuilding, this chapter shifts gear to examine youth participation as a means of cultivating a politicising practice. Moving towards a more politicising orientation places young people as central agents within the process. As young people are so often exposed to or involved in violence within conflicts, their essential role in building peace may well be anticipated; however, it is rarely realised in a substantive way (Simpson, 2018; Lederach, 2020; Akinyetun et al, 2023). Having voice and holding power are central tenets of such participatory processes. For young people to be enabled in this way, democratic philosophy *and* practices need to co-exist and converge.

The role and position of practitioners, policy makers, influencers, and young people are central to growing a politicised peacebuilding ecosystem. This chapter explores stories and models of youth participation to crystallise what makes a radical and authentic form of youth activism in peacebuilding.

A story of voice and change

Youth work which advocates increasing and elevating youth voices is widespread, but having a voice without action and change is demoralising and frustrating for young people. In a recent participative peacebuilding initiative, young people across Northern Ireland and the border counties of Ireland saw tangible returns through their co-production role in devising the priorities for the most recent European Union funding for young people. Through their involvement in 'Young Voices' (McArdle et al, 2020), a participative democracy framework for young people to speak to powerholders, their recommendations to aggressively intervene in the youth mental health crisis resulted in the European Union increasing this funding stream from €20,000,000 to €25,000,000 from 2021 to 2027 (SEUPB, 2021).

Words, words, words

The language of user-empowerment is a myriad of smoke and mirrors. A recently developed lexicon has emerged from marketing and management to describe processes that engage and involve 'the user'. The 'user as subject' has a markedly different input and impact to the 'user as partner' (Whicher and Crick, 2019: 291). The prefix 'co-' has been overlaid on all aspects of a planning and implementation cycle to involve interested participants in the development and delivery of policy, services, and decisions. Co-creation, co-design, and co-production are terms often used interchangeably, but with subtle differences in their emphasis and a diverse range of participatory actions for each process. Vargas et al (2022) describe co-creation as 'value co-creation' where the involvement of stakeholders is seen to add psychological, economic, or social value depending on the focus under scrutiny. In 'value co-creation', stakeholder input is not merely a tokenistic measure but positively correlated to 'added value and impact' (Vargas et al, 2022: 2). Co-creation is a holistic process of stakeholder engagement, from identifying the problem, to creating a responsive solution, through to planning and deploying resources within a strategy. Co-design involves stakeholders in generating solutions and solving a problem, with involvement limited to this distinct phase and outside the scope of identification of the issue or implementation of solutions. Co-production is focused on the action-oriented phase, where stakeholders are engaged on issues of delivery, including the allocation of resources and the optimum approach to implementing an already agreed strategy. All three processes engage differently with stakeholders and can inject important insights at crucial moments that can shape and redirect interventions.

A world of co-creation

To develop and use a co-creation system that is context-specific requires an analytical, responsive tool. Eckhardt et al (2021) present such a heuristic model, evolved from the SISCODE project and drawing on the knowledge gleaned from 135 co-creation cases from across Europe. This model allows for the disaggregation of interrelated factors and components impacting and involved in the 'Eco-system of co-creation' (Eckhardt et al, 2021: 1). Although Eckhardt et al (2021: 3) describe co-creation as a process that pursues 'a nonlinear logic, which embodies a multi-dynamic and multi-contextual process', they bring form and shape to explain this complex process within an onion model. Four 'context' layers are considered, and effort is made to understand the macro-, meso- and micro-domains. The *context of norms* is an exploration of accepted societal standards, either explicit in legislative or regulatory codes or implicit in general consensus on acceptable behaviours. The *context of structures* can have a limiting or enabling effect on co-creation due to the rigidity of existing institutions and institutional policies. These structures may have political, economic, or technological constraints that bear down on the autonomy of functions, actors, and roles. The *context of actors and roles* is an analysis of stakeholders and beneficiaries, considering their ideologies, motivations, capacities, and interrelatedness. The *context of functions* explores the operational processes related to co-creation, with reflection on methodologies, stages of user involvement, and accountability processes.

Using Eckhardt's analytical tool reveals how easily and insidiously co-creation can be constrained. The specific stage of policy and service development open to co-creation has fundamental implications for the radical nature of the change opportunity on offer. The power, roles, and dynamics of the full range of animateurs, actors, and change agents inform the directions and scope of social action. The boundaries of participatory action can be framed and unnecessarily inhibited by these social actors, who do not fully consider or confront their own orientations and positionality.

This chapter focuses on how to broaden the boundaries of participatory action by and with young people. In Chapter 8, the Hamardle model ostensibly promotes a critical analysis of the viewpoints of youth sector peace practitioners. However, through this exploration, the practitioner also subconsciously questions the social norms for peacebuilding in Northern Ireland and the emergent peacebuilding policies and funding. The insights generated provide an understanding of the enabling and challenging forces in the co-creation environment. Once these ideological positions are understood, the practitioner turns to identifying methodologies and approaches to maximise youth engagement in peacebuilding.

What is youth participation?

While a raft of recent literature on co-design proliferates (Whicher and Crick, 2019; Eckhardt et al, 2021; Vargas et al, 2022; Dunlop et al, 2023), the language of this speaks more to policy makers and marketing executives than to community youth work practitioners. While there is value in speaking a common language between practitioners and policy makers, of greater value is the recognition that the principles of youth involvement in decision-making are deeply embedded in the fabric of community youth work with an authoritative canon on 'youth participation'. It is this body of work which informs youth sector peacebuilding locally and holds such promise on a global scale.

In community youth work, the term for young people involved in decision-making is 'youth participation'. As this is such a well-understood, common-sense term, its discipline-specific nature is often lost and misinterpreted. The distinction here between the discipline-specific 'participation' and the 'common-sense' definition is that the latter is about young people TAKING PART while the former is about young people TAKING POWER. For youth workers, youth participation is understood as a process for the involvement of young people in decisions that may impact their lives. This can range from influencing what sweets are sold in the youth club tuck shop to having a voice about government education policy and fiscal spending. A series of youth participation models, approaches, and perspectives have found prominence across the discipline of Community Youth Work. While debates on the efficacy of one model over another can be instructive (similar to the debates earlier on the language of creation), these cerebral or theoretical deliberations can undermine the central driving ambition of young people having voice and agency over decisions that impact them directly or indirectly.

The international legislative framework for youth participation is well-versed and enshrined within the United Nations Convention on the Rights of the Child (UN, 1989). While the entirety of the legislation is not enacted in UK law, the articles are regularly used to guide domestic law, practice, and court proceedings. Article 3.1 proposes the 'best interest' principle, which is followed up with the assertion that this 'best interest' is best represented by the child as the central actor in their own decisions rather than as the subject. Article 12.1 states that: 'States Parties shall assure to the child who is capable of forming his or her own views the right to express those views

Figure 10.1: Drivers of effective youth participation

freely in all matters affecting the child, the views of the child being given due weight in accordance with the age and maturity of the child' (UN, 1989: 5).

The existence of a universal right can give rise to as much tokenism and political correctness as it can the full realisation of said right. For youth participation to be most effective, there are three equally important drivers: the motivations for youth participation, the processes of youth participation, and the efficacy of the outcomes, as illustrated in Figure 10.1. There is a clear, strong connection between the motivations and the outcomes of youth participation, often driven by the passion and belief of a practitioner. Vision holds all of the participants on course towards the outcomes and requires an energised, clear-thinking practitioner. The methodologies are the thread between motivation and outcomes, which can open up effective youth participation or shut it down.

Corney et al (2020), in discussing the rationale for youth participation within youth work, identify two starkly contrasting motivators. Where a strongly weighted adult-centric attitude prevails, this presupposes that young people are ill-equipped to act wisely on their own behalf (Holdsworth, cited in Corney et al, 2020). In response to this, therefore, youth participation processes could be considered as affirmative action or as an antidote to this stereotype, thus equalising the balance of power between young and older. The motivation is a political one that proposes a challenge to the power and status of adulthood and presents a methodology for young people to take their place and exercise their decision-making skills beside adults.

Another motivator is effectiveness. The development and delivery of services pivots on the concept of delivery agents being effective in responding to needs and being efficient in terms of delivery. The participation of young people in service and policy creation brings a different perspective to proceedings, which can lead to more effective futureproofing of services and innovative ways to meet need (Patton et al, 2016). This driver has gained traction with state parties and civil servants who have efficiency in mind but can miss a vital component of youth participation with such a unilateral motivator. Not only are the *ideas* of young people important in this context, but the *process* allows policy makers to gain unique insights into the lives and perspectives of young people. The insights which can be gained from listening can lead to an understanding of the 'hidden things' which young people consider when accessing services and programmes. These may be tacitly understood by young people but not necessarily explicitly expressed. The listener listens for the tacit.

In terms of outcomes, the policy and service-development results of youth participation can be stimulating for some young people, but the personal and social outcomes may have more universal appeal. Research into the health benefits of youth participation (Kirby and Bryson, 2002; Wilson, 2023) indicates that people live longer and have healthier lives if they are active participants in their communities and in decisions that impact upon their lives. Effective youth participation further correlates to stronger communities, with young people and adults collaborating and problem-solving together on local issues and future planning.

The real prize of youth participation is the political engagement of young people. The rewards of youth political participation have the potential to not only influence societal challenges but also to address chronic global challenges. Such youth political engagement is stimulated not to cascade the range of society's problems onto young people's shoulders but to engage a new constituent (and perspective) alongside adults in intransigent issues that have evaded resolution by the current adult population. A raft of terminology exists to describe the range of political participation, such as social activism, political education, social justice, and political development. Within each of these concepts is the juxtaposing of conscientisation and action, with differences in the proportion of one process to the other. The individual engages cerebrally and empathically to consider issues of justice and injustice. But the raising of consciousness of itself does not spur action. In fact, it can lead to a learned helplessness, whereby acceptance and apathy is the prevailing mood. The work of youth participation lies in a cognitive awakening to be accompanied by the practice of action skills and an understanding of what Snyder (2003) terms *waypower* – the ability to find pathways towards your goals. This combination of thought and action can access power and influence.

Models of youth participation

Models of youth participation proliferate (Karsten, 2012; McCready and Dilworth, 2014), with certain models that resonate more within a specific discipline than in others. Research indicates models of different shapes, with ladders, Venn diagrams, yin-yang, wheels, triangles, or cubes. Similar elements recur, but the saturation of material on the involvement of children, young people, and adults is noteworthy in itself. The voluminous material suggests that outside Article 12 of the UN Convention on the Rights of the Child, no one seminal work has been 'adopted' or enacted universally. This is troublesome, as cognitive energy can be wasted in comparing, contrasting, and evaluating various models of youth participation rather than focusing on enacting common principles and methodologies. Many of the models juxtapose the power-full and the power-less (McCready and Dilworth, 2014), a language and critique that can alienate those who inhabit positions and systems of the greatest power. Models of youth participation are fundamentally underpinned by structural analysis of power, oppression, and barriers to participation, which will appeal to some social actors more than others. Furthermore, it may well be that the body of work addresses too many different audiences, with young people, practitioners, and policy makers all drawn to different ideas and elements that fit within their own paradigms. The notion of positionality is worthy of some introspection, and the concept of practitioner reflexivity is relevant to identify our vantage point on youth participation. The Community Youth Work lens is grounded in a strengths-based approach, whereby young people are viewed as and with assets rather than a set of problems to be solved. The three models selected here nestle within this viewpoint.

The Lundy model for youth participation, shown in Figure 10.2, has been tested in practice and policy over at least 15 years (Lundy, 2007). Framed within Article 12 of the UN Convention on the Rights of the Child, Lundy proposes that the full implementation of states' responsibilities regarding how the views of the child are gathered and actioned requires four elements – namely, Space, Voice, Influence, and Audience.

Lundy presents a chronology of activity – with *Space* and *Voice* being developed first, for the child to understand their right to voice and then explore and articulate the world from their perspective. *Audience* and *Influence* come next, preparing the landscape for those who are expected to listen to give due weight to what has been said and to be taken on board in directing

Figure 10.2: Lundy's (2007) model of participation

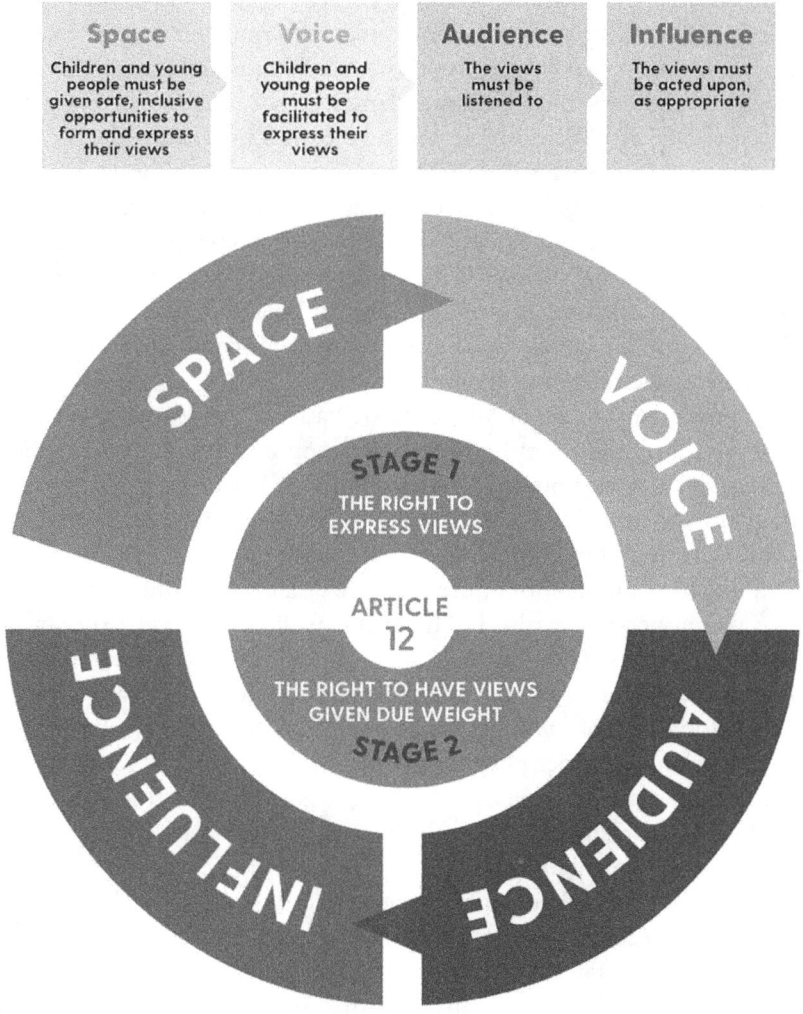

Source: Department of Children, Equality, Disability, Integration & Youth (2021: 8)

any subsequent action. Lundy refers to the 'right to audience' as an underlying principle to place the weight of statutory duty on having mechanisms for speakers to talk to listeners. This element emphasises the need for participation structures that are recognised and used by adults and decision-makers to ensure that children and young people are not speaking into a void. Influence underlines the need for children and young people to have real power to enact their voice. Lundy refers to the nuances of influence and the various manipulations which adults can use to undermine the voice of young people while simultaneously presenting the façade of youth participation. Legislation offers some protections for young people but is slow in combating tokenism. The promotion of feedback loops to young people who have expressed their views is an effective way to build greater accountability into this youth participation system. Like the Hawthorne effect in research, which highlights that simply being observed creates a change in behaviour, where adults are expected to report back on how youth voice has influenced decisions and policy, the very act of being answerable encourages greater effort and integrity. The Lundy model has gained traction with national and international policy makers and practitioners (see Lundy, 2021: 3). This momentum may have been generated as the model has been widely piloted and evaluated by practitioners across the child and youth sector in Northern Ireland. The simplicity of the message has public appeal, while the complex processes that underlie the model attracts the reflective practitioner.

In an Australian study of youth participation, Wierenga et al's (2003) Venn diagram model identified three philosophical themes or qualities as co-requisites for efficacious youth participation. They propose that for youth participation to have integrity and effectiveness, it must have substantial meaning, control, and connectedness for young people.

First, *meaning*. This is about purpose. The task or focus must have salience for the young people involved. There may well be a connection between the young person's story and the task at hand, adding greater meaning. Identifying the connection between the personal and political adds to the intrinsic motivation of a young person and builds unwavering commitment. *Meaning* can link to wider purpose outside the self, which is reminiscent of Seligman's differentiation between living 'the good life' (cultivating signature strengths and characteristics) and the meaningful life (emphasising a belief in something greater than oneself).

Next, *control*. This relates to both the outcomes and the methodologies. Wierenga et al (2003) propose that the process is most effective if young people can see the tangible results of their efforts. Feedback mechanisms and regular debriefing can enhance control. In terms of methodologies, a sense of control emerges from 'doing things that acknowledge, draw upon and extend their strengths; and being/ becoming resourced/ equipped to do the task properly' (Wierenga et al, 2003: 42). Control refers to an inclusive modus operandi which maximises reach, voice, and impact. The role of the animateur in this process will be explored later in this chapter.

Then, *connectedness*. The connection here is to peers first, and then connection to a wider community. In Wierenga et al's (2003: 43) study, one young person, Philip, shows how this connection can lead to a sense of appreciation and value by wider society: 'It is about recognition, existing, having a place and being acknowledged.' These notions of connectedness echo the concept of youth work as a place to 'foster fellowship and associational life' (Jeffs and Smith, 2005: 4). Through connectedness, we not only build the skills of navigating social relationships and communication but also practice our social role within a network, trialling the role and contribution we make in the 'purposeful world'.

For Wierenga et al, the presence of two elements without the third (across all combinations) is insufficient for meaningful and motivated youth participation. Where the model is partially implemented, the propensity for manipulation or tokenism of young people is heightened.

Wierenga et al's model is youth-centric, driven by youth perspectives and insights. It synthesises the lessons extracted from young people involved across a range of participatory formats and structures. This leads to a set of practical adjustments and considerations that can be made to format and structure to 'tip the balance in favour of young people' (Davies, 2021: 8). While the theme of '*meaning*' alludes to the engagement with the policy and political agenda, the explicit role, positioning, and mechanisms of engaging with adult decision-makers is given less prominence in this model. The emphasis is on the young people's motivation and engagement.

In contrast, Andersson (2017) is critical of the developmental psychology ideology which underpins many of the prominent participation models. This school of thought presupposes young people as objects in need of skills development before engaging in political processes, undermining their status as full democratic citizens and disregarding their existing political activity (Biesta, 2011, cited in Andersson, 2017). The status is of insufficiently formed adults, driven by implicit paternalism with the emphasis on the transmission of knowledge and values from adult to young person. Andersson proposes the 3P-M (the *p*edagogical *p*olitical *p*articipation *m*odel) to counter the 'adult-bias' inherent in other established models. The *contingent approach* recognises young people's political engagement as both 'being and becoming', whereby communication reveals the extent of their political participation. This approach considers the political as concomitant with *all* human organisation and society rather than as a separate discreet subset. Figure 10.3 presents Andersson's 3P-M typology.

Andersson's (2017) model is relational between group A (decision-makers) and group B (young people) but is set within a context of the 'pedagogical leadership style' that the A-power uses to establish or maintain different socialisation environments. This typology draws on the work of Pellerin (2005), who identifies and evaluates the characteristics of four parenting styles (authoritative, authoritarian, permissive, and indifferent) used for student teaching and learning within the classroom setting. This model embraces the interaction of environmental, pedagogical, and power factors.

The *informed* position places A as the primary decision-maker, merely informing young people of decisions made. The pedagogical style here is authoritarian, with A-power dominant and domineering. In the *voiced* position, B is expressed and listened to, but the impact of this voice is in

Figure 10.3: Andersson's (2017) typology of youth political participation

TYPOLOGY OF YOUTH POLITICAL PARTICIPATION				
Informed →	Voiced ⇌	Concerted ⇔	Supportive ⇠⇢	Independent ◯
A-power				B-power

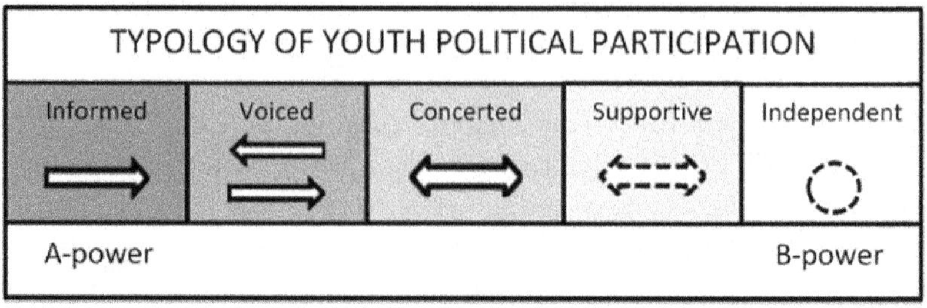

the gift of A. A holds the power and can decide what B can comment on. The pedagogical leadership style is somewhat authoritarian, with traces of the authoritative style that balances clear, firm boundaries with a respectful response to children's rights. An attempt is made by A to listen, but A is limited by its perceptions of B's capacity or 'correctness' in their decision-making.

The *concerted* position is where 'people work in concert with each other' (Woods, 2005: 33, cited in Andersson, 2017: 1356), with B and A communicating responsively with each other towards shared decision-making. This position is characterised by strong decision-making structures based on distributive leadership and co-learning, which have emerged from a purely authoritative pedagogical leadership style.

The *supportive* position rests power firmly with B, while A provides support when explicitly requested to do so. B sees the value of A as a resource to them and makes judgements on how best to deploy B for their own use. The permissive pedagogical style is most prominent here, with A highly responsive to the needs of B, with few terms and conditions on A. Ultimately, the *independent* position allows for B to hold and exercise full power, with A outside the locus of control. There is neither communication nor co-learning between A and B, and the pedagogical style is permissive or indifferent, with a laissez-faire environment offered by A.

The model is limited in its range and scope, with Andersson calling for further research to pilot his work in different contexts and the need for a deeper understanding of the pedagogical and socialisation theories that underpin the 3P-M. However, in mapping the power dynamic between A and B, and the pedagogical context created by the youth sector peacebuilder, it dovetails with the Hamardle model on the orientations of the youth sector peacebuilder.

The map won't get us there

Understanding the nature of youth sector peacebuilding is not enough. Clarity on the orientations of youth sector peacebuilding offers an awareness of the values and principles that drive practitioners and organisations, but in and of itself, this provides insight as opposed to engagement and action. Stanton's (2021) research into peacebuilding in Northern Ireland grapples with this space between theory and practice, where she articulates how peacebuilding acts and actions are created and how a unique 'practice knowledge' becomes the driver that inhabits this liminal space. Through interviewing peacebuilding practitioners, Stanton (2021: 10) pursued the question, 'whose knowledge was considered valuable and what types of knowledge counted within professionalised peacebuilding theory and practice?' This empirical research found a comfortable foundation in the 'lost' Aristotelian virtue of 'phronesis'. The concept of 'episteme' is considered as knowledge closest to 'scientific knowledge' which is context-independent and valued for its objectivity. 'Techne' is understood as skills, craftsmanship or artistry; with an emphasis on knowledge that is practised. Both are well regarded in modern learning and have derivatives in contemporary language. Phronesis has not. 'Phronesis is the intellectual activity most related to praxis' (Flyvbjerg, 2011: 30). This is a practical wisdom that is built and developed through reflective practice, which takes into account context and skill. Phronesis is 'a form of experience-based practical knowledge gained about how to make judgements in a "particular" situation that are deemed necessary in shifting, complex and unstable contexts' (Stanton, 2021: 11). Stanton proposes that in reviving and prizing phronesis, greater status would be afforded to local knowledge and lived experience. This concept appreciates how individual judgements have been instigated or devised to navigate the messy, dangerous contexts of peacebuilding. This gives prestige to stakeholders and users for the practice wisdom they have developed for 'everyday' peacebuilding practices.

Methodologies for a contemporary peacebuilding practice

The nature of political action is distinct from political acts: 'Political actions include voting, paying taxes, constitutional decision making and other established habitual actions and practices. Political acts, on the other hand, are human doings, ruptures or beginnings' (Andersson, 2017: 1351). Andersson supports Isin's (2008: 36) assertion that political acts involve a *rupture* to the accepted institutionalised politics and ways of being. Inherent in this notion is a generational challenge where young people disrupt the political norms that have been accepted and practised by their parents. The adage that 'young people are not interested in politics' is challenged when faced with the proliferation of alternative methods of youth political engagement (Pontes et al, 2018: 3). The political acts of young people have therefore evolved.

The #feesmustfall campaign from post-apartheid South Africa offers a glimpse into contemporary political acts by young people. This student movement, charted by Maringira et al (2022), ran between 2015 and 2017, with a wave of protests across many universities, and was ostensibly a dispute about student-fee increases proposed and implemented by the government. The protests, however, featured mainly young black working-class students in an educational system that restricted them due to their socio-economic profile. Students were being excluded due to their inability to pay, and these Black working-class students not only challenged *this* economic exclusion but asked the question of *why* their parents lacked the financial means to pay. Therefore, what began as a single economic and educational issue evolved into deeper questions on the long-lasting legacy of colonialism and institutional racism. A key indicator of this metamorphosis was an early alliance with general workers across South African universities whose services had been outsourced to private companies. Students and outsourced workers took part in joint demonstrations and connected the issue of fees inequality to broader economic inequality, derived from a feeble transitional justice arrangement that focused on injustices of the past without considering deep colonial issues of racial injustice (Maringira et al, 2022: 110). The #feesmustfall protests symbolised a call for inclusive transitional justice processes.

Maringira et al (2022: 103) caution against the view that tackling socio-economic rights is, by proxy, a peacebuilding act and activity. However, their analysis illustrates a different psyche and tempo by young people in contemporary political activism. The term 'waithood' (Honwana, cited in Maringira et al, 2022: 104) best describes this temporal limbo position of many young people in societies emerging from conflict. 'Waithood' is the period where the political, social, and economic systems are somewhat static but dysfunctional; whereby the weight and expectations for change lie with the young people, whether they chose this path or not. For Honwana, the state of 'waithood' is not characterised as a plateau which is hopeless and inactive. It ebbs and flows, with young people at moments engaged in flurries of activity and amplified voice and, at other times, despondent or disappointed at the scale of the challenges they face. The 'fallist' movement in South Africa exemplifies the creativity and verve of 'waithood' activism at its height.

For Northern Ireland, the waithood generation is of 'the peace babies' born post-ceasefire and in the wake of the 1998 agreement, who inherited a fragile peace alongside institutions that were established to stabilise society and dampen down a culture of violence. The institutions are not designed for building a flourishing socio-economic society, nor are they fit for this purpose without transformation. However, transformation in a post-conflict period has a different timbre than before. For war and conflict, the connection is between activism and violence, but in post-conflict societies, peace and activism are non-violent expressions of discontent. The nature of quiet resistance by young people has perhaps emerged as an antidote to the violence of the past, but this is somehow exhorted by older generations as passivity. Like waithood, it is the antithesis of violence but is often misinterpreted as being inactive or apathetic.

Mac Ionnrachtaigh (2021) sketches out the political acts of a contemporary world of young people locally. 'An Dream Dearg' is Gaelic for 'The Red Gathering', described as an open movement of Irish language activists whose contemporary activities began with 'An La Dearg' in 2017, a large-scale protest to support the introduction of the Irish Language Act in Northern Ireland. This movement has gathered around language but has also intersected with a growing body of Irish-medium youth work and centres across the North (McArdle and Neill, 2023). Political activism is well established in youth work generally but for Irish-medium youth work, its existence and strength are tangible and a defining feature of this sector and its modus operandi. Neill and McArdle, through their long partnership with the sector (2014–2023) connect the political engagements of the young people with their heightened sense of belonging and a strong cultural identity. 'The birth of the political' (Neill and McArdle, 2016: 15) refers to the moments where young people realised their youth club was under threat of closure and they felt a responsibility to act. With the support of 'An Dream Dearg' the young Gaels mobilised at protest marches at the Education Authority Headquarters in Belfast, the statutory funders of the youth services. In and of itself, this is unremarkable, but moments like these built acute consciousness of social justice and fine-tuned political skills. The young Irish activists, like Emma, describe how political awareness was grown through the approaches within their Irish-medium youth club, Glór na Móna:

> It's not that you come in here and politics is shoved down your throat. A lot of the people that work here are political, and they don't tell you that this is right, and this is wrong. They let you have a chance to, like, understand things that you wouldn't normally. (Neill and McArdle, 2016: 15)

What began as a protest to save Irish-medium youth services, morphed into further political support for the introduction of an Irish Language Act; and built further 'awareness of and empathy towards other social justice causes' (Neill and McArdle, 2022: 28) such as marriage equality. The political fire in the belly, in the Irish-medium youth work setting, was cultivated through indigenous youth work approaches. These amalgamate youth work skills of programming and informal learning activities with ancient notions of kinship, community, association, and notions of a cultural (rather than individualised) identity. For culture and community to have modern relevance for young people, it needs to be reimagined with contemporary connection for these young Irish Gaels. The processes of dialogue, making banners, writing letters, taking part and taking power, while building their Irish social world in the Irish-medium youth club, gave them political skills but more significantly a hallowed place to foster and pass on an Irish-speaking world to new generations.

Methodology matters

The influence of social media on revolution and mass mobilisation is evident from the Arab Spring's beginnings in 2010 to 'An Dream Dearg' movement. Beaumont, in the *Guardian* (25 February 2011, cited in Mac Ionnrachtaigh, 2021) suggests that '[t]he medium that carries the message shapes and defines, as well as the message itself'. The spontaneity of social platforms taps into the zeitgeist of young people. The messages are crafted and coordinated by digital natives for maximum influence but more so to 'motivate fence-sitters to join in' (Clarke and Kocak, 2020: 1026). The 'Twitter effect' or the 'Facebook revolution' suggests that these social media platforms were major contributing factors in mobilising people, but the medium without a salient message is unlikely to persuade – 'The skilful use of social media twinned with clear goals propelled the campaign to public prominence' (Mac Ionnrachtaigh, 2021: 395). However, the methodology that connects with the pace, tone, and goals of young people's lives is crucial to engage and agitate. The digital native uses shorthand to match a social media platform to a specific function: 'We use Facebook to schedule the protests, Twitter to coordinate and YouTube to tell the world. #egypt #jan25' (@Fawaz Rashed, Twitter post, 18 March 2011).

Similarly, youth participation methodologies are not randomly implemented but chosen for specific effects. Interactivity is a core feature to generate discussion and dialogue, particularly drawing out voices that are intimidated by the written word. Face-to-face work allows for greater subtlety and intimacy than online and electronic approaches. Young people are stimulated by the visceral sensations a practitioner can generate, and debriefing is used to make sense of these encounters.

The Hunger for Peace Games was developed by YouthAction Northern Ireland as an experiential event for young people (Boyd et al, 2021). Designed in opposition to the Hunger Games novels, the aim of this version is not a fight to the death; here, the objective is towards peace. 'Districts' accrue points, which culminates in an award ceremony. This day-long immersive event facilitates a series of group exercises involving tribal identity, conflict, traitors and infiltrators, and an unfair system of justice. The hour-long debrief allows for reflection on the personal and group actions taken within this controlled environment and their impact on self and others. Competition, cooperation, loyalty, and disloyalty are explored. Questions abound of how to move forward while acknowledging the hurts caused. This methodology was used with 341 young people in spring 2022, and the commentary generated through the debrief was collated into the 'Peace summit: a call to action' report launched in May 2023 (Hamber et al, 2023). This document identifies 12 peacebuilding actions for government and civil society and triggered the development of two new networks to drive these proposals forward. The 'Hunger for Peace Games' allowed young people to generate empathy and understanding for those within conflict and to gather their insights into future-facing actions.

For the capacity building of young people, a peer learning methodology may be most appropriate to stretch their skills and knowledge. The rationale for the 'Peace, Youth and Security' seminar series (a partnership between the Hume Foundation and Ulster University) aligns with UN Resolution 2250, recognising the underrated asset of young people in building sustainable peace. The seminar format begins with a private small-scale facilitated session between young local and global leaders, to share perspectives, actions, and skills. This format recognises the reticence of some young leaders to comfortably express themselves in the public adult-dominated space and presents an alternative.

To mobilise towards action requires methodologies that connect the personal and the political. Methods here integrate three approaches: connection, analysis, and action. To generate a discussion on the role of women in peacebuilding, the practitioner reveals an array of childhood toys, asking young people to choose the toy that they relate to most. This leads to an analysis of the messages implicit in the toys, the longevity of these ideas, and their impact on current and future actions. The arising 'change action' can be small or incremental – writing a 'postcard to Rosa' to be sent to your political representative or joining a lobby or march building solidarity and conviction.

Methodology and the Hamardle model

Within the Hamardle model, the different tone and intention within each quadrant is mirrored in the matching methodologies (Figure 10.4).

For viewpoint 1, critical thinking and dialogue, 'Thinking and challenge methodologies' allow for questioning of accepted norms and seeking wider perspectives. Sessions on fake news and fake photographs from Project Real (ca. 2024) give young people an acute awareness of how information can be manipulated and tools to challenge these. Within viewpoint 2, mutual understanding, the use of 'Connecting and empathy-building methodologies' promotes contact and sharing. Much cross-community work from Northern Ireland used these methodologies – particularly useful as a pragmatic bridge-builder among communities that are systemically, physically, and psychologically segregated. For viewpoint 3, social cohesion

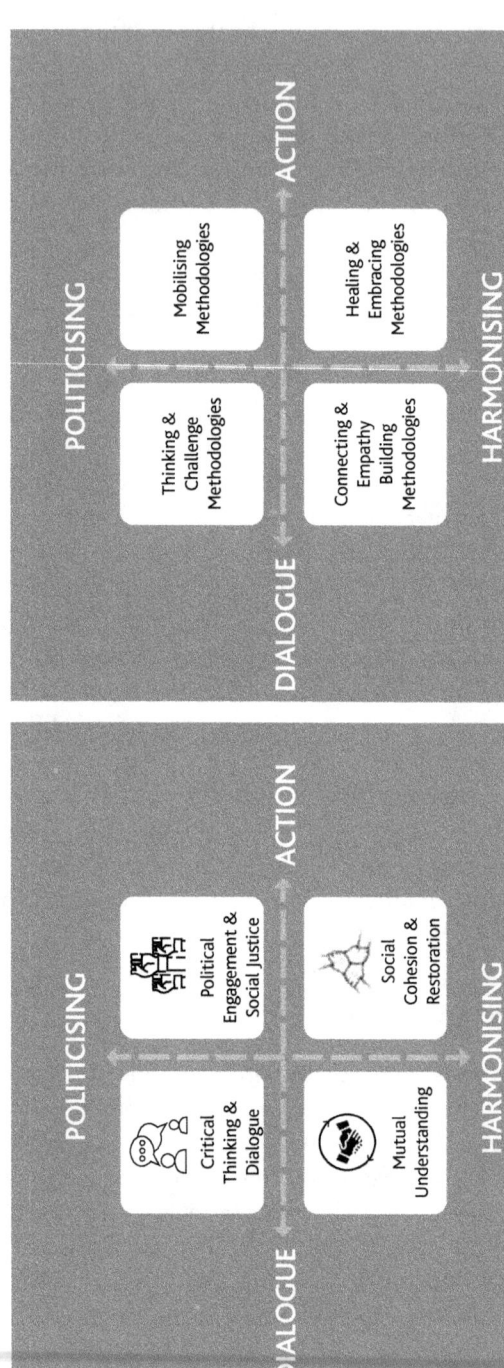

Figure 10.4: Methodologies for the Hamardle model

and restoration, 'Healing and embracing methodologies' simultaneously encourage letting go of the past and embracing new communities and new ways of life. These methodologies are therapeutic or invigorating, such as the Guardians of the Flame (2023) events on forgiveness and healing. The fourth viewpoint, political engagement and social justice, aligns with 'Mobilising methodologies' whereby action is central and joining with collectives is a prominent feature. An example of this methodology in action can be seen in the work of Jacinta Hamley in creating and running an annual climate festival for young people called 'Climate Craic' or through environmental peacebuilding, championed by Rosalind Skillen.

Conclusion

This chapter is presented as a boundary object to traverse the two interdependent communities of practice of youth peace practitioners and policy makers. An explanation of two different languages allows for philosophical viewpoints to be understood, and an exposition of traditional and contemporary methodologies for youth empowerment encourages mutual appreciation of new typologies for youth political participation.

Language has either the power to clarify or cloud meaning. For policy makers, the language of youth engagement and inclusion is expressed as co-creation, co-design, and co-production, each gaining traction over the past decade. On the other hand, youth practitioners are soaked in the practices of youth participation, methodologies of youth empowerment, and promoting political engagement. Much of this youth practitioner language has fallen out of favour for policy makers as fears of radicalisation have surpassed the vision for youth political engagement. Often, language can obfuscate a shared intention, and the intention that connects these interrelated communities of practice is towards youth engagement and peace activism. In remembering and reclaiming the 'antiquated' language of phronesis, the status and wisdom of the wily practitioner is elevated and given greater value in policy circles.

Youth sector peacebuilding is a further arena of divergence, with traditional and contemporary methodologies using different approaches, often reflecting different power paradigms. Transformative youth sector peacebuilding methodologies are interactive, capture voice, and are both action- and reflection-focused. The methodology must inspire as much as or more than the issue. Peacebuilding table talk and mutual understanding have their place, but by using the Hamardle model, we identify matching methodologies for each of the four orientations. To tip the balance in favour of young people, the language and methodologies of practitioners and policy makers require convergence and synergy.

11

Conclusion: Reclaiming a political practice

> Peacebuilding could be a form of radicalisation because you're radical – you're fuelled by a mission to do something. (YW22)

Youth sector peacebuilding holds the capacity to harness the agency, freedom, and creativity of youth to transform societies marked by violent conflict. It has also played pivotal roles in less ambitious goals of containing conflict, reducing prejudice, and diverting young people from violence. Ultimately, we argue that youth sector peacebuilding is a powerful practice that merits more substantive research, scholarship, and policy and practice development. While optimistic about youth sector peacebuilding, we recognise limitations and opportunities to forging a more transformative, emancipatory, and politically engaged approach with young people. In this concluding chapter, we present key takeaways from our analysis and critique of youth sector peacebuilding.

1. Peacebuilding is contested

Achieving consensus on the role, purpose, and direction of peacebuilding with young people in contested societies is neither likely nor, from our perspective, desirable. As demonstrated through the typology of peacebuilding discussed in Chapter 5, multiple concepts feed into perspectives on peacebuilding, which actors and agencies prioritise in different ways. The concepts of reconciliation, intergroup contact, justice, human rights, citizenship, and wellbeing are each surrounded by multiple interpretations and critiques. Practitioners, organisations, and policy makers construct different understandings of peacebuilding shaped by their context and the communities of practice they exist within.

As explored in Chapter 4, the influence of a neoliberal state agenda has swayed peacebuilding policies and practices towards the imposition of short-term programmes with prescribed targets and outcomes that can be coded and quantified. The prescription of peacebuilding outcomes shuts down the space for practitioners to use professional judgement or to discuss and negotiate the purpose of peacebuilding.

An ongoing dialogue with funders and young people is required that recognises peacebuilding as an iterative process that, through sustained engagement, reaches tipping points for change that are not easily predicted in advance. Pre-defining peacebuilding and its outcomes positions young people as consumers of initiatives and programmes rather than inviting localised visions of peace to be developed and pursued with and by young people.

2. Practitioner parlance refresh

This book presents a new vernacular and parlance for the youth sector concerning peacebuilding that has the potential of connecting communities of practice working in different local, regional, and international settings. Furthermore, this new language seeks to aid clarity and dialogue across the policy, practice, and research nexus regarding different approaches and trajectories in peacebuilding work with youth. The four viewpoints of critical thinking and dialogue, mutual understanding, social cohesion and restoration, and political engagement and social justice outlined in Chapter 7 help to distinguish different priorities, assumptions, and ambitions of practice. The Hamardle model, presented in Chapter 8, with the harmonising–politicising vertical axis and dialogue–action horizontal axis, offers a new way to frame and locate oneself within the field of youth sector peacebuilding.

A refreshed language for youth sector peacebuilding enables clarity in situating and differentiating priorities and approaches. This shared terminology can also be utilised to facilitate more focused and insightful conversations within and across sectors, such as policing, community work, formal education, and engagement with funders and policy makers. As such, the Hamardle model offers a preliminary vocabulary for wider civic society peacebuilding in local and global contexts, including post-colonial settings and places experiencing the rise of the far right. Alongside the Hamardle model, a typology of peacebuilding, presented in Chapter 5, helps practitioners reflect on the range of concepts and tensions with which peacebuilders grapple.

3. From criticism to critique

Practice, policy, and research can easily be criticised for their respective shortfalls. Concerns are routinely raised regarding academic over-intellectualism (Elzinga, 2021; Vahid, 2023), practice-based anti-intellectualism (Seal, 2014a; Medvetz, 2018), or the pragmatic imposition of policy through targeted programmes that are experienced as restrictive and unrealistic (Knox et al, 2023). This book attempts to move beyond criticism that tends to polarise the communities of policy, practice, and research. Instead, we aspire to regenerate a critique of youth sector peacebuilding that will stimulate critical dialogue between actors within and across varied domains.

4. The place of young women

While a gender lens is not a primary focus of this text, our findings raise concerns about how the contribution of girls and young women is too often neglected in peacebuilding (Swaine et al, 2019; Simpson and Holdaway, 2023). One of the 48 statements used in our research explicitly referenced acknowledging the historical and contemporary role of women in peacebuilding. The statement did not appear positively across any of the four viewpoints. Wider research points to the crucial role of women in driving and sustaining peacebuilding (Potter, 2004; Muganda, 2021). This gap across all four of our viewpoints reinforces the need to promote the voice and experiences of young women intentionally and proactively in youth sector peacebuilding.

5. Re-politicising practice

Where peacebuilding programmes and policies aimed at young people are sponsored by state actors, there has been a tendency to pursue less radical approaches that prioritise harmonisation over politicisation. This book calls for counter-narratives that challenge the peripheral place that politicising approaches to practice generally experience. Across all four viewpoints identified in our research, a collective and critical engagement of the sector involving young people, practitioners, funders, and policy makers could progress an intentional resistance to aspects of funding that curtail the emancipatory potency of youth work.

Concluding thoughts

Building peace with young people is not a straightforward or linear process. Northern Ireland is illustrative of this complexity and lagging pace of change. As with other places of ethno-territorial conflict, peacebuilding raises questions of competing histories and identities, borders and citizenship, culture and allegiance, violence and trauma, perpetrator and victim, right and wrong, retribution and forgiveness, commonality and difference, apathy and activism, and much more. Cultivating peace requires engaging with emotions and taking risks. It is both deeply personal and profoundly political. The four youth work processes of conversation, relationship building, participation, and experiential learning are essential in youth sector peacebuilding. As architects and facilitators of this skilled work, practitioners need to examine their motivations, priorities, and orientations to peacebuilding with young people. We hope this book provides practitioners with conceptual, theoretical, and reflexive tools to support an ongoing critical analysis of their practice.

Conclusion

To avoid acting as accomplices of a neoliberal peacebuilding industry, practitioners ought to individually and collectively critique the philosophies that underpin their practice. The book invites engagement with notions of individual and collective interests where agents not only criticise power structures but reflect on the complicitous ways in which we each reproduce the prevailing common sense of youth sector peacebuilding. To maximise the efficacy of this reflexivity in bringing about change, dialogical spaces should be established, bringing together young people, youth workers, researchers, funders, and policy makers.

A central argument of this text, based on empirical research, theoretical analysis, and the authors' reflexivity, is that politicising orientations to peacebuilding are the most undervalued yet hold the most liberating potential. These perspectives are inclined to challenge common-sense funding and policy directions. They contain insights to build more collectivist and emancipatory approaches to peacebuilding with young people premised on democratic participation and support for peace activism. The Hamardle model offers a new language and framework to move beyond harmonising approaches and cultivate more politicising approaches that focus on critical dialogue and peace activism with and by youth.

Appendix

No.	Statement
1	Encouraging young people to recognise and tolerate the existence of Unionist/Loyalist and/or Nationalist/Republican views they fundamentally disagree with
2	Encouraging young people to see the value of forgiveness in helping them and others move forward
3	Focusing on commonalities
4	Addressing the needs of young people most alienated from their communities
5	Encouraging young people to be activists and campaign for societal change
6	Supporting young people to challenge the power structures in their community and society
7	Creating a human rights culture where young people know and stand up for their rights and the rights of others
8	Encouraging young people to take responsibility and make amends when they cause harm to others
9	Offering diversionary activities for young people during particularly contentious periods, for example, marching season
10	Cultivating a pacifist culture underpinned by a moral commitment to non-violence
11	Creating opportunities for young people to meet with ex-combatants to better understand the Troubles and the peace process
12	Promoting trust in policing to deliver justice
13	Welcoming newcomers into Northern Ireland
14	Identifying with young people a link between sectarianism and other forms of prejudice and discrimination, for example, racism, sexism, homophobia, and so on
15	Promoting the rights of young people to express their cultural identities, for example, through Irish-medium youth work, participation in marching bands, bonfire building, and so on
16	Diverting young people from radicalisation
17	Promoting the use of and appreciation for the Irish language
18	Acknowledging with young people the atrocities inflicted by Republican and Loyalist paramilitaries and state forces during the Troubles
19	Challenging notions of masculinity that place an emphasis on violence
20	Create neutral spaces where young people from all backgrounds feel safe and accepted
21	Creating opportunities for young people to contribute through helping other people in their community and encouraging volunteering
22	Single identity work with young people within their own communities where they can critically reflect on their own identity and community background within the safety of a group who share similar values and beliefs
23	Intentionally organising non-violent resistance to force, coercion or government policy, for example, through protests, demonstrations, boycotts, and so on

Appendix

No.	Statement
24	Working with young people to expand their mobility and sense of safety within and beyond their immediate community
25	Supporting young people to hold political and institutional representatives to account (for example, politicians, police)
26	Creating safe spaces for dialogue where young people can voice disagreements regarding other people's ideas about religion and politics
27	Promoting 'Northern Irish' as an inclusive identity for all living here
28	Ensuring young people from minority groups have fair access to services
29	Encouraging young people to embrace conflict as an opportunity for change
30	Challenging young people's traditional community biases, for example, not voting along Unionist/Nationalist lines; going to a school or living in an area where they are a minority
31	Creating environments where friendships flourish across lines of division
32	Exploring with young people social and political events of the past that fuelled violence
33	Promoting a sense of global citizenship where young people recognise they belong to a global community and have rights and responsibilities that reflect this reality
34	Challenging gender-based violence and discrimination experienced primarily by women and LGBT+ individuals and groups
35	Addressing transgenerational trauma and poor mental health affecting young people
36	Working non-violently to prevent paramilitary style attacks on young people
37	Supporting young people to engage in politics and creating platforms for young people's voices to be heard by political institutions
38	Developing young people's self-awareness and recognition of oppression and injustice faced by others, and themselves
39	Encouraging young people to embrace restorative rather than retributive ideas of justice
40	Encouraging young people to open up their cultural traditions to 'outsiders' and to embrace cultural traditions of others
41	Fostering empathy and understanding with those who hold different political beliefs and cultural traditions
42	Emphasising the historical and contemporary role of women in peacebuilding
43	Promoting educational attainment and aspirations in working-class communities
44	Promoting the view that social cohesion between Loyalists/Unionists and Republicans/Nationalists is sustainable
45	Supporting young people to step beyond notions of single identity and embrace multiple identities
46	Investing in the leadership capacity of young people equipping them to be community leaders who can articulate and act for the needs of their community
47	Enabling bonds of trust to be formed in place of hostility
48	The pursuit of truth-telling and victims' rights to see those responsible for acts of violence, oppression and injustice held to account

Notes

Chapter 1
1. The choice of terminology is political. Northern Ireland is a constituent part of the United Kingdom, along with England, Scotland, and Wales. Northern Ireland is the state comprising six counties created in 1921 to house a Protestant and Unionist majority population and become separate from the mostly Catholic 26 counties of the Republic of Ireland. This process is referred to as the partition of Ireland and is the constitutional question at the centre of 'the Troubles'. The use of 'the north of Ireland' is a rejection of the legitimacy of the state of Northern Ireland and an avowal of the legitimacy of the island of Ireland as a free state.

Chapter 7
1. For further detail on the Q methodological procedures, see Hamilton and Hammond (2023).
2. As outlined in Chapter 6, to aid reflexivity one of the authors (Hamilton) also took part in the Q methodology sorting exercise as part of the research and was aligned with viewpoint 1. Therefore, while there were 43 practitioners in the study, after an initial analysis Hamilton also completed a Q sort and aligned with viewpoint 1, meaning there are 44 Q sorts that make up our findings.
3. See the Appendix for the full list of 48 statements.
4. A Q sort is the sorting grid completed by each participant. In our study there were 44 participants who each sorted 48 statements on a sorting grid from +5 to -5, therefore there were 44 Q sorts.

References

Akhavan, P. (2009) 'Are international criminal tribunals a disincentive to peace? reconciling judicial romanticism with political realism', *Human Rights Quarterly*, 31(3): 624–654.

Akinyetun, T., Bakare, K. and Adedini, S. (2023) 'Youth and peacebuilding: policy implications of conflict resolution in Africa', *Journal of Contemporary Sociological Issues*, 3(1): 68–88.

Allport, G.W. (1954) *The nature of prejudice*, Cambridge, MA: Addison Wesley.

Alternatives (ca. 2024) *About* [online], Belfast: Alternatives, https://alternativesrj.co.uk/about/

Anderson, I., Rossi, R. and Hubloue, I. (2022) 'Community-level mental health and psychosocial support during armed conflict: a cohort study from the Democratic Republic of Congo, Mali, and Nigeria', *Frontiers*, 10: 1–16.

Andersson, E. (2017) 'The pedagogical political participation model (the 3P-M) for exploring, explaining and affecting young people's political participation', *Journal of Youth Studies*, 20(10): 1346–1361.

Andrieu, K. (2010) 'Civilizing peacebuilding: transitional justice, civil society and the liberal paradigm', *Security Dialogue*, 41(5): 537–558.

ARK (2023a) *Northern Ireland Life and Times survey (NILT)* [online], ARK, https://www.ark.ac.uk/ARK/nilt

ARK (2023b) *Young Life and Times survey (YLT) 2023* [online], ARK, www.ark.ac.uk/ylt

Arnstein, S. (1969) 'A ladder of citizen participation', *Journal of the American Institute of Planners*, 35(4): 216–224.

Ashe, F. (2012) 'Gendering war and peace: militarized masculinities in Northern Ireland', *Men and Masculinities*, 15(3): 230–248.

Ashe, F. (2019) *Gender, nationalism and conflict transformation: new themes and old problems in Northern Ireland politics*, London: Routledge.

Auld, J., Gormally, B., McEvoy, K. and Richie, M. (1997) *'The Blue Book' designing a system of restorative community justice in Northern Ireland: a discussion document*, Belfast: The Authors.

Baker, C. and Obradovic-Wochnik, J. (2016) 'Mapping the nexus of transitional justice and peacebuilding', *Journal of Intervention and Statebuilding*, 10(3): 281–301.

Bakhtin, M.M. (1981) *The dialogic imagination*, Austin: University of Texas Press.

Bakhtin, M.M. (1986) *Speech genres and other late essays*, Austin: University of Texas Press.

Baldridge, B.J. (2020) 'The youthwork paradox: a case for studying the complexity of community-based youth work in education research', *Educational Researcher*, 49(8): 618–625.

Ball, S. (2008) *The education debate*, Bristol: Policy Press.
Banks, S. (2010) *Ethical issues in youth work* (2nd edn), London: Routledge.
Batsleer, J. (2008) *Informal learning in youth work*, London: SAGE.
Batsleer, J. (2013) 'Youth work, social education, democratic practice and the challenge of difference: a contribution to debate', *Oxford Review of Education*, 39(3): 287–306.
Beck, D. and Purcell, R. (2010) *Popular education for youth and community development work*, Exeter: Learning Matters.
Beck, D. and Purcell, R. (2020) *Community development for social change*, New York: Routledge.
Begley, C. (2019) 'Troubles, transformation and tension: education policy, religious segregation and initial teacher education in Northern Ireland', *Profesorado, Revista de Currículum y Formación de Profesorado*, 23(4): 8–25.
Beirne, M. and Knox, C. (2014) 'Reconciliation and human rights in Northern Ireland: a false dichotomy?', *Journal of Human Rights Practice*, 6(1): 26–50.
Belfast Telegraph (2023) '25 facts you may not know about the Orange Order' [online], *Belfast Telegraph*, 11 July, https://www.belfasttelegraph.co.uk/news/northern-ireland/25-facts-you-may-not-know-about-the-orange-order/41829112.html
Berents, H. (2018) *Young people and everyday peace: exclusion, insecurity, and peacebuilding in Colombia*, Oxon: Routledge.
Borer, T.A. (2004) 'Reconciling South Africa or South Africans? Cautionary notes from the TRC', *African Studies Quarterly*, 8(1): 19–38.
Bourdieu, P. (1977) *Outline of a theory of practice*, Cambridge: Cambridge University Press.
Bourdieu, P. (1986) 'The forms of capital', in J. Richardson (ed) *Handbook of theory and research for the sociology of education*, New York: Greenwood, pp 241–258.
Bourdieu, P. (1989) 'Social space and symbolic power', *Sociological Theory*, 7(1): 14–25.
Bourdieu, P. (1990) *Logic of practice* (R. Nice, trans), Cambridge: Polity Press.
Bourdieu, P. (1994) *In other words: essays towards a reflexive sociology* (M. Adamson, trans), Cambridge: Polity.
Bourdieu, P. (2000) *Pascalian meditations* (R. Nice, trans), Cambridge: Polity Press.
Bourdieu, P. (2014) *On the state: lectures at the College de France, 1989–1992*, edited by P. Champagne, R. Lenoir, F. Poupeau and M.-C. Riviere (D. Fernbach, trans), Cambridge: Polity Press.
Bourdieu, P. and Wacquant, L. (1992) *An invitation to reflexive sociology*, Cambridge: Polity.
Boutros-Ghali, B. (1992) *An agenda for peace: preventive diplomacy, peacemaking and peace-keeping. Report of the Secretary-General pursuant to the statement adopted by the Summit Meeting of the Security Council on 31 January 1992*, New York: United Nations.

References

Boyd, P., Toner, K. and McMullan, M. (2021) *Hunger for peace games*, Belfast: YouthAction Northern Ireland.

Brewer, J. (1992) 'Sectarianism and racism and their parallels and differences', *Ethnic and Racial Studies*, 15(3): 352–64.

Brewer, J.D., Teeney, F., Dudgeon, K., Mueller-Hirth, N. and Lal Wijesinghe, S. (2018) *The sociology of everyday life peacebuilding*, London: Palgrave Macmillan.

Bright, G. and Pugh, C. (2019) 'Youth work and cartographic action: re-naming paradoxes – mapping utopian futures', in G. Bright and C. Pugh (eds) *Youth work: global futures*, Boston: Brill Sense, pp 62–80.

British and Irish Governments (1998) *Agreement between the government of the United Kingdom of Great Britain and Northern Ireland and the government of Ireland (annex to the agreement reached in the multi-party negotiations – the Belfast Agreement/the Good Friday Agreement)*, 10 April, Belfast: NIO, https://www.gov.uk/government/publications/the-belfast-agreement

Brown, M.A., Boege, V., Clements, K.P. and Nolan, A. (2010) 'Challenging statebuilding as peacebuilding – working with hybrid political orders to build peace', in O.P. Richmond (ed) *Palgrave advances in peacebuilding: critical developments and approaches*, Hampshire: Palgrave Macmillan, pp 99–115.

Brown, S.R. (1980) *Political subjectivity: application of Q methodology in political science*, New Haven: Yale University Press.

Browne, B.C. and Bradley, E. (2021) 'Promoting Northern Ireland's peacebuilding experience in Palestine–Israel: normalising the status quo', *Third World Quarterly*, 42(7): 1625–1643.

Bruce, S. (2002) *God is dead: secularization in the West*, Oxford: Blackwell Publishing.

Büber, M. (1970) *I and thou* (W. Kaufman, trans, 3rd edn), Edinburgh: T & T Clark.

Buchroth, I. and Husband, M. (2015) 'Youth work in the voluntary sector', in G. Bright (ed) *Youth work: histories, policy and contexts*, London: Palgrave Macmillan, pp 102–124.

Buchroth, I. and Connolly, D. (2019) 'Dichotomous voluntary futures', in G. Bright and C. Pugh (eds) *Youth work: global futures*, Boston: Brill Sense, pp 146–165.

Bunting, L., Montgomery, L., Mooney, S., MacDonald, M., Coulter, S., Hayes, D., et al (2019) *Developing trauma informed practice in Northern Ireland: key messages*, Belfast: Queen's University Belfast.

Bunyan, P. and Ord, J. (2012) 'The neoliberal policy context of youth work management', in J. Ord (ed) *Critical issues in youth work management*, London: Routledge, pp 19–29.

Burrell, G. and Morgan, G. (1979) *Sociological paradigms and organisational analysis: elements of the sociology of corporate life*, London: Heinemann Educational.

Bush, K. and Houston, K. (2011) *The story of peace: learning from EU PEACE funding in Northern Ireland and the Border Region*, Belfast: INCORE.

Byrne, J., Hamber, B., Morrow, D., Dougherty, B. and Gallagher, G. (2016) *Political violence and young people: exploring levels of risk, motivations and targeted preventative work*, Belfast: Ulster University.

Byrne, S. and Nadan, A. (2011) 'The social cube analytical model and protracted ethnoterritorial conflicts', in T. Matyok, J. Senei and S. Byrne (eds) *Critical issues in peace and conflict studies*, Maryland: Lexington Books, pp 61–80.

CAIN (Conflict Archive on the Internet) (2023a) *Fact sheet on the conflict in and about Northern Ireland* [online], Belfast: Ulster University CAIN Web Service, https://cain.ulster.ac.uk/victims/docs/group/htr/day_of_reflection/htr_0607c.pdf

CAIN (Conflict Archive on the Internet) (2023b) *A draft chronology of the conflict – 1994* [online], Belfast: Ulster University CAIN Web Service, https://cain.ulster.ac.uk/othelem/chron/ch94.htm

Carpenter, S. (2017) '"Modeling" youth work: logic models, neoliberalism, and community praxis', *International Studies in Sociology of Education*, 26(2): 105–120.

Carr, S. (2022) 'And someone to talk to: the role of therapeutic youth work', *Youth & Policy* [online], https://www.youthandpolicy.org/articles/and-someone-to-talk-to-the-role-of-therapeutic-youth-work/

Carter, C. (2004) 'Education for peace in Northern Ireland and the USA', *Theory and Research in Social Education*, 32(1): 24–38.

Chandler, D. (2017) *Peacebuilding: the twenty years crisis, 1997–2017*, Cham: Springer Nature.

Chapman, T., Campbell, H., Wilson, D. and McCready, P. (2018) 'Working across frontiers: community based restorative justice in Northern Ireland', in I. Vanfraechem and I. Aertsen (eds) *Action research in criminal justice: restorative justice approaches in intercultural settings*, Oxon: Routledge, pp 117–141.

Clarke, K. and Kocak, K. (2020) 'Launching revolution: social media and the Egyptian uprising's first movers', *British Journal of Political Science*, 50(3): 1025–1045.

Coakley, J. (2021) 'Is a middle force emerging in Northern Ireland?' *Irish Political Studies*, 36(1): 29–51.

Coburn, A. and Gormally, S. (2017) *Communities for social change: practicing equality and social justice in youth and community work*, New York: Peter Lang.

Cochrane, F. (2013) *Northern Ireland: the reluctant peace*, New Haven: Yale University Press.

Community NI (2019) *NIFHA and housing associations integration project host first ever formal visit to north by Fine Gael NI engagement group* [online], Belfast: NICVA, https://www.communityni.org/news/nifha-and-housing-associations-integration-project-host-first-ever-formal-visit-north-fine

Conner, J.O., Ober, C.N. and Brown, A.S. (2016) 'The politics of paternalism: adult and youth perspectives on youth voice in public policy', *Teachers College Record*, 118(8): 1–48.

Connolly, P. (2000) 'What now for the contact hypothesis? Towards a new research agenda', *Race, Ethnicity and Education*, 3(2): 169–193.

Cooper, N., Turner, M. and Pugh, M. (2011) 'The end of history and the last liberal peacebuilder: a reply to Roland Paris', *Review of International Studies*, 37(4): 1995–2007.

Cooper, T. (2012) 'Models of youth work: a framework for positive sceptical reflection', *Youth & Policy*, 109: 98–117.

Cooper, T. (2013) 'Institutional context and youth work professionalization in postwelfare societies', *Child and Youth Services*, 34(2): 112–124.

Cooper, T. (2018) 'Defining youth work: exploring the boundaries, continuity and diversity of youth work practice', in P. Alldred, F. Cullen, K. Edwards and D. Fusco (eds) *The SAGE Handbook of Youth Work Practice*, London: SAGE, pp 3–17.

Cooper, T. and White, R. (1994) 'Models of youth work practice', *Youth Studies Australia*, 13(4): 30–35.

Cooperstein, S.E. and Kocevar-Weidinger, E. (2004) 'Beyond active learning: a constructivist approach to learning', *Reference Services Review*, 32(2): 141–148.

Corney, T., Williamson, H., Holdsworth, R., Broadbent, R., Ellis, K., Shier, H., et al (2020) *Approaches to youth participation in youth and community work practice: a critical dialogue*, Victoria: Youth Workers Association.

Corney, T., Marion, J., Baird, R., Welsh, S. and Gorman, J. (2023) 'Youth work as social pedagogy: toward an understanding of non-formal and informal education and learning in youth work', *Child & Youth Services*, 45(3): 345–370.

Costa, C. and Murphy, M. (2015) 'Bourdieu and the application of habitus across the social sciences', in C. Costa and M. Murphy (eds) *Bourdieu, habitus and social research: the art of application*, Basingstoke: Palgrave Macmillan, pp 3–17.

Costa, C., Burke, C. and Murphy, M. (2019) 'Capturing habitus: theory, method and reflexivity', *International Journal of Research & Method in Education*, 41(1): 19–32.

Coulter, C. and Shirlow, P. (2023) 'Northern Ireland 25 years after the Good Friday Agreement: an introduction to the special issue', *Space and Polity*, 27(1): 1–16.

Coulter, C., Flaherty, E. and Shirlow, P. (2023) '"Seismic" or stalemate? The (bio)politics of the 2021 Northern Ireland Census', *Space and Polity*, 27(1): 57–77.

Council of Europe (2000) *Recommendation 1437 (2000): non formal education*, Strasbourg: Council of Europe Parliamentary Assembly.

Coyles, D., Hamber, B. and Grant, A. (2023) 'Hidden barriers and divisive architecture: the role of "everyday space" in conflict and peacebuilding in Belfast', *Journal of Urban Affairs*, 45(6): 1057–1080.

Crick, B. (2004) 'Politics as a form of rules: politics, citizenship and democracy', in A. Leftwich (ed) *What is politics*, Cambridge: Polity Press, pp 67–85.

Crick, B. (2007) 'Citizenship: the political and the democratic', *British Journal of Educational Studies*, 55(3): 235–248.

CRJI (Community Restorative Justice Ireland) (2020) *Who we are* [online], Belfast: CRJI, https://www.crjireland.org/who-we-are

Crownover, J. (2009) 'Youth work in south east Europe: youth transitions and challenges in a post conflict environment', *Youth & Policy*, 102: 67–79.

Daoudy, M. (2009) 'State-building', in V. Chetail (ed) *Post-conflict peacebuilding: a lexicon*, Oxford: Oxford University Press, pp 350–358.

Darby, J. (ed) (1983) *Northern Ireland: the background to the conflict*, Belfast: Appletree Press.

Davies, B. (2010) 'What do we mean by youth work?', in J. Batsleer and B. Davies (eds) *What is youth work?*, London: Learning Matters, pp 1–6.

Davies, B. (2015) 'Youth work: a manifesto for our times – revisited', *Youth & Policy*, 115: 96–117.

Davies, B. (2021) 'Youth work: a manifesto revisited: at the time of Covid and beyond', *Youth & Policy* [online], https://www.youthandpolicy.org/articles/youth-work-manifesto-revisited-2021/

Davies, B. and Merton, B. (2009) 'Squaring the circle: the state of youth work in some children and young people's services', *Youth & Policy*, 103: 5–24.

Davies, B. and Taylor, T. (2019) 'On critical beginnings: how we got to where we are', in G. Bright and C. Pugh (eds) *Youth work: global futures*, Boston: Brill Sense, pp 1–17.

DE (Department of Education) (1997) *Youth work: a model for effective practice*, Bangor: Department of Education.

DE (Department of Education) (2005) *Strategy for the delivery of youth work in Northern Ireland (2005–2008)*, Bangor: Department of Education.

DE (Department of Education) (2015) *Sharing works: a policy for shared education*, Bangor: Department of Education.

Deer, C. (2014) 'Doxa', in M. Grenfell (ed) *Pierre Bourdieu: key concepts* (2nd edn), Oxon: Routledge, pp 114–125.

Del Felice, C. (2008) 'Youth criminality and urban social conflict in the city of Rosario, Argentina', *International Journal of Conflict and Violence*, 2(1): 72–97.

Department of Children, Equality, Disability, Integration & Youth (2021) *Final review of the National Strategy on Children and Young People's Participation in Decision-making 2015–2020*, Dublin: Department of Children, Equality, Disability, Integration & Youth.

de St Croix, T. (2016) *Grassroots youth work: policy, passion and resistance in practice*, Bristol: Policy Press.

de St Croix, T. (2018) 'Youth work, performativity and the new youth impact agenda: getting paid for numbers?', *Journal of Education Policy*, 33(3): 414–438.

References

de St Croix, T. and Doherty, L. (2023) '"It's a great place to find where you belong": creating, curating and valuing place and space in open youth work', *Children's Geographies*, 21(6): 1029–1043.

Devine, P., Early, E., Minchen, L. and Schubotz, D. (2023) *Assessing demand for integrated education*, Belfast: Queen's Policy Engagement.

Dewey, J. (1997) *Experience and education*, New York: Touchstone.

Dewey, J. (2007) *Democracy and education*, Teddington: Echo Library.

Diamond, P. and Colfer, B. (2023) 'Irish unification after Brexit: old and new political identities?', *The Political Quarterly*, 94: 104–114.

Dillon, M. (1991) *The dirty war*, London: Arrow Books.

Dixon, J., Durrheim, K. and Tredoux, C. (2005) 'Beyond the optimal contact strategy: a reality check for the contact hypothesis', *American Psychologist*, 60(7): 697–711.

Doebler, S., McAreavey, R. and Shortall, S. (2018) 'Is racism the new sectarianism? Negativity towards immigrants and ethnic minorities in Northern Ireland from 2004 to 2015', *Ethnic and Racial Studies*, 41(14): 2426–2444.

DoJ (Department of Justice) (2023) *About the Department of Justice*, Belfast: Department of Justice, https://www.justice-ni.gov.uk/about-department-justice

DoJ (Department of Justice) (ca. 2024) *Register of community based restorative justice schemes*, Belfast: Department of Justice, https://www.justice-ni.gov.uk/articles/register-community-based-restorative-justice-schemes

Doxtader, E. (2003) 'Reconciliation: a rhetorical concept/ion', *Quarterly Journal of Speech*, 89: 267–92.

Doyle, M.W. (1986) 'Liberalism and world politics', *American Political Science Review*, 80(4): 1151–1169.

Dudai, R. (2018) 'Transitional justice as social control: political transitions, human rights, norms and the reclassification of the past', *The British Journal of Sociology*, 69(3): 691–711.

Dunlop, L., Rushton, E.A.C., Atkinson, L., Blake, C., Calvert, S., Cornelissen, E., et al (2023) 'An introduction to the co-creation of policy briefs with youth and academic teams', *Journal of Geography in Higher Education*, 47(1): 149–159.

Eckhardt, J., Kaletka, C., Kruger, D., Maldonado-Mariscal, K. and Schulz, A.C. (2021) 'Ecosystems of co-creation', *Frontiers in Sociology*, 6: 1–11.

Elzinga, B. (2021) 'Intellectualizing know how', *Synthese*, 198: 1741–1760.

Evans, M. (2016) 'Structural violence, socioeconomic rights, and transformative justice', *Journal of Human Rights*, 15(1): 1–20.

Ewert, G.D. (1991) 'Habermas and education: a comprehensive overview of the influence of Habermas in educational literature', *Review of Educational Research*, 61(3): 345–378.

Farnsworth, V., Kleanthous, I. and Wenger-Trayner, E. (2016) 'Communities of practice as a social theory of learning: a conversation with Etienne Wenger', *British Journal of Educational Studies*, 64(2): 139–160.

Feeney, B. (2014) *A short history of the Troubles*, Dublin: The O'Brien Press.

Femia, J.V. (1981) *Gramsci's political thought: hegemony, consciousness, and the revolutionary process*, Oxford: Clarendon Press.

Fenwick, T.J. (2000) 'Expanding conceptions of experiential learning: a review of the five contemporary perspectives on cognition', *Adult Education Quarterly*, 50(4): 243–272.

Firchow, P. (2018) *Reclaiming everyday peace: local voices in measurement and evaluation after war*, Cambridge: Cambridge University Press.

Fisher, D. (1984) 'A conceptual analysis of self-disclosure', *Journal for the Theory of Social Behaviour*, 14: 277–296.

Flinders, M. and Buller, J. (2006) 'Depoliticisation: principles, tactics and tools', *British Politics*, 1: 293–318.

Flinders, M. and Wood, M. (eds) (2015) *Tracing the political: depoliticisation, governance and the state*, Bristol: Policy Press.

Flyvbjerg, B. (2011) 'Making social science matter', in G. Papanagnou (ed) *Social science and policy challenges: democracy, values and capacities*, Paris: UNESCO Research and Policy, pp 25–56.

Fordham, P. (1993) 'Informal, non-formal and formal education programmes', in *ICE301 lifelong learning: unit 1, approaching lifelong learning*, London: YMCA George Williams College.

Forrest, D. (2010) 'The cultivation of gifts in all directions: thinking about purpose', in T. Jeffs and M.K. Smith (eds) *Youth work practice*, Basingstoke: Palgrave Macmillan, pp 54–69.

Freeden, M. (1996) *Ideologies and political theory*, Oxford: Clarendon Press.

Freeden, M. (2013a) 'The morphological analysis of ideology', in M. Freeden, L.T. Sargent and M. Stears (eds) *The Oxford handbook of political ideologies*, Oxford: Oxford University Press, pp 115–137.

Freeden, M. (2013b) *The political theory of political thinking: the anatomy of a practice*, Oxford: Oxford University Press.

Freire, P. (1970) *Pedagogy of the oppressed* (M.B. Ramos, trans), New York: Herder and Herder.

Freire, P. (1996) *Pedagogy of the oppressed* (new revised edn), London: Penguin Books.

Freire, P. (2007) *Education for critical consciousness*, New York: Continuum.

GAA (Gaelic Athletic Association) (2023) *About the GAA*, Dublin: GAA, https://www.gaa.ie/the-gaa/about-the-gaa/

Gallie, W.B. (1956) 'Essentially contested concepts', *Proceedings of the Aristotelian Society*, 56: 167–198.

Galtung, J. (1964) 'An editorial', *Journal of Peace Research*, 1(1): 1–4.

References

Galtung, J. (1975) 'Three approaches to peace: peacekeeping, peacemaking, and peacebuilding', in J. Galtung (ed) *Peace, war and defence: essays in peace research*, Copenhagen: Christian Ejlers, pp 282–304.

Galtung, J. (1990) 'Cultural violence', *Journal of Peace Research*, 27(3): 291–305.

Galtung, J. (2000) *Conflict transformation by peaceful means (the transcend method)*, Geneva: United Nations Disaster Management Training Programme.

Gaudette, T., Scrivens, R. and Venkatesh, V. (2022) 'The role of the internet in facilitating violent extremism: insights from former right-wing extremists', *Terrorism and Political Violence*, 34(7): 1339–1356.

Gilmartin, N. and Browne, B.C. (2022) *Refugees and forced displacement in Northern Ireland's Troubles: untold journeys*, Liverpool: Liverpool University Press.

Giroux, H.A. (1988) 'Critical theory and the politics of culture and voice: rethinking the discourse of educational research', in R.R. Sherman and R.B. Webb (eds) *Qualitative research in education: focus and methods*, London: Falmer Press, pp 190–210.

Giugni, M. and Grasso, M.T. (2020) 'Talking about youth: the depoliticization of young people in the public domain', *American Behavioral Scientist*, 64(5): 591–607.

Goetze, C. and Guzina, D. (2008) 'Peacebuilding, nationbuilding, statebuilding: turtles all the way down?', *Civil Wars*, 10(4): 319–347.

Gomersall, O. (2024) *Young people and PEACE: a conflict transformation positioned analysis of EU PEACE Programme youth programming in Northern Ireland and the Irish border region*, Belfast: Queens University Belfast.

Gonzalez-Vicente, R. (2020) 'The liberal peace fallacy: violent neoliberalism and the temporal and spatial traps of state-based approaches to peace', *Territory, Politics, Governance*, 8(1): 100–116.

Govan, D.H. (2021) 'Towards a religious understanding of the Orange Order: Belfast 1910 to 1914', *Irish Studies Review*, 29(4): 501–514.

Government of Ireland (2020) *Policy information: PEACE IV programme (Ireland/Northern Ireland)*, Dublin: Irish Government, https://www.gov.ie/en/policy-information/0dbc6f-irish-border-counties-peace-programme/

Govier, T. (2009) 'A dialectic of acknowledgement', in J.R. Quinn (ed) *Reconciliation(s): transitional justice in post-conflict societies*, Montreal: McGill-Queen's University Press, pp 36–50.

Gramsci, A. (1971) *Selections from the prison notebooks of Antonio Gramsci*, New York: International Publishers.

Grand Orange Lodge of Ireland (2022) *Home page: welcome*, Belfast: Grand Orange Lodge of Ireland, https://www.goli.org.uk/

Grant, D. (2019) 'A practitioner's response to resilience in the face of trauma: implications for service delivery', *Irish Probation Journal*, 16: 95–106.

Grasso, M.T. and Bessant, J. (2018) *Governing youth politics in the age of surveillance*, London: Routledge.

Grattan, A. and Morgan, S. (2007) 'Youthwork in conflict societies: from divergence to convergence', in D. Magnuson and M. Baizerman (eds) *Work with youth in divided and contested societies*, Rotterdam: Sense Publishers, pp 165–177.

Gray, A.M., Hamilton, J., Kelly, G., Lynn, B., Melaugh, M. and Robinson, G. (2018) *Northern Ireland peace monitoring report: number five*, Belfast: Community Relations Council.

Gray, A.M., Hamilton, J., Hetherington, G., Kelly, G., Lynn, B., Devine, P., et al (2023) *Northern Ireland peace monitoring report: number 6*, Belfast: Community Relations Council.

Gready, P. and Robins, S. (2014) 'From transitional to transformative justice: a new agenda for practice', *International Journal of Transitional Justice*, 8(3): 339–361.

Grenfell, M. (ed) (2014) *Pierre Bourdieu: key concepts* (2nd edn), Oxon: Routledge.

Guardians of the Flame (2023) *Workshops* [online], Newry: Guardians of the Flame, https://www.guardiansoftheflame.org/workshops

Habermas, J. (1984) *The theory of communicative action, volume 1*, Boston: Beacon Press.

Habermas, J. (1987) *The theory of communicative action, volume 2*, Boston: Beacon Press.

Hamber, B. and Kelly, G. (2005) 'A place for reconciliation? Conflict and locality in Northern Ireland', *Democratic Dialogue*, 18: 1–80.

Hamber, B. and Gallagher, E. (2014) 'Ships passing in the night: psychosocial programming and macro peacebuilding strategies with young men in Northern Ireland', *Intervention*, 12(1): 43–60.

Hamber, B. and Kelly, G. (2018) 'Northern Ireland: case study', in Interpeace, *Challenging the conventional: making post-violence reconciliation succeed*, Geneva: Kofi Annan Foundation, pp 98–148.

Hamber, B., Gallagher, E. and Ventevogel, P. (2014) 'Narrowing the gap between psychosocial practice, peacebuilding and wider social change: an introduction to the special section in this issue', *Intervention*, 12(1): 7–15.

Hamber, B., Erwin, D. and McArdle, E. (2023) *The unfinished business of peace and reconciliation: a call to action*, Belfast: The John and Pat Hume Foundation.

Hamilton, A. (2022) *Theorising youth sector peacebuilding: youth workers' orientations within the politics of peacebuilding*, PhD thesis, Belfast: Ulster University.

Hamilton, A. and McArdle, E. (2020) *Young people and peacebuilding: challenges and opportunities*, Belfast: ARK.

Hamilton, A. and Hammond, M. (2023) 'Harmonising or politicising: youth sector peacebuilding in contested societies', *Irish Journal of Sociology*, 31(2): 203–228.

Hammond, M. (2008) 'Cross community youth work training in a divided and contested society', *Youth & Policy*, 97&98: 47–56.

Hammond, M. (2018) *The point of encounter: an investigation into the purpose, processes and theory underpinning youth work practice*, PhD thesis, Belfast: Ulster University.

Hammond, M. and Harvey, C. (2021) *Reclaiming youth work: a return to the founding principles of youth work during the covid-19 pandemic*, Belfast: ARK.

Hammond, M. and McArdle, E. (2024) 'Conversation in youth work: a process for encounter', *Child & Youth Services*, 45(1): 140–160.

Hansson, U. and Roulston, S. (2021) 'Integrated and shared education: Sinn Féin, the Democratic Unionist Party and educational change in Northern Ireland', *Policy Futures in Education*, 19(6): 730–746.

Hargie, O., Dickson, D. and Nelson, S. (2003) 'A lesson too late for the learning? cross-community contact and communication among university students', in O. Hargie and D. Dickson (eds) *Researching the Troubles: social science perspectives on the Northern Ireland conflict*, Edinburgh: Mainstream Publishing, pp 86–106.

Harland, K. (2009) 'From conflict to peacebuilding: reflections and descriptions of youth work practice in the contested spaces of Northern Ireland', *Youth & Policy*, 102: 7–20.

Harland, K. (2011) 'Violent youth culture in Northern Ireland: young men, violence, and the challenges of peacebuilding', *Youth & Society*, 43(2): 414–432.

Harland, K. and McCready, S. (2014) 'Rough justice: considerations on the role of violence, masculinity, and the alienation of young men in communities and peacebuilding processes in Northern Ireland', *Youth Justice*, 14(3): 269–283.

Harvey, D. (2005) *A brief history of neoliberalism*, New York: Oxford University Press.

Hatton, K. (2018) 'Youth work and social pedagogy: reflections from the UK and Europe', in P. Alldred, F. Cullen, K. Edwards and D. Fusco (eds) *The SAGE handbook of youth work practice*, London: SAGE, pp 154–167.

Haydon, D. and Scraton, P. (2008) 'Conflict, regulation and marginalisation in the north of Ireland: the experiences of children and young people', *Current Issues in Criminal Justice*, 20(1): 59–78.

Haydon, D., McAlister, S. and Scraton, P. (2012) 'Young people, conflict and regulation', *The Howard Journal of Criminal Justice*, 51(5): 503–520.

Hayward, K. (2018) 'The pivotal position of the Irish border in the UK's withdrawal from the European Union', *Space and Polity*, 22(2): 238–254.

Hayward, K. (2021) *What do we know and what should we do about the Irish border?*, London: SAGE.

Hayward, K. and McManus, C. (2019) 'Neither/nor: the rejection of Unionist and Nationalist identities in post-Agreement Northern Ireland', *Capital & Class*, 43(1): 139–155.

Hayward, K. and Komarova, M. (2022) 'The protocol on Ireland/Northern Ireland: past, present, and future precariousness', *Global Policy*, 13(Suppl. 2): 128–137.

Heathershaw, J. (2008) 'Unpacking the liberal peace: the dividing and merging of peacebuilding discourses', *Millennium: Journal of International Studies*, 36(3): 597–621.

Henao-Izquierdo, L. (2021) *Political transition, reintegration, and the challenges of reconciliation in Colombia from the perspective of youth*, Geneva: Interpeace.

Henderson, G.P. (2006) 'The public and peace: the consequences for citizenship of the democratic peace literature', *International Studies Review*, 8(2): 199–224.

Hewstone, M., Lolliot, S., Swart, H., Myers, E., Voci, A., Ramiah, A., et al (2014) 'Intergroup contact and intergroup conflict', *Peace and Conflict: Journal of Peace Psychology*, 20(1): 39–53.

HMSO (1972) *Education and libraries (Northern Ireland) 1972 order*, London: HMSO.

Hughes, J. (2018) 'Agency versus structure in reconciliation', *Ethnic and Racial Studies*, 41(4): 624–642.

Hughes, J. and Loader, R. (2015) '"Plugging the gap": shared education and the promotion of community relations through schools in Northern Ireland', *British Educational Research Journal*, 41(6): 1142–1155.

Hughes, J. and Loader, R. (2023) 'Shared education: a case study in social cohesion', *Research Papers in Education*, 38(3): 305–327.

Hurley, L. and Treacy, D. (1993) *Models of youth work: a sociological framework*, Dublin: Irish YouthWork Press.

Husband, M. (2020) 'Tracking technology: youth work in a society of control', *Youth & Policy* [online], https://www.youthandpolicy.org/articles/tracking-technology-youth-work-in-a-society-of-control/

Hvidsten, A.H. and Skarstad, K.I. (2018) 'The challenge of human rights for peace research', *International Theory*, 10(1): 98–121.

IDYW (In Defence of Youth Work) (2012) *This is youth work: stories from practice*, In Defence of Youth Work with UNISON.

IDYW (2014) *IDYW statement 2014* [online], https://indefenceofyouthwork.com/idyw-statement-2014/

Irish News (2022) *Games changing: beyond the playing field in GAA*, Belfast: Irish News.

Isin, E.F. (2008) 'Theorizing acts of citizenship', in E.F. Isin and G.M. Nielsen (eds) *Acts of citizenship*, London: Zed Books, pp 15–43.

James McAdams, A. and Piccolo, S. (eds) (2024) *Far-right newspeak and the future of liberal democracy*, London: Routledge.

Jeffs, T. and Smith, M.K. (2005) *Informal education: conversation, democracy and learning* (revised edn), Nottingham: Education Heretics Press.

Jeffs, T. and Smith, M.K. (eds) (2010) *Youth work practice*, Basingstoke: Palgrave Macmillan.

Jeffs, T. and Smith, M.K. (2011) 'What is informal education?', *The Encyclopaedia of Pedagogy and Informal Education* [online], https://infed.org/mobi/what-is-informal-education

Jeffs, T., Coburn, A., Scott-McKinley, A. and Drowley, S. (2019) 'Contrasting futures? Exploring youth work across the UK', in G. Bright and C. Pugh (eds) *Youth work: global futures*, Boston: Brill Sense, pp 18–61.

Jessop, B. (2015) 'Repoliticising depoliticisation: theoretical preliminaries on some responses to the American fiscal and Eurozone debt crises', in M. Flinders and M. Wood (eds) *Tracing the political: depoliticisation, governance and the state*, Bristol: Policy Press, pp 95–116.

Jones, T.S. (2004) 'Enhancing collaborative tendencies: extending the single identity model for youth conflict education', *New Directions for Youth Development*, 102: 11–34.

Joppke, C. (2023) 'Explaining the populist right in the neoliberal west', *Societies*, 13(5): 110–130.

Kagoyire, M., Kangabe, J. and Ingabire, M. (2023) ' "A calf cannot fail to pick a colour from its mother": intergenerational transmission of trauma and its effect on reconciliation among post-genocide Rwandan youth', *BMC Psychol* 11(104): 1–17.

Karsten, A. (2012) *A potpourri of participation models – updated* [online], Nonformality, https://www.nonformality.org/2012/11/participation-models/

Kirby, P. and Bryson, S. (2002) *Measuring the magic? Evaluating and researching young people's participation in public decision making*, London: Carnegie UK Trust.

Knox, C. (2011a) 'Tackling racism in Northern Ireland: "the race hate capital of Europe"', *Journal of Social Policy*, 40(2): 387–412.

Knox, C. (2011b) 'Cohesion, sharing, and integration in Northern Ireland: environment and planning', *Government and Policy*, 29(3): 548–566.

Knox, C., O'Connor, K., Ketola, M. and Carmichael, P. (2023) 'EU PEACE funding: the policy implementation deficit', *European Policy Analysis*, 9: 290–310.

Laclau, E. and Mouffe, C. (2014) *Hegemony and socialist strategy: towards a radical democratic politics*, London: Verso.

Lagana, G. (2021) *The European Union and the Northern Ireland peace process*, Cham: Palgrave Macmillan.

Lambourne, W. (2009) 'Transitional justice and peacebuilding after mass violence', *International Journal of Transitional Justice*, 3(1): 28–48.

Lave, J. and Wenger, E. (1991) *Situated learning: learning in doing: social, cognitive and computational perspectives*, Cambridge: Cambridge University Press.

Lederach, A.J. (2020) 'Youth provoking peace: an intersectional approach to territorial peacebuilding in Colombia', *Peacebuilding*, 8(2): 198–217.

Lederach, J.P. (1995) *Preparing for peace: conflict transformation across cultures*, New York: Syracuse University Press.
Lederach, J.P. (1997) *Building peace: sustainable reconciliation in divided societies*, Washington, DC: United States Institute of Peace Press.
Lederach, J.P. (2003) *The little book of conflict transformation*, New York: Good Books.
Ledwith, M. (2016) *Community development in action: putting Freire into practice*, Bristol: Polity Press.
Ledwith, M. (2020) *Community development: a critical and radical approach* (3rd edn), Bristol: Policy Press.
Li, M., Liedner, B., Petrović, N., Orazani, S.N. and Rad, M.S. (2018) 'The role of retributive justice and the use of international criminal tribunals in post-conflict reconciliation', *European Journal of Social Psychology*, 48(2): 0133–0151.
Little, A. (2006) 'Theorizing democracy and violence: the case of Northern Ireland', *Theoria: A Journal of Social and Political Theory*, 111: 62–86.
Little, A. (2011a) 'Debating peace and conflict in Northern Ireland: towards a narrative approach', in K. Hayward and C. O'Donnell (eds) *Political discourse and conflict resolution: debating peace in Northern Ireland*, Oxon: Routledge, pp 209–223.
Little, A. (2011b) 'Disjunctured narratives: rethinking reconciliation and conflict transformation', *International Political Science Review*, 33(1): 82–98.
Little, A. and Maddison, S. (2017) 'Reconciliation, transformation, struggle: an introduction', *International Political Science Review*, 38(2): 145–154.
Littler, J. (2018) *Against meritocracy: culture, power and myths of mobility*, Oxon: Routledge.
Lohmeyer, B.A. (2017a) 'Restorative practices and youth work: theorizing professional power relationships with young people', *Young*, 25(4): 375–390.
Lohmeyer, B.A. (2017b) 'Youth and their workers: the interacting subjectification effects of neoliberal social policy and NGO practice frameworks', *Journal of Youth Studies*, 20(10): 1263–1276.
Lohmeyer, B.A. (2018) 'Youth as an artefact of governing violence: violence to young people shapes violence by young people', *Current Sociology*, 66(7): 1070–1086.
Lundy, L. (2007) 'Voice is not enough: conceptualising Article 12 of the United Nations Convention on the Rights of the Child', *British Educational Research Journal*, 33(6): 927–942.
Lundy, L. (2021) *Briefing paper to Northern Ireland Assembly: promoting child and youth engagement in Northern Ireland*, Belfast: Queen's University Belfast [online] https://www.niassembly.gov.uk/globalassets/documents/committees/2017-2022/education/my-life-and-learning-in-lockdown/2.-20210426-professor-lundy-briefing-paper.pdf

Lundy, P. and McGovern, M. (2006) 'Participation, truth and partiality: participatory action research, community-based truth-telling and post-conflict transition in Northern Ireland', *Sociology*, 40(1): 71–88.

Lundy, P. and McGovern, M. (2008) 'Whose justice? Rethinking transitional justice from the bottom up', *Journal of Law and Society*, 35(2): 265–292.

Lundy, P., Gilmartin, N., McDermott, P., Finegan, R. and Murphy, R. (eds) (2021) *Dealing with the legacy of conflict in Northern Ireland through engagement and dialogue*, Glencree: The Glencree Centre for Peace and Reconciliation.

Mac Ginty, R. (2008) 'Indigenous peacemaking versus the liberal peace', *Cooperation and Conflict*, 43(2): 139–162.

Mac Ginty, R. (2011) *International peacebuilding and local resistance: hybrid forms of peace*, Basingstoke: Palgrave.

Mac Ginty, R. (2012) 'Routine peace: technocracy and peacebuilding', *Cooperation and Conflict*, 47(3): 287–308.

Mac Ginty, R. (2014) 'Everyday peace: bottom–up and local agency in conflict-affected societies', *Security Dialogue*, 45(6): 548–564.

Mac Ginty, R. (2021) *Everyday peace: how so-called ordinary people can disrupt violent conflict*, New York: Oxford University Press.

Mac Ginty, R. and Richmond, O.P. (2013) 'The local turn in peacebuilding: a critical agenda for peace', *Third World Quarterly*, 34(4): 763–783.

Mac Ginty, R. and Richmond, O.P. (2016) 'The fallacy of constructing hybrid political orders: a reappraisal of the hybrid turn in peacebuilding', *International Peacekeeping*, 23(2): 219–239.

Mac Ionnrachtaigh, F. (2021) 'Promoting sedition: the Irish language revival in the north of Ireland – power, resistance and decolonization', in N.C. Gibson (ed) *Fanon today: reason and revolt of the wretched of the earth*, Wakefield: Daraja Press, pp 365–414.

MacMillan, J. (2004) 'Whose democracy; which peace? Contextualizing the democratic peace', *International Politics*, 41: 472–493.

Magnuson, D. (2007) 'The perils, promise and practice of youth work in conflict societies', in D. Magnuson and M. Baizerman (eds) *Work with youth in divided and contested societies*, Rotterdam: Sense Publishers, pp 3–10.

Maringira, G., Ndelu, S., Gukurume, S. and Langa, M. (2022) '"We are not our parents" – beyond political transition: historical failings, present angst and future yearnings of South African youth', *International Journal of Transitional Justice*, 16(1): 101–117.

Maton, K. (2014) 'Habitus', in M. Grenfell (ed) *Pierre Bourdieu: key concepts* (2nd edn), Oxon: Routledge, pp 48–64.

McAlister, S., Haydon, D. and Scratton, P. (2014) 'Childhood in transition: growing up in "post-conflict" Northern Ireland', *Children's Geographies*, 12(3): 297–311.

McAlister, S., Corr, M.-L., Dwyer, C. and Drummond, O. (2021) 'It didn't end in 1998': examining the impacts of conflict legacy across generations, Belfast: Queen's University Belfast.

McAlister, S., Neill, G., Carr, N. and Dwyer, C. (2022) 'Gender, violence and cultures of silence: young women and paramilitary violence', Journal of Youth Studies, 25(8): 1148–1163.

McArdle, E. and Morgan, S. (2020) 'Long walk from the door', in S. McCready and R. Loudon (eds) Investing in lives: the history of the youth service in Northern Ireland (1973–2017), volume 2, Belfast: Youth Council for Northern Ireland, pp 419–432.

McArdle, E. and Neill, G. (2023) 'The making and shaping of the young Gael: Irish-medium youth work for developing indigenous identities', Social Inclusion, 11(2): 223–231.

McArdle, E., McConville, L. and Stainsby, J. (2020) YouthPact evaluation: relationship, relevance and rigour to maximise impact within Peace4Youth, Belfast: YouthPact.

McAtackney, L. and Ó Catháin, M. (eds) (2024) The Routledge handbook of the Northern Ireland conflict and peace, Oxon: Routledge.

McBride, S. (2019) Burned: the inside story of the 'cash-for-ash' scandal and Northern Ireland's secretive new elite, Newbridge: Merrion Press.

McCandless, E. (2010) 'The UN's tripartite peace architecture amidst promises and challenges for sustaining peace', in J. Johansen and J.Y. Jones (eds) Experiments with peace: a book celebrating peace on Johan Galtung's 80th birthday, Cape Town: Pambazuka Press, pp 201–213.

McCready, S. (2020) 'A statutory youth service: the troubles and keeping young people safe (1973–1979)', in S. McCready and R. Loudon (eds) Investing in lives: the history of the youth service in Northern Ireland (1973–2017), volume 2, Belfast: Youth Council for Northern Ireland, pp 9–64.

McCready, S. and Dilworth, J. (2014) Youth participation literature review, Belfast: YouthAction Northern Ireland.

McCready, S. and Loudon, R. (eds) (2020) Investing in lives: the history of the youth service in Northern Ireland (1973–2017), volume 2, Belfast: Youth Council for Northern Ireland.

McEvoy-Levy, S. (2012) 'Youth spaces in haunted places: placemaking for peacebuilding in theory and practice', International Journal of Peace Studies, 17(2): 1–32.

McGarry, J. and O'Leary, B. (2016) 'Power-sharing executives: consociational and centripetal formulae and the case of Northern Ireland', Ethnopolitics, 15(5): 497–519.

McGlynn, C., Niens, U., Cairns, E. and Hewstone, M. (2004) 'Moving out of conflict: the contribution of integrated schools in Northern Ireland to identity, attitudes, forgiveness and reconciliation', Journal of Peace Education, 1(2): 147–163.

McGrattan, C. (2021) '"They never went looking for war": three understandings of the Northern Ireland civil rights movement', *Práticas da História, Journal on Theory, Historiography and Uses of the Past*, 13: 55–85.

McKittrick, D. and McVea, D. (2012) *Making sense of the troubles: a history of the Northern Ireland conflict*, London: Viking.

McLafferty, M., Armour, C., O'Neill, S., Murphy, S., Ferry, F. and Bunting, B. (2016) 'Suicidality and profiles of childhood adversities, conflict related trauma and psychopathology in the Northern Ireland population', *Journal of Affective Disorders*, 200: 97–102.

McMullan, M. (2018) *Sectarianism and separation in Northern Ireland: a perspective-based evaluation on the contribution of youth work*, PhD thesis, University of Southampton.

McVeigh, R. and Rolston, B. (2007) 'From Good Friday to good relations: sectarianism, racism, and the Northern Ireland state', *Race and Class*, 48(4): 1–23.

Medvetz, T. (2018) 'Bourdieu and the sociology of intellectual life', in T. Medvetz and J.J. Sallaz (eds) *The Oxford handbook of Pierre Bourdieu*, New York: Oxford University Press, pp 454–478.

Mezirow, J. (2003) 'Transformative learning as discourse', *Journal of Transformative Education*, 1(1): 58–63.

Milliken, M. (2020) 'The development and delivery of community relations through youth work', in S. McCready and R. Loudon (eds) *Investing in lives: the history of the youth service in Northern Ireland (1973–2017), volume 2*, Belfast: Youth Council for Northern Ireland, pp 433–456.

Milliken, M. and Roulston, S. (2022) *How education needs to change: a vision for a single system*, Coleraine: Ulster University.

Mitchell, G. (2000) *Making peace*, Berkeley: University of California Press.

Moon, C. (2006) 'Narrating political reconciliation: truth and reconciliation in South Africa', *Social & Legal Studies*, 15(2): 257–275.

Morrow, D. (2011) 'After antagonism? The British–Irish ethnic frontier after the Agreement', *Irish Political Studies*, 26(3): 301–312.

Morrow, D. (2015a) 'Acknowledging religious and cultural diversity in an antagonistic society: the challenge of Northern Ireland', in I. Honohan and N. Rougier (eds) *Tolerance and diversity in Ireland, north and south*, Manchester: Manchester University Press, pp 211–231.

Morrow, D. (2015b) 'Northern Ireland: breaking the inheritance of conflict and violence', in P. Antonello and P. Gifford (eds) *Can we survive our origins? Readings in Rene Girard's theory of violence and the sacred*, East Lansing, MI: Michigan State University Press, pp 169–190.

Morrow, D. (2017) 'Reconciliation and after in Northern Ireland: the search for a political order in an ethnically divided society', *Nationalism and Ethnic Politics*, 23(1): 98–117.

Morrow, D. (2019) *Sectarianism in Northern Ireland: a review*, Belfast: Ulster University.

Morrow, D. (2020) *Fog in Belfast: a hundred years of uneasiness, and no end in sight*, London: London School of Economics.

Morrow, D. and Wilson, D. (1996) *Ways out of conflict: resources for community relations work*, Belfast: Corrymeela Press.

Muganda, W. (2021) 'Charting a feminist present and future: young women's leadership in building peace and promoting gender equality, Palestine – Israel', *Journal of Politics, Economics, and Culture*, 26(1): 7–13.

Murphy, M.C. and Evershed, J. (2022) 'Contesting sovereignty and borders: Northern Ireland, devolution and the Union', *Territory, Politics, Governance*, 10(5): 661–677.

Murray, C. (2023) *Young men, masculinities and imprisonment: an ethnographic study in Northern Ireland*, Cham: Palgrave Macmillan.

Murray, M., Payne, B., Morrow, D., Byrne, J. and Walsh, C. (2019) *Results and analysis of the local policing review 2018 consultation: your police service, your views*, Belfast: Ulster University.

Neill, G. and McArdle, E. (2016) *A model of Irish-medium youth work*, Belfast: Glór na Móna.

Neill, G. and McArdle, E. (2022) *Squeezed in and squeezed out: lessons from Irish-medium youth work*, Belfast: Glór na Móna.

Newman, E., Paris, R. and Richmond, O.P. (eds) (2009) *New perspectives on liberal peacebuilding*, New York: United Nations University Press.

NIECD (Northern Ireland Council for Educational Development) (1988) *Education for mutual understanding: a guide*, Belfast: NICED.

Nilan, P. (2021) *Young people and the far right*, Singapore: Palgrave Macmillan.

NISRA (Northern Ireland Statistics and Research Agency) (2021) *Results: information on census 2021 and supporting materials* [online], Belfast: NISRA, www.nisra.gov.uk/statistics/2021-census/results

The Nobel Peace Prize (2023) 'Full text of Alfred Nobel's will' [online], Stockholm: The Nobel Foundation, https://www.nobelprize.org/alfred-nobel/full-text-of-alfred-nobels-will-2/

Nolan, P. (2012) *Northern Ireland peace monitoring report: number one*, Belfast: Community Relations Council.

Nolan, P. (2013) *Northern Ireland peace monitoring report: number two*, Belfast: Community Relations Council.

Nolan, P. (2014) *Northern Ireland peace monitoring report: number three*, Belfast: Community Relations Council.

NYA (National Youth Agency) (2000) *Ethical conduct in youth work: a statement of values and principles from the National Youth Agency*, Leicester: National Youth Agency.

O'Mahony, D., Doak, J. and Clamp, K. (2012) 'The politics of youth justice reform in post-conflict societies: mainstreaming restorative justice in Northern Ireland and South Africa', *Northern Ireland Legal Quarterly*, 63(2): 269–290.

O'Neill, S. (2015) *Towards a better future: the trans-generational impact of the troubles on mental health*, Belfast: Commission for Victims and Survivors/Ulster University.

Ord, J. (2016) *Youth work process, product and practice: creating an authentic curriculum in work with young people* (2nd edn), London: Routledge.

O'Toole, F. (2010) *Enough is enough: how to build a new republic*, London: Faber & Faber.

Paffenholz, T. (2009) 'Civil society', in V. Chetail (ed) *Post-conflict peacebuilding: a lexicon*, Oxford: Oxford University Press, pp 60–73.

Paffenholz, T. (2015) 'Unpacking the local turn in peacebuilding: a critical assessment towards an agenda for future research', *Third World Quarterly*, 36(5): 857–874.

Parlevliet, M. (2017) 'Human rights and peacebuilding: complementary and contradictory, complex and contingent', *Journal of Human Rights Practice*, 9: 333–357.

Patten, C. (1999) *A new beginning: policing in Northern Ireland – the report of the independent commission on policing for Northern Ireland*, Norwich: HMSO.

Patton, G.C., Sawyer, S.M., Santelli, J.S., Ross, D.A., Afifi, R., Allen, N.B., et al (2016) 'Our future: a Lancet commission on adolescent health and wellbeing', *Lancet*, 387(10036): 2423–2478.

Peck, J. and Tickell, A. (2002) 'Neoliberalizing space', *Antipode*, 34(3): 380–404.

Peck, J., Brenner, N. and Theadore, N. (2018) 'Actually existing neoliberalism', in D. Cahill, M. Cooper, M. Konings and D. Primrose (eds) *The SAGE handbook of neoliberalism*, London: SAGE, pp 3–15.

Pellerin, L.A. (2005) 'Applying Baumrind's parenting typology to high schools: towards a middle-range theory of authoritative socialization', *Social Science Research*, 34: 283–303.

Pettigrew, T.F. (2010) 'Commentary: South African contributions to the study of intergroup relations', *Journal of Social Issues*, 66(2): 417–430.

Pettigrew, T.F. and Tropp, L.R. (2006) 'A meta-analytic test of intergroup contact theory', *Journal of Personality and Social Psychology*, 90(5): 751–783.

Pierson, C. (2018) 'Gendering peace in Northern Ireland: the role of United Nations Security Council Resolution 1325 on women, peace and security', *Capital & Class*, 43(1): 57–71.

Podd, W. (2010) 'Participation', in J. Batsleer and B. Davies (eds) *What is Youth Work?* Exeter: Learning Matters, pp 20–32.

Pontes, A., Henn, M. and Griffiths, M.D. (2018) 'Towards a conceptualisation of young people's political engagement: a qualitative focus group study', *Societies*, 8(1): 1–17.

Potter, M. (2004) *Women, civil society and peacebuilding: paths to peace through the empowerment of women*, Belfast: Training for Women Network.

Project Real (ca. 2024) *Project Real* [online], www.projectreal.co.uk.

PSNI (Police Service of Northern Ireland) (2024) *Workforce composition statistics* [online], Belfast: PSNI, https://www.psni.police.uk/about-us/our-publications-and-reports/our-publication-scheme/who-we-are-and-what-we-do/workforce

Ransome, P. (1992) *Antonio Gramsci*, Hertfordshire: Harvester Wheatsheaf.

Rawolle, S. and Lingard, B. (2013) 'Bourdieu and educational research', in M. Murphy (ed) *Social theory and educational research*, Oxon: Routledge, pp 117–137.

Reicher, S. (1986) 'Contact, action and racialization: some British evidence', in M. Hewstone and R. Brown (eds) *Contact and conflict in intergroup encounters*, Oxford: Basil Blackwell, pp 152–168.

Reicher, S. (2007) 'Rethinking the paradigm of prejudice', *South African Journal of Psychology*, 35: 412–432.

Reynolds, M. (2017) 'The Gaelic Athletic Association and the 1981 H-Block hunger strike', *The International Journal of the History of Sport*, 34(3–4): 217–235.

Reysen, S. and Katzarska-Miller, I. (2017) 'Superordinate and subgroup identities as predictors of peace and conflict: the unique content of global citizenship identity', *Peace and Conflict: Journal of Peace Psychology*, 23(4): 405–415.

Reysen, S., Larey, L.W. and Katzarska-Miller, I. (2012) 'College course curriculum and global citizenship', *International Journal of Development Education and Global Learning*, 4(3): 27–39.

Richardson, N.L. (1997) *Education for mutual understanding and cultural heritage* [online], Belfast: CAIN, https://cain.ulster.ac.uk/emu/emuback.htm

Richmond, O.P. (2005) *The transformation of peace*, Hampshire: Palgrave Macmillan.

Richmond, O.P. (2009) 'Becoming liberal, unbecoming liberalism: liberal-local hybridity via the everyday as a response to the paradoxes of liberal peacebuilding', *Journal of Intervention and Statebuilding*, 3(3): 324–344.

Richmond, O.P. (2010) 'A genealogy of peace and conflict theory', in O.P. Richmond (ed) *Palgrave advances in peacebuilding: critical developments and approaches*, Hampshire: Palgrave Macmillan.

Richmond, O.P. (2011a) 'Critical agency, resistance and a post-colonial civil society', *Co-operation and Conflict*, 46(4): 419–440.

Richmond, O.P. (2011b) *A post-liberal peace*, Oxon: Routledge.

Richmond, O.P. and Tellidis, I. (2020) 'Analogue crisis, digital renewal? Current dilemmas of peacebuilding', *Globalizations*, 17(6): 935–952.

Roberts, D. (2011) 'Post-conflict peacebuilding, liberal irrelevance and the locus of legitimacy', *International Peacekeeping*, 18(4): 410–424.

References

Rogan, J. (2016) *Young people's participation in peacebuilding: a practice note*, Geneva: United Nations Inter-Agency Network on Youth Development, Working Group on Youth and Peacebuilding and PeaceNexus Foundation.

Rogers, C. (1967) 'The interpersonal relationships in the facilitation of learning', in J. Harrison, F. Reeve, A. Hanson and J. Clarke (eds) *Supporting lifelong learning: perspectives on learning*, New York: The Open University, pp 25–39.

Rosher, B. (2022) '"And now we're facing that reality too": Brexit, ontological security, and intergenerational anxiety in the Irish border region', *European Security*, 31(1): 21–38.

Ruane, J. and Todd, J. (1996) *The dynamics of conflict in Northern Ireland: power, conflict and emancipation*, Cambridge: Cambridge University Press.

Sandel, M.J. (2021) *The tyranny of merit: what's become of the common good?*, Dublin: Penguin.

Sanders, A. (2019) *The long peace process: the United States of America and Northern Ireland, 1960–2008*, Liverpool: Liverpool University Press.

Schubotz, D. (2023) *Young Life and Times (YLT) survey: summary of results – 2023*, Belfast: ARK.

Schubotz, D. and McArdle, E. (2014) *Young people and mental health, policy, and research review*, Belfast: ARK.

Scott-McKinley, A. (2020) 'Curriculum and youth work', in S. McCready and R. Loudon (eds) *Investing in lives: the history of the youth service in Northern Ireland (1973–2017), volume 2*, Belfast: Youth Council for Northern Ireland, pp 396–408.

Seal, M. (2014a) 'Youth work is common sense, you just have to trust your instincts', in M. Seal and S. Frost (eds) *Philosophy in youth and community work*, Dorset: Russell House Publishing, pp 8–22.

Seal, M. (2014b) 'I treat everyone as an individual', in M. Seal and S. Frost (eds) *Philosophy in youth and community work*, Dorset: Russell House Publishing, pp 112–131.

Seal, M. (2016) 'Critical realism's potential contribution to critical pedagogy and youth and community work: human nature, agency and praxis revisited', *Journal of Critical Realism*, 15(3): 263–276.

Seal, M. and Frost, S. (eds) (2014) *Philosophy in youth and community work*, Dorset: Russell House Publishing.

SEUPB (2018) *Children & young people: quality and impact body*, Belfast: SEUPB.

SEUPB (2021) *Peace plus programme 2021–2027: programme overview*, Belfast: SEUPB.

Shaull, R. (1996) 'Foreword', in P. Freire, *Pedagogy of the oppressed*, London: Penguin Books, pp 11–16.

Shultz, L. (2009) 'Conflict, dialogue and justice: exploring global citizenship education as a generative social justice project', *Journal of Contemporary Issues in Education*, 4(2): 3–13.

Simpson, G. (2018) *The missing peace: independent progress study on youth, peace and security*, New York: United Nations.

Simpson, R. and Holdaway, L. (2023) 'Between rhetoric and reality: reclaiming the space for locally led peacebuilding that responds to conflict dynamics in violent and hateful extremism programming', *Conflict, Security & Development*, 23(5): 385–400.

Smith, A. (2003) 'Citizenship education in Northern Ireland: beyond national identity?', *Cambridge Journal of Education*, 33(1): 15–32.

Smith, A. and Robinson, A. (1996) *Education for mutual understanding: the initial statutory years*, Coleraine: University of Ulster.

Smith, A., O'Connor, U., Bates, J. and Milliken, M. (2019) *Research update: citizenship practices and political literacy in young people*, Belfast: ARK.

Smyth, M. and Hamilton, J. (2003) 'The human costs of the troubles', in O. Hargie and D. Dickson (eds) *Researching the troubles: social science perspectives on the Northern Ireland conflict*, Edinburgh: Mainstream Publishing, pp 15–36.

Smyth, P. (2017) *Stop attacks – beyond the societal shrug: addressing paramilitary attacks on young people in Northern Ireland*, Belfast: Wiseabap Engagement.

Snyder, C.R. (2003) *The psychology of hope: you can get there from here*, New York: Free Press.

Spencer, G. (ed) (2011) *Forgiving and remembering in Northern Ireland: approaches to conflict resolution*, London: Continuum International.

Sriram, C.L. (2009) 'Transitional justice and the liberal peace', in E. Newman, R. Paris and O.P. Richmond (eds) *New perspectives on liberal peacebuilding*, New York: United Nations University Press, pp 112–129.

Stanton, E. (2021) *Theorising civil society peacebuilding: the practical wisdom of local peace practitioners in Northern Ireland, 1965–2015*, Oxon: Routledge.

Stevenson, C. and Sagherian-Dickey, T. (2018) 'Territoriality and migration in a divided society: lay theories of citizenship and place in Northern Ireland', *Qualitative Psychology*, 5(1): 135–154.

Susen, S. (2014) 'Reflections on ideology: lessons from Pierre Bourdieu and Luc Boltanski', *Thesis Eleven*, 124(1): 90–113.

Susen, S. (2016) 'The sociological challenge of reflexivity in Bourdieusian thought', in D. Robbins (ed) *The anthem companion to Pierre Bourdieu*, London: Anthem Press, pp 49–93.

Swaine, A., Spearing, M., Murphy, M. and Contreras-Urbina, M. (2019) 'Exploring the intersection of violence against women and girls with post-conflict statebuilding and peacebuilding processes: a new analytical framework', *Journal of Peacebuilding & Development*, 14(1): 3–21.

Swartz, D.L. (2013) *Symbolic power, politics, and intellectuals: the political sociology of Pierre Bourdieu*, Chicago, IL: University of Chicago Press.

Tajfel, H. (1982) *Social identity and intergroup relations*, New York: Cambridge University Press.

Taylor, T. (2017) 'Treasuring not measuring: personal and social development' [online], *Youth and Policy*, https://www.youthandpolicy.org/articles/treasuring-not-measuring/

Taylor, T., Connaughton, P., de St Croix, T., Davies, B. and Grace, P. (2018) 'The impact of neoliberalism upon the character and purpose of English youth work and beyond', in P. Alldred, F. Cullen, K. Edwards and D. Fusco (eds) *The SAGE handbook of youth work practice*, London: SAGE, pp 84–97.

TEO (2013) *Together: building a united community*, Northern Ireland: The Executive Office.

Thompson, N. (2016) *Anti-discriminatory practice* (6th edn), London: Palgrave.

Tiffany, G. (2001) 'Relationships and learning', in L. Deer Richardson and M. Wolfe (eds) *Principles and practice of informal education*, Oxon: Routledge Falmer, pp 93–105.

Tolbert, D. (2009) 'International criminal law: past and future', *University of Pennsylvania Journal of International Law*, 30(4): 1281–1294.

Tonge, J. (2020) 'Beyond unionism versus nationalism: the rise of the Alliance party of Northern Ireland', *The Political Quarterly*, 91(2): 461–466.

Townsend, D., Taylor, L.K., Merrilees, C.E., Furey, A., Goeke-Morey, M.C., Shirlow, P., et al (2020) 'Youth in Northern Ireland: linking violence exposure, emotional insecurity, and the political macrosystem', *Monographs of the Society for Research in Child Development*, 85(4): 1–122.

UN (United Nations) (1989) *Convention on the rights of the child*, New York: United Nations.

UN (United Nations) (2000) *Report of the panel on UN peace operations (The Brahimi Report), A/55/305 – S/2000/809*, New York: United Nations, 21 August.

UNSC (United Nations Security Council) Res 1325 (31 October 2000) UN Doc S/RES/1325.

UNSC (United Nations Security Council) Res 2250 (9 December 2015) UN Doc S/RES/2250.

Vahid, H. (2023) 'Reason, reasoning, and the taking condition', *European Journal of Philosophy*, 1–11.

Vargas, C., Whelan, J., Brimblecombe, J. and Allender, S. (2022) 'Co-creation, co-design and co-production for public health: a perspective on definitions and distinctions', *Public Health Research & Practice*, 32(2): e3222211.

Verkoren, W. and van Leeuwen, M. (2013) 'Civil society in peacebuilding: global discourse: local reality', *International Peacekeeping*, 20(2): 159–172.

Verwoerd, W. (2021) ' "Building" and "cultivating" peace: practitioner reflections on the sustainable peace network project', *Glencree Journal*, 238–248.

Veugelers, W. (2011) 'The moral and the political in global citizenship: appreciating differences in education', *Globalisation, Societies and Education*, 9(3–4): 473–485.

Wacquant, L. (2008) 'Pierre Bourdieu', in R. Stones (ed) *Key sociological thinkers* (2nd edn), Basingstoke: Palgrave Macmillan, pp 261–277.

Wacquant, L. and Akçaoğlu, A. (2017) 'Practice and symbolic power in Bourdieu: the view from Berkeley', *Journal of Classical Sociology*, 17(1): 55–69.

Watts, S. and Stenner, P. (2012) *Doing Q methodological research: theory, method and interpretation*, London: SAGE.

Welch, M. (2020) 'Signs of trouble: semiotics, streetscapes, and the Republican struggle in the north of Ireland', *Crime Media Culture*, 16(1): 7–32.

Wenger, E. (1998) *Communities of practice: learning, meaning, and identity*, New York: Cambridge University Press.

Wenger-Trayner, E. (2013) 'The practice of theory: confessions of a social learning theorist', in V. Farnsworth and Y. Solomon (eds) *Reframing educational research: resisting the 'what works' agenda*, London: Routledge, pp 105–118.

Wenger-Trayner, E. and Wenger-Trayner, B. (2014) 'Learning in landscapes of practice: a framework', in E. Wenger-Trayner, M. Fenton-O'Creevy, S. Hutchinson, C. Kubiak and B. Wenger-Trayner (eds) *Learning in landscapes of practice: boundaries, identity, and knowledgeability*, London: Routledge, pp 13–30.

Whicher, A. and Crick, T. (2019) 'Co-design, evaluation and the Northern Ireland innovation lab', *Public Money & Management*, 39(4): 290–299.

Whitehouse, P. (1990) 'Education for mutual understanding: a guide', *Journal of Curriculum Studies*, 22(5): 493–499.

Whyte, N. (2002) *The 1998 referendums* [online], Belfast: ARK, https://www.ark.ac.uk/elections/fref98.htm

Wierenga, A., Wood, A., Trenbath, G., Kelly, J. and Vidakovic, O. (2003) *Sharing a new story: young people in decision-making*, Melbourne: Australia Youth Research Centre.

Williamson, H. (2015) *Finding common ground*, Brussels: Council of Europe European Youth Work Convention.

Williamson, H. (2020) *Cornerstone challenges for European youth work and youth work in Europe making the connections and bridging the gaps: some preparatory thoughts for planning the 3rd European youth work convention and implementing the European youth work agenda*, Brussels: Council of Europe European Youth Work Convention.

Wilson, A. (2023) 'The benefits and challenges of participation for children and young people', in H. Sharp and L. Walker (eds) *Participation in children and young people's mental health*, New York: Routledge, pp 44–57.

Wilson, R. (2016) *Northern Ireland peace monitoring report: number four*, Belfast: Community Relations Council.

Woolford, A. and Ratner, R.S. (2003) 'Nomadic justice? Restorative justice on the margins of law', *Social Justice*, 30(1): 177–194.

Wright, F. (1987) *Northern Ireland: a comparative analysis*, Dublin: Gill & Macmillan.

Wright, F. (1996) *Two lands on one soil*, Dublin: Gill & Macmillan.

Wright, S.C. and Lubensky, M. (2009) 'The struggle for social equality: collective action vs prejudice reduction', in S. Demoulin, J.P. Leyens and J.F. Dovidio (eds) *Intergroup misunderstandings: impact of divergent social realities*, New York: Psychology Press, pp 291–310.

Wright, S.C. and Baray, G. (2012) 'Models of social change in social psychology: collective action or prejudice reduction? Conflict or harmony?', in J. Dixon and M. Levine (eds) *Beyond prejudice: extending the social psychology of conflict, inequality, and social change*, Cambridge: Cambridge University Press, pp 225–247.

YLT (Young Life & Times) (2023) *20 years of the Young Life and Times (YLT) survey* [online], Belfast: ARK, https://www.ark.ac.uk/ARK/node/998

Index

3P-M model 155–156

A
active citizenship 116
activism
  grassroots approaches 43, 47
  peacebuilding as 90, 91, 146–163
  radical 54, 141
  rights activism 75
  for social change 116
  transformative justice 79–80
adjacent concepts 90–91
adverse childhood experiences 112, 128, 129
  see also trauma
advocacy 55, 56
agency
  citizenship education 124
  critical pedagogy 12
  democracy 65
  experiential learning 29
  failure to recognise 63
  liberalism 61
  participation 13, 57, 149
  politicisation 82, 146
  reconciliation 71
  structural restrictions on 41
  structure versus agency 84–85
Alliance Party 8
Allport, G. 72, 126
'An Dream Dearg' 159
Andersson, E. 155–156
Ashe, F. 76
'at risk' young people 55, 62, 127, 139
Australia 12, 154
aversive acknowledgement 70
avoidance cultures, breaking down 102
awards and prizes 44–45

B
Bakhtin, M.M. 31
Belfast Good Friday Agreement 7, 16, 19, 34, 66
'best interest' principle 149
Blue Book 66
bonfire building 102
border zones of political ideologies 87–88
bottom-up peacebuilding 55–56, 58, 119
boundary objects 38, 50, 140, 163
Bourdieu, P. 35, 38–44, 45–47, 48–50, 60, 84, 87, 92, 124–125, 131, 135–136, 139, 142, 144, 145
Brexit 8
Bruce, S. 21

Büber, M. 30
Byrne, S. 21, 22, 23

C
capacity building 83, 84, 161
capital (Bourdieu) 44–47, 49, 51, 135–136
capitalism 59, 91
  see also neoliberalism
Catholic
  demographics of research participants 95–96
  education system 21
  and partition 18
  police 20
  religious and cultural traditions 21–23
centrist politics 24
Chandler, D. 57, 58
child exploitation 110
citizenship
  constructing unity discourses 126
  education 130
  education system 53, 124
  neoliberalism 62
  political engagement and social justice 116
  social cohesion and restoration 110, 112
  transformative justice 79–80
  typology of peacebuilding 80–82
civic consciousness 134
civil society 58, 61
co-creation 48, 92, 143, 145, 146–163
co-design 147
cognitive dissonance 101, 123
collective action 12, 53, 74, 81, 87, 115, 124, 130
collective resistance model 74
colonialism 6, 17, 59, 137, 138
common ground 31, 89, 106, 126, 134
communities of practice
  and boundary objects 38
  definition 35–36
  morphological analysis 87
  in peacebuilding field 42, 50, 163
  power 39, 51
  radical peacebuilding 141, 142, 143, 144
  regimes of competence 139–140
community relations 2, 24, 71, 105
Community Restorative Justice Ireland 138, 139
Community Youth Work 149, 152
compliance, incentivisation of 136–138
conflict legacies 6, 7, 16, 24, 66, 71, 77, 85, 110–115, 158
confounded Q sorts 118

Index

conscientisation
  versus action 151
  critical pedagogy 26
  critical thinking 28, 32, 114–115
  dialogue 30, 122
  political consciousness 101, 134, 140, 144, 151
consensus 36, 53, 68, 144
contact hypothesis 72–73, 126
contested terms 'peacebuilding' and 'youth work' 10–13, 164–165
conversation and dialogue processes 28, 29–32
Cooper, T. 12, 53–54, 55, 56, 134
co-production 147
core, adjacent and peripheral concepts 90–92
Corney, T. 150
Costa, C. 142
Coulter, C. 23, 24
counter-discourses 64, 137
Craig, W. 18
Crick, B. 130
critical consciousness 12, 30, 31, 32, 100, 102–103
critical peace studies 57, 59, 86
critical pedagogy 12, 26, 81, 100, 101, 122
critical thinking 28, 32, 100–105, 115, 122–125, 141, 143, 161
cross-community contact 65–66
cultural adjacency 91
cultural capital 44, 135, 139
cultural identities 102
cultural violence 75, 79, 131
culture wars 9, 17

D

de St Croix, T. 28, 62, 64
decontestation 87
dehumanisation 3, 59, 122, 124
democracy 12, 29, 59, 75, 131, 146
demographics of research participants 95, 103–104, 109, 112–113, 117
depoliticisation of practice 63, 65
devolution 17–18, 19, 20
Dewey, J. 29
dialogue
  critical thinking and dialogue viewpoint 100–105, 122–125, 126, 143, 161
  harmonisation 134
  morphological analysis 89
  radical peacebuilding 141
  typology of peacebuilding 79
  youth work processes 28, 29–32
diversionary work 101, 111
diversity 66, 80, 81, 126
Dixon, J. 73

Downing Street Declaration 34
doxa 136, 143, 144

E

Eckhardt, J. 148
economic capital 44, 46, 47, 135
Education for Mutual Understanding (EMU) 66, 126
education system 20–21, 65, 66–67, 81, 123, 126
emancipatory potential 9, 13, 31–32, 58, 61, 102–103, 123–124, 141–142
empathy 31, 102, 161
employability programmes 47, 62, 84
empowerment 55, 56, 113–117, 131, 147
equality 12, 30–31, 59, 64, 75, 81, 91, 158
equity 23, 25, 66, 85, 91
ethnic frontier lens 16–17, 18–24
European Union (EU) 7, 34, 67, 95, 104, 109, 147
evaluations 49, 62, 118
everyday peacebuilding 60–62
experiential learning 29, 55
extremism 9–10, 111

F

factor analysis 97, 98, 117–118
family resemblances 87–88, 121–122
far-right extremism 9–10
feedback loops 154
#feesmustfall 157–158
Femia, J.V. 58, 136, 137
feminism 77
field (Bourdieu) 42–44, 48, 49, 139, 143
Fisher, D. 73, 126
forgiveness 110, 128, 163
Forrest, D. 13
Freeden, M. 87–88, 89, 90, 91, 92, 93
Freire, P. 12, 26, 28, 30, 31, 81, 114–115, 121, 122, 124, 141
friendships, building 105–109, 126, 127
funding
  continuity of 119
  driving social change 108
  evaluations 49
  field (Bourdieu) 141
  focus on economic capital 44, 46–47
  grassroots approaches 47, 144
  incentivising compliance 136–138
  instrumental outcomes 52
  investment in peacebuilding 34–35, 44
  meta-capital 135
  outcomes-focused 38, 48, 63, 119, 127, 137, 164
  P4Y ('Peace4Youth') funding stream 95, 104, 109, 117, 119
  'playing the game' 141
  product-oriented 55

refusing 64
resistance 133
targets 52

G

Gaelic Athletic Association (GAA) 22
Gallie, W.B. 86
Galtung, J. 10, 55, 75, 76, 79, 110, 131
gender 76–77, 102, 129, 166
Giroux, A. 126
global citizenship 80, 81
Good Friday Agreement *see* Belfast Good Friday Agreement
Govier, T. 70
Gramsci, A. 58, 136
grassroots approaches
  funding 47, 144
  legitimacy 43–44
  peacebuilding 1, 35
  political engagement and social justice viewpoint 116, 119
  resistance 64
  and the state 47–48
  transformative justice 79
  United Nations (UN) 58
  veneer of 61
  youth work processes 1, 13, 145
Green versus Orange 115–116

H

Habermas, J. 30, 31
habitus 40–42, 48, 49, 50–51
Hamardle model of youth sector peacebuilding 121–132, 133, 142, 144, 148, 161–163, 165
Hamber, B. 69–70
Hamilton, Andy 5–6, 32, 93, 95, 100, 124
Hammond, Mark 2–3, 27, 28, 29, 30, 31, 32, 93, 100
Hargie, O. 73, 126, 127
harmonious living 105, 123, 125–127
harmonisation 127–129, 138–139, 140, 145, 162
harmonising versus politicising 133–135
hegemony 58, 61, 133, 136, 137, 142
history, engaging with 102
history of Northern Ireland 6–9, 17–19
Home Rule 17–18
housing, segregated 21
human rights 75–77, 130
Hunger for Peace Games 160–161
Hvidsten, A.H. 75

I

ideational structures 89–91, 92, 99
impact 49, 62
  see also outcomes
In Defence of Youth Work 141
individualism 53, 63, 124

ineliminable features 90
informal education 12, 26, 53, 124
interdependence 38, 39, 42, 66, 100, 126, 137
intergroup contact 72–75, 84, 89, 123, 125–126, 134
intersectionality 68
investment in peacebuilding 34–35, 44
  see also funding
IRA (Irish Republican Army) 18, 19, 34
Irish language 102, 159

J

Jeffs, T. 26, 30, 154
July 12 marches 22
justice 77–80
  see also social justice
justice system 24, 129, 139
  see also police

K

Kaptein, R. 17
Kelly, G. 69–70

L

Laclau, E. 136
Lave, J. 35–36, 50, 51, 87, 139, 144
law and order 20
Ledwith, M. 12, 60, 122, 133
legacies of conflict 6, 7, 16, 24, 66, 71, 77, 85, 110–115, 158
legitimising the illogical 91
liberalism 57, 58, 87, 90–91, 126
  see also neoliberalism
limitations of youth work 103
listening 31, 151
Little, A. 59, 71
'local turn' 61, 68, 86
logic of practice 39
logical adjacency 90–91
Lohmeyer, B.A. 79, 128, 131, 138
Loyalists *see* Unionists
Lundy model for youth participation 152–153, 154

M

Mac Ionnrachtaigh, F. 159, 160
managerialism 61, 64
Maringira, G. 158
masculine perspectives 76, 127, 129
McArdle, E. 3–5, 33, 66, 147, 159
McKittrick, D. 17, 18, 19
McVea, D. 17, 18, 19
meaning making 29, 37–38, 39, 87, 154
mental health 82–83, 103, 107, 112, 147
meritocracy 62, 91, 124, 137, 142–143
meta-capital 47, 135–136, 139, 143
Mezirow, J. 28, 29, 31, 32
middle ground/centrist parties 24

Milliken, M. 21, 25
morphological analysis 86–98, 121
Morrow, D. 17, 18
Mouffe, C. 136
multiculturalism 80, 81, 126
mutual understanding 65–67, 89, 105–109, 125–127, 135–136, 142–143, 161

N

Nadan, A. 21, 22, 23
national identities 81, 96, 106
Nationalists
and Catholicism 18, 22
history of Northern Ireland 7, 8, 17
law and order 20
mutual understanding viewpoint 137
NEETs (not in education, employment or training) 116
negative peace 75, 110
negotiation of meaning 37–38, 39, 87
Neill, G. 159
neoliberalism 52, 57, 59–65, 118–120, 137, 138, 139, 141, 164, 167
neutrality 101, 105, 106, 108, 134
NI Alternatives 139
non-violence 91, 110, 143, 158
Northern Irish identity 81, 105, 106

O

Orange Order 22
outcomes 52, 63, 75, 78, 118–119, 127, 137, 151
out-groups 72–73, 125

P

P4Y ('Peace4Youth') funding stream 95, 104, 109, 117, 119
paramilitarism
and dissent 65
harmonisation work 127, 129
history of Northern Ireland 7, 65, 77
ongoing 9, 82, 110–112
restorative justice 89
participants in study 93–96
participation
communities of practice 35–36, 50
embedded notions of co-creation 92
health benefits of 151
models of 152–156
negotiation of meaning 37–38
participation processes 28–29
peace activism 146–163
what is youth participation 149–152
youth participation in political arenas 103
partition 4, 6–7, 18
Patten report 3, 20
PEACE IV programme 67, 95, 104, 108, 119

peace walls 24
peacebuilding
as contested concept 10–11, 164–165
and conversation 32
covert 10, 19
top-down versus bottom-up 55–59
typology 69–85, 165
peacebuilding theory 25
peacekeeping 10
peacemaking 10
peace-versus-war dualism 55, 57
peer learning 161
performance targets 48, 52, 62, 104, 118–119, 127, 141, 164
peripheral concepts 92
personal development 27, 54, 83, 85, 106–108, 142–143
personal versus political 53, 122, 143
Pettigrew, T.F. 73, 74
phronesis 157, 163
Pierson, C. 77
'plug and play' approach 39
police 2–3, 20, 84, 103, 110, 111–112, 138–139
policy/practice divide 38, 52
political consciousness 101, 134, 140, 144, 151
political education 66
political elites 59, 60, 67, 68
political engagement 113–117, 129–131, 141, 143, 151–152, 157–158, 163
political identities 22–23, 24, 95–96
political ideologies 55, 60, 87, 89
political literacy 81–82
political thinking 87–98
politicisation 133–135, 140, 143, 145, 146–163, 166
politicising dialogue 100–105, 122–125
populism 9–10
positionality 2–6, 95, 112, 133, 142, 148, 152
positive peace 75, 110
post-liberal peacebuilding 60–62
power
addressing power imbalances 103
and agency 124
Bourdieu, P. 38–39, 43–44
conversation and dialogue processes 30–31
equality between youth worker and young person 26
models of youth participation 152
and money 34
participation as taking power 149
political engagement 114–115
radicalising youth sector peacebuilding 133–145
regimes of competence 140–141
reification 37

restorative justice 79
symbolic capital/symbolic power 45, 47–50, 135–136, 139, 140, 142
power-sharing government 7, 19, 77
practical knowledge 40, 121
practice capital 45, 46, 143
praxis 121, 124, 157
pro-social behaviours 110
Protestant
  demographics of research participants 95–96
  education system 21
  Orange Order 22
  and partition 18
  religious and cultural traditions 21–23
psychosocial programming 82–83

Q

Q methodology 86, 92–98, 99–100, 117–118, 120, 144

R

racism 71–72
radical change 53–55, 66, 89, 103, 116
radical democratic practice 131
radical peacebuilding 141–142
radicalisation 103, 111, 124, 127, 129, 133–145, 166
Ratner, R.S. 138
reconciliation 69–72, 84, 123
reflexivity 43, 48–51, 121, 124–125, 132–133, 142–144
'regimes of competence' 35–36, 41, 50, 139–141
Reicher, S. 74
reification 37–38, 50
rejuvenating youth work 64–65
relationship-building processes 27, 29–30, 100–101, 105–109, 126, 161
religious and cultural traditions 18, 21–23
  see also Catholic; Protestant
re-politicisation of practice 166
Republic of Ireland 8, 18
Republicans 17
  see also Nationalists
research methods 92–98
researcher positionality 2–6, 95
resilience 129
resistance
  antidote to violence 158–159
  collective resistance model 74
  as core youth work process 89, 90, 91
  political engagement and social justice viewpoint 103, 116, 141, 143
  post-liberal peacebuilding 60–62
  rejection of funding as 46
  rejuvenating youth work 64–65
restorative justice 34, 70, 78–79, 89, 103, 110–113, 138

restorative principles 127–129, 138–139, 143
retaliation cycles 110
Richmond, O.P. 60, 61
rights realisation gap 76, 130
Roulston, S. 21
'rules of the game' 41, 42, 137, 142

S

safe spaces 101, 105, 106, 127
'schemes of perception' 41, 42, 51, 87
schools 65–67, 126
Seal, M. 26
sectarianism 9, 66, 71, 102, 112, 115, 124, 143
segregation 7, 9, 20, 21, 65–66, 124
self-disclosure 73
shared education 66–67
short-termism 55, 118
single-identity work 73, 92, 107, 126, 140
Sinn Féin 8
SISCODE project 148
Skarstad, K.I. 75
small-p politics 115
Smith, A. 126–127
Smith, M.K. 26, 30, 154
social capital 45, 135
social class 6, 77, 113, 115
social cohesion 56, 58, 67, 80, 84, 92
social cohesion and restoration viewpoint 110–113, 127–129, 138–139, 143
social control versus social change 53–55, 128, 138
social identity theory 72
social justice 63, 77, 91, 113–117, 129–131, 141, 143, 163
social media 160–161
social pedagogy 12, 26
sociology of radical change 53, 54
South Africa 158
Stanton, E. 157
starting points, meeting young people at 116
state-building 57
statutory youth work policies 25
structural violence 75, 131
superordinate identities 80, 106
surveillance 84, 118
symbolic capital/symbolic power 45, 47–50, 135–136, 139, 140, 142
symbolic violence 131

T

Tajfel, H. 72, 125
taken-for-granted assumptions 14, 48, 100, 131, 133
targets 48, 52, 62, 104, 118–119, 127, 141, 164
technocracy 60, 137, 141
territoriality 112, 127

theories of change 37, 47
theory of practice (Bourdieu) 38–50
'thinking tools' 39–44, 144
Tiffany, G. 26, 28
tokenism 67, 81, 119, 147, 150, 154, 155
top-down versus bottom-up 14, 35, 52, 55, 58, 61, 68, 86, 108, 118, 119, 146
transformative justice 79–80
transformative learning 28, 30
transgenerational trauma 82, 112, 128
transitional justice 77, 78
trauma 82, 83, 103, 112, 128
Tropp, L.R. 73
'Troubles' 7, 16, 24
trust, reciprocity of 126, 127
Trust Attraction Hypothesis 73, 126

U

Unionists 7, 8, 17, 18, 20, 22
United Nations Convention on the Rights of the Child 149, 152
United Nations (UN) 11, 57, 78, 161
United Nations Youth, Peace, and Security Resolution (UNSC Res 2250, 2015) 67, 76
United Network of Youth Peacebuilders 129

V

Vargas, C. 147
Verwoerd, W. 10

victim–perpetrator distinctions 70
voice 147–148, 149, 152

W

'waithood' 158
waypower 152
wellbeing 82–83, 103, 107, 112
Wenger, E. 35–36, 37, 38, 50, 51, 87, 139, 144, 146
Wenger-Trayner, E. 36, 39
'Where were you when?' exercise 2
Wierenga, A. 154, 155
women 77, 91, 102, 129, 161, 166
Woolford, A. 138
working classes 6, 113, 115
Wright, F. 16–17, 18–19, 20, 21, 22, 23, 33

X

xenophobia 66, 112

Y

Young Life and Times surveys (YLT) 24
Young Voices 147
youth work
  description of 25–27
  four modes of 53
  as ill-defined practice 11–13
  neoliberalisation of 62
  political models of 55, 56
  processes 27–32
  social control versus social change 53–55

www.ingramcontent.com/pod-product-compliance
Lightning Source LLC
Chambersburg PA
CBHW051545020426
42333CB00016B/2102